OECD Digital Government Studies

Digital Government Review of Norway

BOOSTING THE DIGITAL TRANSFORMATION OF THE PUBLIC SECTOR

OECD
BETTER POLICIES FOR BETTER LIVES

This work is published under the responsibility of the Secretary-General of the OECD. The opinions expressed and arguments employed herein do not necessarily reflect the official views of OECD member countries.

This document and any map included herein are without prejudice to the status of or sovereignty over any territory, to the delimitation of international frontiers and boundaries and to the name of any territory, city or area.

Please cite this publication as:
OECD (2017), *Digital Government Review of Norway: Boosting the Digital Transformation of the Public Sector*, OECD Digital Government Studies, OECD Publishing, Paris.
http://dx.doi.org/10.1787/9789264279742-en

ISBN 978-92-64-27973-5 (print)
ISBN 978-92-64-27974-2 (PDF)

Series: OECD Digital Government Studies
ISSN 2413-1954 (print)
ISSN 2413-1962 (online)

Photo credits: Cover © Grisha Bruev/Shutterstock.com

Corrigenda to OECD publications may be found on line at: *www.oecd.org/about/publishing/corrigenda.htm*.

Foreword

Norway has laid solid foundations for the development of a national digital government. These foundations are based on sustained efforts to use technology to improve the organisational efficiency of public sector institutions. This has led to high levels of citizen satisfaction with public services in areas such as health care and education that are well above the OECD average. The creation of an electronic identification system (eID), citizens' digital mailboxes, one-stop-shop portals for citizens and businesses and the development of inclusive digital strategies and services are all results of the government's commitment to improving and simplifying the relationship between the public sector and the Norwegian population. A system of basic data registries, as well as the adoption of digital government principles, such as not asking users to provide the same data more than once, have also made it easier for public institutions to share data and become more closely integrated.

This *Digital Government Review of Norway* is designed to support the Norwegian government in harnessing digital technologies for more efficient, inclusive, open and citizen-driven public policies. The Review was prepared by the Reform of the Public Sector Division of the Public Governance Directorate of the OECD at the request of the Norwegian Ministry of Local Government and Modernisation (Kommunal-og moderniseringsdepartementet, KMD).

The review's policy recommendations provide insights on important policy areas such as the governance of digital government, a strategic approach to commissioning digital goods and services, the development of digital skills inside public sector institutions, and developing a public sector that recognises the social, economic and strategic value of government data.

The review underlines the high digitalisation level of Norway's economy and society, which creates favourable conditions for digital government within the public sector. Nonetheless, it urges the government to capitalise on the important results achieved so far to ensure the continuous contribution of digital government to public sector productivity, business innovation and social engagement in Norway. It is crucial to promote "systems thinking" across the Norwegian public sector to overcome a siloed and sectoral organisational culture, and the development of agency-specific solutions to over-arching policy challenges. This requires a governance framework that supports a participatory, co-ordinated and coherent design and implementation of digital government initiatives across the public sector.

This Digital Government Review takes stock of the results of previous collaboration efforts between the OECD and the Norwegian government, and in particular, the 2005 e-Government study of Norway. The Review is based on the analytical frameworks for digital government, open government data, and a data-driven public sector developed by the OECD based on the 2014 OECD Recommendation of the Council on Digital Government Strategies. The OECD undertook a peer-review mission to Oslo in

November 2016 - with the participation of peers from the Netherlands, New Zealand and the United Kingdom - and met with public officials from Norwegian ministries and agencies as well as with actors from the local level of government, the private and third sectors. Two online surveys were administered across the Norwegian public sector for the purpose of this review.

The main assessment and recommendations of the review were presented to public sector officials during the Nordic-Baltic Ministerial Conference on Digitalisation (25 April 2017), Norwegian public officials during the Norwegian Digitalisation Conference in Oslo (8-9 June 2017), and to OECD delegates of the OECD Working Party of Senior Digital Government Officials. This review contributes to the OECD "Going Digital" horizontal project, which aims to guide countries in developing a coherent and effective policy framework for making the digital transformation of public sectors, economies and societies work for growth and well-being.

Acknowledgements

This *Digital Government Review of Norway* was prepared by the Public Governance (GOV) Directorate of the OECD. The mission of the Public Governance Directorate is to help governments at all levels design and implement strategic, evidence-based and innovative policies to strengthen public governance, respond effectively to diverse and disruptive economic, social and technological challenges and deliver on government's commitments to citizens.

This review was produced under the supervision of Barbara-Chiara Ubaldi, heading GOV's work on Digital Government, Open Government Data and Data-Driven Public Sector. Strategic directions were provided by Edwin Lau, head of the Public Sector Reform Division in GOV, and Luiz de Mello, Deputy Director of the Public Governance Directorate.

Chapters 1 and 5 were written by Jacob Arturo Rivera Perez, Policy Analyst in the GOV Public Sector Reform Division. Chapters 2, 3 and 4 were written by João Ricardo Vasconcelos, also Policy Analyst in the GOV Public Sector Reform Division. All chapters benefited from contributions and revisions provided by Barbara-Chiara Ubaldi.

The national peer reviewers from the Netherlands, New Zealand and the United Kingdom provided very valuable contribution and orientation to the review:

- For the Netherlands, Mr. John Kootstra, Policy Department Information Society and Government, Dutch Ministry of the Interior and Kingdom Relations.
- For New Zealand, Mr. Tim Occleshaw, Government Chief Technology Officer, Department of Internal Affairs.
- For the United Kingdom, Mr. Sanmuganathan Rahulan, former Senior Technology Adviser at the Office of the Chief Technology Officer, Government Digital Service, UK Cabinet Office.

This review would not have been possible without the commitment and support of the Norwegian Ministry of Local Government and Modernisation (KMD). We are particularly thankful to Mr. Jan Hjelle, Director General at the Department of Information and Communications Technology (ICT) Policy and Public Sector Reform, KMD; Mr. Timothy Szlachetko, Senior Adviser at the Department of ICT Policy and Public Sector Reform, KMD; and Mr. Espen Sjovoll, Deputy Director General, Department of ICT Policy and Public Sector Reform, KMD.

Finally, the review team wishes to acknowledge the significant contributions provided by many Norwegian stakeholders from the public sector during interviews and who answered the OECD surveys administered for the purpose of this review.

Table of contents

Tables

Figures

Figures *(continued)*

Figures *(continued)*

Executive summary

The digital transformation of the public sector is imperative to achieve the transition from e-government to a fully developed open, and efficient, digital government. The rapid and pervasive uptake of digital technologies worldwide is generating innovative business models and drastically changing the lives of citizens. Constant access to online products and services, and the increasing convenience and simplicity of digital services has also raised citizens' expectations regarding communications and services in the public sector. Governments need to rapidly capitalise on the availability of new technologies to better serve their constituencies.

The Digital Agenda of Norway, also known as the "White Paper", builds upon the continuous and resilient efforts of the central government in areas such as e-government. It reflects the government's willingness to strategically use technology to streamline inter-agency and sectoral organisational processes, improve public service delivery, spur business innovation, and increase digital inclusion for greater social equality. The Norwegian Digital Agenda underlines the potential benefits of new technologies and related trends – e.g. data analytics and cloud-based solutions to modernise government's activities - as well as open government data published by public sector institutions.

Achieving the Digital Agenda's goals requires strategic actions to enable the systemic and coherent digital transformation of the public sector. Norway enjoys a consensus-based public sector where decision making is the result of collaborative processes among ministries and agencies. However, the vertical administrative culture relies on the role and capacities agencies have to implement digital government policies, resulting in fragmented efforts of sector-specific solutions to systemic policy challenges. This fragmentation undermines the Norwegian public sector's vision of "one government for citizens and businesses" and hinders a broad cost-benefit assessment of investments on digital technology in the Norwegian public sector.

Existing governance arrangements also affect the amount of pressure and incentives available to encourage ministries and agencies to align their decisions with over-arching strategic objectives and policy guidelines. Key institutional actors lack the means to promote the use of common guidelines, standards and digital solutions across policy sectors. There is scope, therefore, for reinforcing the role and leadership of the central government in this effort. There is also an opportunity to align the vision of the central government with that of ministries and agencies and to build skills within public sector institutions to achieve specific objectives included in the Digital Agenda.

Policy recommendations

- Consider developing a dedicated and integrated digital government strategy – including an impact assessment instrument - indicating expected outputs, outcomes and impacts, involving relevant stakeholders from across society and the public, private and third sector in its development, implementation and regular cost-benefit evaluation.

- Develop a clearer and more structured governance framework for digital government, strengthening leadership, reinforcing the mandate of the Agency for Public Management and eGovernment (Difi) and defining clearer roles for actors. This could include the establishment of a national Government Chief Information Officer (GCIO), supported by an agile organisational structure.
- Sustain efforts to ensure the legal and regulatory framework favours the achievement of the Digital Agenda and better responds to changing citizens' and businesses' needs and expectations.
- Strengthen co-ordination and synergies with local government through more regular and stable co-ordination mechanisms, e.g. greater involvement of KommIT through the regular participation of representatives of different municipalities, and promoting the use of digital government key enablers across municipalities.
- Reinforce the role of the Digitisation Council (*Digitaliseringsrådet*), strengthening its position as a recognised collective body guaranteeing a sound and agile evaluation of all proposed projects or investments in the digital arena.
- Reinforce the applicability of general digital standards and guidelines - to provide a more coherent, interoperable and resilient digital government infrastructure - through ICT project evaluation and establishing a standard business case model for ICT projects for mandatory use across sectors and levels of government.
- Leverage the use of Difi's project management platform – the Project Wizard – for the implementation of inter-institutional, standardised and comparable management practices.
- Increase the priority assigned to the development of digital and data-related leadership and skills across the public sector through a dedicated information and communications technology (ICT) human resources policy, regularly mapping needs across the administration, and improving the attractiveness of civil service roles in digital government.
- Develop a specific strategy for the commissioning of digital technologies in the public sector, expanding demand-aggregation processes to the procurement of digital goods and services, exploring synergies and increasing the public sector's negotiating capacities with private suppliers, reinforcing the adoption of existing common standards, and enhancing the transparency, tracking and accountability of public ICT expenditures.
- Establish an integrated service delivery policy within the new Digital Government Strategy to reinforce the effectiveness and sustainability of the public sector's efforts to deliver high-quality services.
- Consider prioritising the development of Norway's role as promoter of cross-border services among Nordic and Baltic countries, through the country's active support for the development of a common area for cross-border digital services in the public sector.
- Define a formal open government data strategy (part of the data governance and management strategy) in collaboration with private, public and third-sector actors. Such a strategy should have a clear roadmap with milestones, including the development of a formal open data infrastructure – supported by a consultation

process - drawing upon the current data categories identified by the Norwegian government.

- Simplify and streamline data sharing practices across the public sector to break down data silos and enable further efficiency within the public sector as well as data re-use by external actors. Data needs to be easily found, understood and used by all systems.
- Define a roadmap for the development of a data-driven public sector. This should include the development of skills as a core element of the Digital Government Strategy and backbone of the overall public data governance and management strategy, capitalising on both the willingness of the central government to exploit the use of data science and big data and opportunities identified by public sector instititutions for the development of data-driven services and foresight activities.

Assessment and recommendations

On the path to digital transformation in Norway

Background: Capitalising on a privileged context

Norway, together with other Nordic countries, is well placed on the path to digital transformation, when compared with its European peers. That position is reflected in several international monitoring instruments, namely the European eGovernment Benchmark[1] and the UN E-Government Survey (see also Figure 0.1).[2] OECD instruments such the OECD OURdata Index (which benchmarks open data policies across OECD countries and partners) have also placed Norway among the top-ten OECD countries on open government data (see Figure 0.2).

The sustainability of this self-earned, privileged positioning in international rankings would require, however, not only the continuous development of structural conditions demanding permanent improvements, but also building a sense of urgency within the Norwegian context to maintain the drive for further advancing the overall digital transformation of the public sector. This would be necessary to better respond to the continuously evolving needs and expectations of digitally sophisticated and "ready" businesses and citizens, and to strategically tackle future challenges related to welfare financing, social inclusion and economic growth. Building up this sense of urgency would also contribute to strengthening Norway's position in relation to its participation in regional collaboration mechanisms, such as the Nordic Council and the European Economic Area.

The public sector is no exception to the digital transformation that is permeating and spreading across the Norwegian economy and society. In this context, the challenge for the Norwegian government is neither to introduce new digital technologies into public sector activities nor to adopt technology within the framework of traditional public sector business models.

Figure 0.1. **Digital Economy and Society Index (DESI) 2017 ranking: Norway**

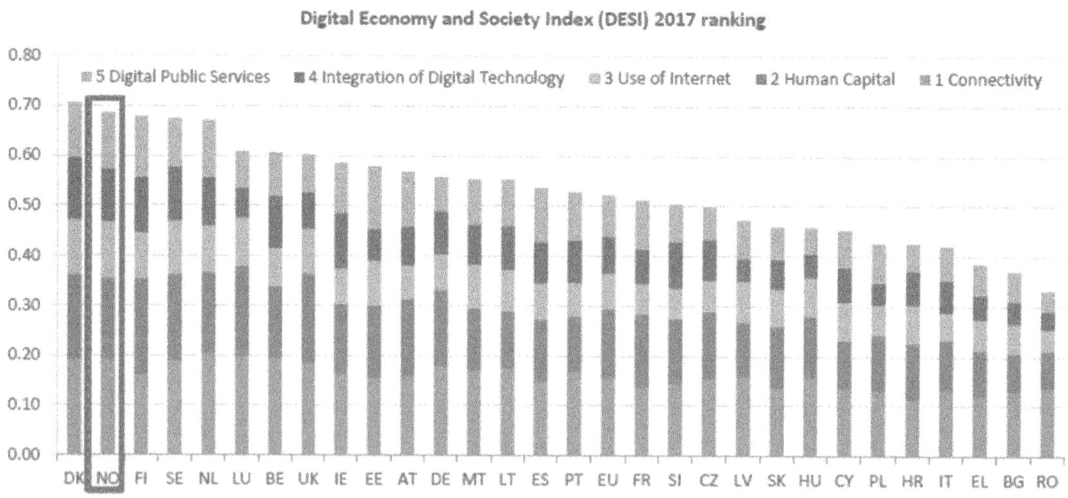

Source: European Commission (2017), "Digital Economy and Society Index 2017: Norway", Digital Single Market, https://ec.europa.eu/digital-single-market/en/scoreboard/norway.

Figure 0.2. **Open-Useful-Reusable Government Data Index (OURdata), 2017**

OECD countries and partners

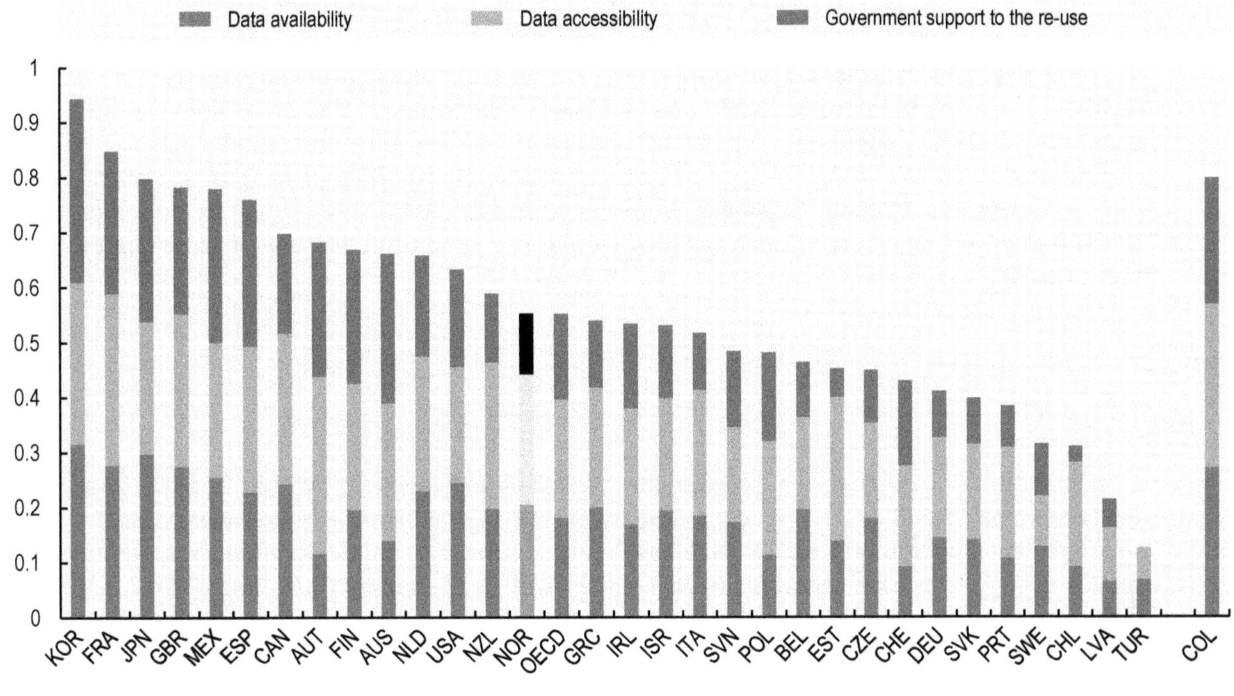

Notes: Data for Hungary, Iceland and Luxembourg are not available. Denmark does not have a central/federal data portal and is therefore not displayed in the index. Information on data for Israel: http://dx.doi.org/10.1787/888932315602.

Source: OECD (2017), *Government at a Glance 2017*, OECD Publishing, Paris, http://dx.doi.org/10.1787/gov_glance-2017-en.

Key and strategic actions should focus on further integrating digital technologies by design into the government's modernisation efforts. This would require transforming the working dynamics and processes of public administrations across all policy areas - and at all levels of government – and drive organisational change in close collaboration with citizens, businesses and local governments.

As a result, the Norwegian government could progress towards a public sector capable of delivering innovative services and opportunities digitally by default, which would further increase public sector efficiencies, and respond to the demands of a society and an economy that are ready for them.

In order to achieve the transition from e-government to digital government, Norway (as an early implementer of e-government) should overcome legacy problems and improve the coherence of a digital landscape often characterised by the coexistence of digital services and points of access to the public that appear to be littered.

The digital transformation of the Norwegian public sector should take place at all organisational levels

Norwegian public sector institutions, politicians, policy makers and public managers - at the central and local levels - should capitalise on technological developments. To do so, these actors would need to experiment with new technologies (e.g. prototyping) while also using citizens' inputs as drivers of organisational learning and knowledge-based institutions. A cross-cutting strategy to fully reap the opportunities of technology with a more efficient and systemic approach would need to be implemented. Such an approach to the maximisation of digital technologies would also streamline the use of those digital platforms already in place.

Stakeholders from the public sector should acknowledge themselves as agents of transformational change

From this perspective, the Norwegian ministries and agencies would benefit from further exploring and exploiting technology to increasingly engage with networked actors (e.g. citizens, institutions and businesses), rely on inter-operable machines, systems, processes (e.g. machine learning, open source) and data sources (e.g. linked data, big data, inter-institutional and cross-border data sharing). As a whole, these strategic actions would contribute to advancing the digital transformation of Norway's public sector.

The challenge for Norway is to avoid fragmentation, leading to duplication and incoherence

Siloed and decentralised governance models can lead to multiple access points for government services across public sector agencies (e.g. sectoral or domain-specific online platforms, electronic mailboxes, electronic identification system [eID] tools) that, while providing innovative "solutions" that respond to citizens' and businesses' demands, create duplication and limit opportunities for synergies and integrated service delivery.

Leveraging a sense of urgency

General agreement exists among public, private and social stakeholders on the relevance of the current digital agenda as a driver that can help Norwegian public sector institutions realise and fully capitalise on digital technologies - namely in terms of policy making and service delivery effectiveness, efficiency, and inclusiveness. Nonetheless, there is also a lack of a sense of urgency among public sector officials to capitalise on the ecosystems' digital maturity in order to advance digital transformation a step further.

Severe economic crises, leading to scarcity and instability, often function as drivers of change, while administering and managing change in wealthy and healthy environments may require a proactive approach towards the identification of incentives for transformation. The economic crisis that recently affected most OECD member countries – and which has created the sense of urgency in many instances - was not deeply felt in Norway. This is a result of effective "cushion" macroeconomic policies against external shocks, and considerable oil wealth to manage (OECD, 2016).

Similarly, the good level of the existing online public services has not created high levels of dissatisfaction among users so far, as proven by Norway's good placing in international rankings (as mentioned earlier).

The aforementioned results emanate from the contextual advantages and a solid basis in Norway that do not seem to be leveraged at the moment (e.g. high mobile penetration, good examples of data use in the education sector, integrated service delivery in municipalities)

There seems to be a general feeling among stakeholders that the sense of urgency may come soon. Three key examples illustrate some of the concerns and general feelings shared by several stakeholders during the OECD peer review mission to Oslo (26-30 September 2016):

1. **Increasing societal expectations**: Citizens and companies have growing expectations regarding their service experience. Used to top information and communications technology (ICT) service providers like Google, Facebook, Amazon or Uber, public service users expect the same kind of service simplicity, user friendliness, effectiveness and quality that ensure high levels of trust.
2. **Vendor dependence**: The limited efforts in place to co-ordinate ICT procurement in the public sector are generating some vendor dependency problems (e.g. supply-chain risks) at central and local levels.
3. **Unsustainable performance in international rankings**: Although Norway remains in good position in several international rankings, a general concern can be found about the lack of sustainability of the mentioned positions, since other countries are making greater efforts and more strategic investments to advance their digital government performance.

At the same time, the participation of Norway in Nordic-specific co-operation mechanisms underpins the need to do better - from the city to the supranational level.

Regional programmes such as the 2017-20 Nordic Cooperation Programme for Regional Development and Planning and the 2014-17 Nordic Cooperation Programme for Innovation and Business Policy raise, directly or indirectly, issues related to the digital transformation of the public sector.

Data-driven business innovation and entrepreneurship, digital skills, smart cities, smart governments and the sharing economy are widely addressed as part of a common Nordic policy agenda that is clearly levered by digital evolution. The development of shared building blocks such as cross-national and shared services, e.g. eID, and open, sharable and inter-operable government data are at the core of this ambitious agenda.

Leveraging synergies between Norway and other Nordic countries in areas such as digital welfare or business innovation calls for the definition and implementation of specific policies and standards, common to all concerned countries

This would require the Norwegian government to move from procedures that – even when ICT-enabled – were often analogue in design, to the transformation of public sector business models based on the opportunities offered by digital technologies. By doing so, Norway would be able not only to better respond to the demands and needs of the Norwegian population, but could also contribute to maintaining the overall leadership of the Nordic region in terms of digitalisation, and construct a joint leading role for the Nordic countries in relation to the European Single Digital Market.

Governing the digital transformation of the Norwegian public sector

Key assessments

Between 2005 and 2017, Norway adopted several information society and/or digital government agendas (e.g. eNorway plans). While each of these policy documents stressed a different focus, they reflected different policy angles based on changing political priorities, and defined diverse goals; they also drew upon each other's advancements and challenges. As a result, this inter-connected model has created continuity in the policy design and implementation process, which has been useful in placing Norway among the top-ranking countries on digital government policies.

The current Digital Agenda for Norway (2015-16) (also known as the "White Paper") stresses the need to use digital technologies to modernise, simplify and improve public sector processes and external outputs. To make the lives of citizens and businesses easier and enhance their productivity, the White Paper identifies the following government priorities (KMD [Ministry of Local Government and Modernisation], 2016):

1. **User-centric focus**: Use technologies to support a user-centric public administration that provides seamless and integrated public services to its constituents, and simplifies day-to-day life.
2. **ICT as a significant input for innovation and productivity**: Digitise public operations in ways that support the productivity of economic agents, overall digital innovation and business competitiveness.
3. **Strengthen digital competence and inclusion**: Continuously improve digital competence and inclusiveness throughout all life phases, and across all population groups (e.g. migrants, refugees).
4. **Effective digitisation of the public sector**: Embed digital technologies in public sector reform efforts to reduce the complexity of the administration and deliver user-friendly digital services. Develop common solutions and foster their use in the central and local government and facilitate interoperability with European solutions.
5. **Sound data protection and information security**: Conceive data protection and security as integrated elements of ICT development and use. Citizens should, as far as possible, have control over their own data. Ensuring ICT security to maintain trust in digital solutions.

Digital government issues are deeply relevant to the current Digital Agenda, reflecting the commitment of the Norwegian government to address the digital transformation of the public sector. However, an autonomous strategy could bring substantial advantages to the capacity to co-ordinate and monitor the development of digital government. A stand-alone strategy would also benefit from a clearer identification and increased usage potential by the digital government ecosystem.

Improving overall governance

The OECD Recommendation on Digital Government Strategies highlights the need to define clear institutional roles and responsibilities as one of the basic preconditions for sound governance and to sustainably develop and support the digital transformation of the public sector. Considering the complexity of the task to be undertaken, and the need to establish a governance model that enables and strengthens collaboration and co-ordination and tackle silo-based approaches, roles and responsibilities should be clear to all stakeholders involved in the digital transformation process to secure adequate leadership.

Besides the clarification of roles and mandate – supported by adequate power distribution, policy instruments and levers - the establishment of appropriate mechanisms for co-ordination and collaboration are also necessary to ensure multi-stakeholder co-operation and engagement, as well as the co-responsibility of public, private or civil actors. This is also essential to create shared ownership of results, which supports joint and integrated efforts.

A sound governance framework – inclusive of institutional set-up, co-ordination mechanisms, soft or hard policy levers – facilitates decision-making processes in consensus-based organisational cultures, the adoption of agreements within decentralised decision-making and policy-implementation environments, and the co-ordinated definition, observance and enforcement of guidelines in digital government domains

What emerged during the OECD peer review mission was a general consensus among different stakeholders about the central policy co-ordination role of the Ministry of Local Government and Modernisation (KMD) and the strategic, instrumental role of the Agency for Public Management and eGovernment (Difi) in boosting the Digital Agenda for Norway. Significant agreement about the adequacy, urgency and level of ambition of the policy objectives identified also exists, which reflects a high level of maturity of the digital government ecosystem.

However, the results of the peer review mission showed that a governance framework with additional clarity on responsibilities and stronger leadership seems to be required; this view appears to be shared by many stakeholders, including user representatives and private sector institutions, e.g. suppliers.

For instance, the division of responsibilities between KMD (responsible for co-ordinating ICT/digitalisation policies and steering Difi, an agency within the KMD) and the Ministry of Trade, Industry and Fisheries (NFD) (responsible for the Brønnøysund Register Centre, which administers among other things, the Altinn platform) has led to disperse leadership and overlapping roles between these public bodies in areas of utter relevance to the effective implementation of Norway's digital agenda.

The role of Difi is also considered fundamental in the Norwegian public sector, but some doubts exist regarding: 1) its current capacity to provide the right support and leadership at the central and local levels; 2) the agency's levers to lead and sustain progresses in the digital transformation of the Norwegian public sector; and 3) its overall capacity to rapidly internalise and foresee the opportunities brought by the fast-paced digital era.

Difi assumes a central role in setting priorities, tackling the implementation of the digital agenda and developing cross-cutting guidelines and common components (e.g. public sector ICT architecture). However, besides its technical-pedagogical role, Difi lacks some strategic instruments (e.g. evaluation of ICT projects, ICT funding) to better leverage digital government development in Norway.

At the same time, the role and capacities of SKATE (the inter-institutional steering and co-ordination mechanism on digital government chaired by Difi and integrated by 12 public sector organisations) and the Digitisation Council (a multi-stakeholder advisory group providing by-request guidance on ICT projects' cost-benefit analysis and risk management) (see the section, Improving ICT management and strategic planning in Norway, later in this chapter), appear limited to support a coherent policy and effective collaboration in its implementation. For instance, according to some of the SKATE's members interviewed during the peer review mission, the spaced regularity of its meetings and its consensus-based nature makes it a very useful forum for information sharing, but with limited co-ordinating powers.

The limitations of its current governance framework may negatively impact Norway's capacity and opportunity to fully benefit from undergoing digital transformation efforts

The governance framework in place is not the most adequate to provide the right leadership required for supporting effective co-ordination, collaboration and shared efforts within the public sector. This governance model also limits the effectiveness of ministries' intentions and actions (including the impact of specific projects and investments), since fragmented and unarticulated public initiatives tend to respond in a limited way to citizens' and businesses' needs.

A stronger mandate - which could imply and provide, for instance, clearer and stronger responsibilities and levers - and the increase of resources for Difi is fundamental to reinforcing its co-ordinating powers at the national level, but also with respect to the 19 counties and 426 municipalities. Stronger co-ordination seems necessary, moving beyond setting policy objectives and priorities to enable the more effective steering of joint actions towards the achievement of common results and overarching government goals.

Although there isn't a "one-size-fits-all" model to country-specific digital government governance needs, experiences across the OECD provide evidence that the formal identification of a position equivalent to a Government Chief Information Officer (and/or Chief Digital Transformation Officer) could be considered as one of the possible alternatives. This would also help fill the gap mentioned during the peer review mission with regard to a visible "champion" of digital government within the Norwegian public sector.

The scenario above is also relevant with regard to open government data. While Difi holds key responsibilities within the framework of open data policies (e.g. developing open data guidelines), Norway lacks a formal Chief Data Officer in charge of providing strategic guidance on open data policies and initiatives across the country. As a result, this may have direct and indirect negative impacts on the achievement of key overarching policy objectives (e.g. spurring business innovation and furthering the digital economy).

Developing a strategic, system-thinking approach

Developing a system-thinking administration should be at the core of the development of digital government, and assumed as a central priority for the Norwegian public sector. This objective should be pursued by identifying public sector agencies with good examples to replicate, aligning the incentives and the organisational objectives, monitoring practices' alignment to overarching goals, and identifying long-term needs and shared solutions for the whole Norwegian administration.

Encouraging horizontal knowledge sharing is neither an unknown nor a new challenge for the Norwegian public sector. The verticality, top-down and decentralised policy implementation approach of the Norwegian public sector has created "innovation clusters" within leading agencies – often strong and autonomous - and within specific policy sectors (e.g. health, tax, loans). This has led to an unbalanced availability of competencies and capacities across and among ministries and agencies.

A strategic, horizontal knowledge sharing in line with central objectives is also needed. While local governments have given the Norwegian Association of Local and Regional Authorities (KS) a role in order to better co-ordinate on issues related to digital government and innovation (similar to the Dutch Local Governments' KING model), vertical co-funding issues and discrepancies in policy priorities seem to exist between the central government, counties and municipalities. As a result, local governments may make decisions based on their own priorities, thus weakening the capacity of the co-ordinating body to steer a multi-level and structured approach to better achieve national priorities.

Developing a cross-sectoral system-thinking approach would strengthen the Digital Agenda for Norway as a strategic tool to steer decisions and better align priorities with the national political agenda and key policy goals across the whole administration

Norwegian policy makers could benefit from further understanding that digital transformation can only be the result of the interaction and interconnection between public sector institutions, citizens and businesses – relations that are indeed eased and facilitated by digital technologies. Such a collaborative approach should also be considered as a strategic effort to bring "all the voices" to the table, enabling the more structured involvement of citizens, companies and general interest groups, and moving beyond the traditional citizen-centred approach to an evolving citizen-driven approach.

A pervasive strategic system-thinking approach can also accelerate the awareness of the digital journey among public leaders to overcome vertical thinking and increase awareness around the networked role of ICT. Together with a stronger, clearer and more coherent governance framework, this approach could ease the endeavour to ensure the sustained commitment and support of the digital transformation from top political leadership within the central government. Clear fundamental governance and control mechanisms, such as the following, should accelerate the digital journey:

- Orchestrated development and use of key **building blocks** (e.g. eID, eAuthentication, ePayments, eDelivery, eDocuments, eForms, etc.).
- Further **adoption of common standards**, architectures and norms.
- Development of a **common ICT procurement strategy**, aggregating the demand for stronger negotiating power, enabling savings and promoting the adoption of more interoperable solutions across the central and local level public sector institutions.
- Adoption of **common guidelines to support shared efforts** regarding digital service delivery, encouraging the development of more citizen-centred platforms, under the leadership of an existent agency adopting this mandate or role *de facto* (e.g. Difi).
- Strengthened **oversight capacities and mandates** to ensure systemic, strategic, efficient and accountable investments in ICT projects, and discourage siloed and inefficient expenditures. This is highly relevant, particularly in light of potential risks related to economic growth as a result of lower oil revenues and greater need for well-financed and sustainable welfare services.

OECD member country experience in strengthening system-thinking approaches to digital government is very diverse. For some countries, the adoption of effective soft approaches is easier thanks to the consensus culture generally in place in their public sector. Other countries tend to use harder approaches as an answer to more vertical or/and competitive cultures.

Depending on the experience, specific context, policy goals and expectations underway, one of the forthcoming challenges for Norwegian authorities is to adopt a clear and effective governance model – inclusive of the relevant tools and mechanisms - that can help design strategic decisions on policies and investments based on system-thinking dynamics in the public sector, while involving external actors in the process

Proposals for action

Governing the digital transformation of the Norwegian public sector

In light of the key assessments exposed above, which draw on the main findings and analysis included in Chapter 2 of this review, the Norwegian government could consider implementing the following policy recommendations:

1. **Consider the development of an autonomous digital government strategy**, to strengthen the political relevance of the digital transformation of the public sector and to be used as a policy instrument to align decisions and investments to overarching strategic goals, aggregating the commitment, ownership and efforts of the entire digital government ecosystem. A stand-alone strategy can bring several advantages in terms of co-ordination, management and monitoring, namely:
    - ***Reinforce the focus and coherent actions with regard to key strategic issues, goals and priorities*** for the development of digital government, while securing the proper alignment with other relevant strategies, e.g. sector reform, innovation and digital economy.
    - ***Secure the inclusiveness of the policy process*** in the design, development and management stages of the strategy. The involvement of public, private and civil society stakeholders can help reflect different needs and perspectives in the strategy and will also reinforce the commitment, sense of ownership and the development of a system-thinking culture.
2. **Ensure an updated legal and regulatory framework, aligned with the changing needs and increasing expectations of citizens and businesses.** The Norwegian government should maintain its commitment to adapt and advance the regulatory framework for digital government with a system-based rather than a topic-oriented approach, i.e. decisions on laws and regulations are supported by a holistic and cross-sectoral view so that they reach the government as a whole (whole-of-government approach). The assessment of regulatory challenges based on topic-oriented and sector-driven efforts have somehow hindered the faster advancement of the digital agenda in the country (e.g. the Cloud Strategy), which is why Norway would gain from paying particular attention to specific policy areas, such as public sector data governance as a whole (see Chapter 5) to find joint and more efficient solutions to systemic problems.
3. **Consider the development of an impact assessment methodology** based on the expected outputs, outcomes and impacts of the suggested stand-alone digital government strategy. This approach can support a more consistent use of cost-benefit analysis approaches, a structured management of projects consistent with the overarching strategic priorities and an accurate and transparent reporting of the public sector's efforts for digital government development.

Setting up a sound institutional framework for stronger leadership

The Norwegian government should consider implementing the following recommendations relevant to the **development of a clearer, more solid and more structured governance framework**, which would support stronger leadership and the definition of clearer roles for the different actors. This governance framework should:

- involve and commit the relevant actors across the public sector
- outline the diverse attributions for the different actors playing a key role in the governance framework, in particular to strengthen the clarity of roles and the efficiency of the co-ordination between KMD and its subordinate agency, Difi, that would improve synergies and help overcome potential confusion, or current gaps, in terms of responsibilities
- engage with, and communicate efficiently, the responsibilities, as well the progress underway, to key stakeholders across the public sector, the private sector and civil society.

Proposals for action *(continued)*

In line with the above, as well as with relevant OECD member country experience, the Norwegian government may consider implementing the following strategic actions:

4. **Consider the establishment of a national Government Chief Information Officer (GCIO) formally recognised as a public "champion" with a clear mandate and powers to lead the digital transformation of the Norwegian public sector, supported by the adequate governance framework**. The role of the GCIO should be focused on supporting the strategic use of technology within the public sector, driven by efficiency and effectiveness gains, and prioritising user-driven approaches for better value creation to the Norwegian economy and society. The government of Norway could consider:

   – ***Establishing the post of national GCIO*** in the Ministry of Local Government and Modernisation (KMD) with the responsibility to define the digital government strategy for Norway and co-ordinate its implementation, and with a ranking level that would enable direct reporting to the minister. The responsibilities of the national GCIO would include co-ordinating with, and monitoring, the not-yet available position of the Chief Data Officer (CDO), whose establishment is put forward by this review (see Chapter 5). This would ensure that the proposed strategy for the management and governance of the public sector data value chain is at the core of the digital transformation of the Norwegian public sector.

   – ***Envisaging an agile organisational structure supporting the GCIO***, e.g. the Department of ICT Policy and Public Sector Reform (AIF), or a special taskforce within this department, fulfilling this role.

   – ***Reinforcing the mandate of Difi*** as the agency/directorate responsible for carrying out the implementation of the digital government strategy (and overall digital transformation) of the public sector as defined by KMD. The supporting instrumental role of Difi in the operationalisation of the strategy could be strengthened by undertaking the following actions:

     – Assign to Difi the mandate to support the GCIO in the development of a national Digital Government Strategy - based on an inclusive approach bringing on board all relevant actors and stakeholders.

     – Allocate the formal monitoring responsibilities to co-ordinate the implementation of the above-mentioned digital government strategy.

     – Increase the human and financial resources allocated to Difi to enable it to lead and support the development of digital government in Norway, and in particular, to co-ordinate the implementation of the strategy.

     – Broaden the scope of the responsibilities of the Digitisation Council, of which Difi is the secretariat, with regard to the evaluation of ICT projects. The Council should be responsible for evaluating strategic ICT projects - focusing in particular on medium-sized projects - according to common ICT standards and guidelines, to ensure their alignment with the overarching strategic goals set in the national digital government strategy, the efficient commissioning of goods and services and fostering re-use of systems.

     – Consider the establishment of a new mechanism for ICT project evaluation for projects below NOK 10 million. The mentioned mechanism, that should be agile, online-based and non-mandatory, would help the Norwegian government to better follow ICT project development. Under the leadership of KMD, Difi should be responsible for developing and implementing this new mechanism.

Proposals for action *(continued)*

- Reinforce and consolidate the advisory and co-ordination role for strategic ICT procurement, allowing for better alignment of requisites (e.g. common norms and standards) and the exploration of synergies for demand aggregation, in line with the efforts underway with the Government Procurement Center (Statens innkjøpssenter).
- Increase the available funding mechanisms, namely through the expansion of Difi's Co-Financing Mechanisms (Medfinansieringsordningen), enabling the agency to better support and influence the development of strategic projects in the public sector in line with the digital government strategy.
- Assign the mandate to co-ordinate the implementation of a national policy for digital service delivery, to be designed by the GCIO, reinforcing the agency's role in the development of more citizen-driven public services, taking into account that even user-centred approaches are not constantly available across the entire public sector (see the section, Building a data-driven public sector in Norway, later in this chapter).

5. **Reinforce the involvement of relevant stakeholders from across the public sector in the development and implementation of the digital government strategy**. The Norwegian government should consider establishing a new body (e.g. a committee, council, etc.) to secure the regular engagement of key actors from across and within levels of government with the role to steer public sector efforts towards digital transformation. The mandate of the new body would include:
   - ***engaging in the design and in the co-ordination of the implementation of the national digital government strategy***, through the participation in regular meetings that could be held at a higher political and/or top-management level, or at a more operational one, given the specific focus of the meeting's agenda and level of discussion required
   - ***following the development of strategic ICT projects***, i.e. key enablers for digital government development (e.g. digital identification, interoperability and data exchange among base registers, one-stop-shops for digital service delivery), or initiatives with a transversal nature, issuing recommendations for their development.
   - ***following up on the activities of the Digitisation Council***, discussing the recommendations issued by it.
6. In order to ensure the inclusive development of the digital government strategy, **establish a body (e.g. advisory council) that includes representatives from the private sector, academia and civil society** in order to guarantee the integration of more pluralistic views for digital government development in Norway. Meetings should happen regularly, allowing its members to better follow the national efforts underway and contribute, as relevant.
7. **Strengthen the co-ordination and synergies with the local government** through more regular and stable co-ordination mechanisms. This can be achieved by reinforcing local governments' engagement in the development of the Norwegian digital government strategy. The following mechanisms can support better co-ordination across levels of government:
   - ***reinforce the involvement of KommIT*** through the regular participation of direct representatives of different municipalities in the meetings of the ***possibly newly established body*** (see Recommendation 5 above) to secure proper representation of the municipalities
   - ***better promote the use of key enablers across the municipalities*** (e.g. digital identification, interoperability, integrated central-local one-stop-shops for digital service delivery), increasing the capacity of Difi to orient and support the necessary efforts at local level (see the section, From user-focused to user-driven service delivery in Norway, later in this chapter).

Improving ICT management and strategic planning in Norway

Key assessments

The strategic planning and efficient management of ICT investments and projects require organisational knowledge, and the availability of specific skills and competencies among public sector officials. Technologies are becoming increasingly complex, with multiple cost structures and dependencies, connected to more and more diverse variables. Business skills and different business models can be mobilised to guarantee constant organisational learning, develop public sector intelligence and support strategic choices on technology for the overall sustainability of the digital transformation process. The use of business case methodologies to better plan and decide on ICT investments in line with political priorities (side by side with the need to ensure the availability of project management skills) has been assumed by OECD member countries as a fundamental factor in nurturing and sustaining the shift from e-government to digital government (Mickoleit, 2014).

A more frequent use of common business case and project management approaches and tools across an administration can also have a positive impact on better mobilising financial resources and better linking and pooling different funding sources, particularly for joint projects (or for projects requiring process integration and or/sharing). As a result, this could help to prioritise public investment in critical policy sectors (e.g. health, welfare and education), spot and lever potential synergies and encourage an approach to sharing and integration, which is at the core of the digital transformation.

The limited use of common practices to formulate the value proposition for ICT investments, and to manage projects across the Norwegian public sector, inevitably leads to additional hurdles to strategically justify investments

This also limits the capacity to point to tangible benefits for the public sector (at the macro, meso and micro levels), for citizens and businesses. The lack of these common practices can lead to unnecessary and duplicated efforts, to untapped opportunities for synergies with negative consequences in terms of public ICT investment efficiency and effectiveness.

Reinforcing the "cost-benefit" approach

SKATE (the inter-institutional steering and co-ordination mechanism on digital government chaired by Difi) was conceived as a horizontal co-ordination forum for the identification of common needs, actions and solutions across the public sector, with a focus on the prioritisation and coherence of ICT investments. The Digitalisation Council was created to provide advice to public sector agencies on ICT projects. The involvement of stakeholders from the public (at all levels), private and third sectors has been useful to build a strong basis for further capitalising on common synergies, implementing co-ordinated efforts, and ensuring better coherence in terms of priorities to be followed, standards to be applied and goals to be accomplished.

The Norwegian government has put in place the Budget Investment Proposal programme (Statsingsforslag) as an effort to draw upon the provision of additional financial funding (provided by the Ministry of Finance with KMD's strategic advice) to align ICT and digitalisation projects at the ministerial level to central policy goals. In order to obtain these additional funds, government ministries are required to provide "proof" (by filling out a form) of the measurement processes used to assess projects' costs-benefits and benefits realisation. KMD's advice and the information provided by ministries are then used as decision-making elements by the Ministry of Finance to prioritise specific ICT project proposals.

Building capacities across public sector institutions for the widespread use of business cases and/or value proposition approaches (e.g. cost-benefit analysis) can contribute to strengthening ICT project planning and management

Isolated examples of these practices are already available across different policy sectors, with positive impact reported in terms of projects' efficiency, coherence with broader national goals and sustainability. For instance, the Brønnøysund Register, responsible for managing the Altinn platform – that provides important services to citizens and businesses – reported always using business cases methodologies to plan and prioritise investments. Nevertheless, a consensus seems to exist among stakeholders within the Norwegian public sector, namely among the members of the Digitisation Council, on the need for a more structured and articulated approach in this respect.

The existence of mechanisms capable of guaranteeing projects' scrutiny and quality assurance is fundamental to assure adequate coherence of ICT projects and the necessary articulation among public sector stakeholders. Experiences across OECD member countries are diverse in this respect. While in some countries more centralised models are in place - with more linear and institutionalised co-ordination - other countries have adopted more decentralised models, mostly based on consensual and compromise-oriented approaches. In Norway, the second option prevails.

The current *ex ante* evaluation mechanisms of ICT projects in Norway do not seem adequate enough to hold decision makers and implementers fully accountable for ICT investments and results:

- The current threshold (over NOK 750 million) set for the mandatory *ex ante* project cost-benefit assessments (known as KS-ordningen or Quality Assurance Scheme) carried out by the Ministry of Finance (with the support of external consultancy firms) is only applicable to major-scale ICT projects.
- For those ICT projects between NOK 10 million and NOK 750 million, public sector institutions are recommended - yet not obliged - to seek the advice of the Digitisation Council,[3] a multi-stakeholder group chaired by Difi to support agencies on the definition and implementation of cost-efficient ICT projects. Nevertheless, stakeholders highlighted the limitations of this mechanism during the OECD peer review mission as the final recommendations of the Council are neither mandatory nor have a specific impact on the final allocation of resources for ICT projects. Since it is not an obligatory mechanism, the number of projects submitted for review is still substantially low.

In order to address the issues above, the Norwegian government put in place two financial incentives in 2016 to encourage public sector bodies to perform cost-benefit assessments:

- **Difi's co-financing mechanism**:[4] This mechanism aims to reinforce Difi's capacity to better pursue a systemic quality management approach for ICT projects by providing additional budget (up to 50%) for ICT projects with a total cost ranging from NOK 5 million to NOK 50 million. Difi's co-funding is limited to a maximum financial contribution of NOK 15 million.
- **KMD's 2016 Digitalisation Memorandum**:[5] In the 2016 Digitalisation Memorandum, KMD defined a set of actions in key areas (e.g. cloud computing, common components) to be prioritised by public sector organisations with regard to digitalisation. These actions were embedded in the KMD's distribution of the Digitalisation Memorandum that is distributed among ministries and agencies on a yearly basis. The 2016 Memorandum, which superseded a prior memorandum published in 2015,[6] also requires ministries and agencies to use a best practice project management model for projects with a total cost of more than NOK 10 million in order to ensure the cost efficiency of ICT projects. The memorandum recommends the use of **Difi's "Project Wizard" project management platform** (www.prosjektveiviseren.no). The Agency for Financial Management (DFØ)'s guidelines for cost-benefit analysis and benefits realisation have been embedded within the framework of Difi's platform.

Difi's co-financing mechanism and the 2016 Digitalisation Memorandum are evidence of KMD's decision to strengthen its co-ordination capabilities and the levers at its disposal (e.g. financial and legal instruments) to improve the quality of institutional ICT projects. Nevertheless, Norway, like other OECD countries, is striving to find a balance between leveraging the further adoption of cross-cutting, structured ICT project-management approaches and tools, and the need to avoid limiting the agility, rapidity and flexibility required in a context of digital transformation within a highly decentralised public sector.

Enhancing the more frequent use of financial approval mechanisms to strengthen the alignment of projects (e.g. Difi's co-financing model) with national strategic objectives is an opportunity to be fully tapped

The further use of financial policy levers, used in several OECD member countries, can significantly improve the systemic governance of ICT projects, and generate positive impacts regarding project coherence and alignment. In addition, the use of Difi's project management platform should be leveraged to contribute to the implementation inter-institutional, standardised and comparable management practices. This would avoid the proliferation of ICT project-management models that draw upon different project-management frameworks.

As mentioned earlier, establishing a central ICT procurement strategy (comprising the aggregation of demand of ICT products and services, e.g. the "government as a single customer" approach in New Zealand) is also a viable strategy to create stronger public sector negotiating power in relation to private provision of ICT goods and services.

Such a procurement strategy should be framed within a broader, common, standardised and well-structured ICT supply chain strategy that draws upon strategic policy implementation and comprises additional public management elements. For instance, private-public partnerships, knowledge sharing, public sector innovation, risk management, co-responsibility and organisational learning. This common supply chain strategy can lead to considerable improvements in terms of efficiency, and it would indeed enable a more coherent approach to ICT procurement that would result in savings, and stronger negotiating power, leading to better prices offered by vendors and improved alignment with common norms and standards to be followed.

Improving organisational learning on project management

The implementation of ICT projects' common monitoring mechanisms is a fundamental instrument to improve organisational learning across different policy sectors and levels of government. Consolidated metrics can be useful to better follow outputs and monitor the outcomes and impacts of policies underway. Knowledge-sharing practices can also help leverage and spread experiences across different areas of the public sector, and encourage synergies to the extent possible.

Leveraging and sharing organisational knowledge on successes and failures across different sectors and levels of government is pivotal to creating an enviroment that promotes and enables the digital transformation of the public sector

This requires the capacity of different actors to work together, share and integrate processes and resources, leveraging existing assets (e.g. systems, people, data). KMD has given Difi the task of examining how an ICT project catalogue can be created. The objective is to explore how the availability of an ICT project catalogue would contribute to building the government's knowledge of ongoing digitilisation projects and improve organisational learning on project management. However, while there are several examples of good project management practices, interviews held during the peer review mission pointed at the existence of disarticulated practices, and duplicated efforts at the agency level.

This fragmentation and lack of inter-agency co-ordination is visible also within the same ministries. While some ministries have tried to implement a more structured approach in order to better control and monitor projects (e.g. the Ministry of Justice), this is not common practice across Norwegian ministries. As a result, the existing heterogeneity in terms of project management and oversight undermines effective co-ordination and, as a result, leads to missed opportunities of collaboration, efficiencies and synergies.

The above-mentioned incoherent and unarticulated environment is able to create virtuous cycles among those institutions that succeed, generating front-running examples and practices of digital government. However, in the cases of those institutions that don't succeed, a negative cycle is easily generated: lack of required skills, limited leadership capacities and few instruments available to generate, capture and maintain knowledge bring serious limitations to the digital transformation of the public sector.

KMD's Digitisation Memorandum is a sign of the Norwegian government's commitment to improve the public sector performance and will contribute positively to the necessary shift in this area. The requirement to use Difi's "Project Wizard" platform (www.prosjektveiviseren.no) should create new opportunities for coherence, knowledge sharing and synergies among ICT public sector projects.

Developing internal capacities vs. outsourcing

Several OECD member countries prioritise the need to find the right balance between public and private efforts in the promotion of the digital transformation. The lack of ICT skills in the public sector determines that ICT deployment and maintenance mostly rely on external service providers. That creates obvious dependences, namely from big consultancy firms, hardware and mostly software providers.

During the OECD peer review mission to Oslo, Norwegian public officials and private sector actors expressed and stressed concerns about the above-mentioned issues. For example, public officials highlighted the current reliance on external consultancies to assess, conceptualise and prototype ICT projects, whereas private sector representatives underlined, as mentioned above, labour mobility from the private to the public sector. While, in theory, this scenario should have contributed to reducing reliance on external support, the current human resource management (HRM) system in place may lack a strategic ICT-related component that could contribute to building and strengthening public sector institutions' capacities to self-capitalise on technological developments.

The definition and implementation of an effective HRM ICT-focused approach would be useful to attract, employ and retain ICT professionals and champions, and secure the availability of the digital skills required to support Norway's digital transformation

These professionals would bring the right set of skills and competencies to actually build further ICT project management capacity across the whole public sector, while bringing a fresh, forward-looking vision about the opportunities of new technologies to transform public sector activities.

Yet, evidence from the OECD mission also points to the public sector's frequent reluctance to contract external service providers, despite the lack of capacity, in areas where private sector advantages are typically clear (e.g. software development, general information technology [IT] maintenance). This organisational culture may also have a negative impact on the willingness of the Norwegian government to outsource and partner with private sector organisations to ensure timely access and efficient provision of key government services in areas such as welfare and health.

The sustainable digital transformation of the Norwegian public sector would require further clarification of the areas where the government wants to maintain a leading role, and build specific capacities for such a purpose, and those where private sector intervention could broadly and actively contribute to the achievement of specific policy goals (e.g. project design vs. development of technical solutions)

Proposals for action

Improving ICT management and strategic planning in Norway

In light of the key assessments exposed above, which draw on the main findings and analysis included in Chapter 3 of this review, the Norwegian government could consider implementing the following policy recommendations:

8. **Reinforce the role of the Digitisation Council (Digitaliseringsrådet), strengthening its position as a widely recognised public collective body responsible for guaranteeing a sound and agile evaluation of ICT projects.** The Council should continue to be recognised as a crucial body with the mandate to foster coherency, effectiveness and sustainability of ICT projects across the Norwegian public sector. The following actions could reinforce its role in the digital government ecosystem:
   - ***better promote and advertise the responsibilities of the Digitisation Council*** across the Norwegian public sector, clarifying its mission and demonstrating the benefits of the assessment for projects' alignment, efficiency and effectiveness, but also for the public administration as a whole in relation to its capacities to coherently implement digital government
   - ***shift from a non-mandatory to a mandatory approach for reviewing ICT projects (between NOK 10 million and NOK 750 million)***, given the dimension of the projects assessed and their potentially large impact on the Norwegian public sector
   - ***assure the proper financial and human resources*** to support the activity of the Council, and its reinforced mandate.
9. **Reinforce the applicability of general ICT standards and guidelines through ICT project evaluation,** namely the following topics:
   - digital identification and digital signatures
   - common standards and architectures
   - clear language and user involvement
   - information and data openness for transparency and re-use purposes
   - information security and personal data protection
   - digital first and universal design

   ICT project evaluation should be assumed as a strategic policy lever to support a consistent and coherent implementation of the digital government strategy – i.e. currently the Digitalisation Memorandum and eventually a stand-alone digital government strategy across the Norwegian public sector.
10. **Establish a standard business-case model** for mandatory use for ICT projects across sectors and levels of government. The model should be flexible, applicable to different types and sizes of ICT projects and should be properly connected with the Norwegian standardised ICT project management model.
11. **Leverage the use of Difi's project management platform - Project Wizard** – to contribute to the implementation of inter-institutional, standardised and comparable management practices. The use of the platform should not be considered mandatory, but incentives could be provided for its use while also ensuring that public stakeholders are aware of the advantages of using it, avoiding the proliferation of ICT project management practices. The consolidation of Difi's Project Wizard should also be connected with the development of a standardised ICT business case model for the whole Norwegian public sector.

Proposals for action *(continued)*

12. **Increase the level of priority conceded to the development of leadership and digital professional skills across the public sector** through the adoption and strategic management of an ICT human resources policy. The need to satisfy the internal demand for ICT professionals capable of responding to the rising complexity of users' needs and associated with the rapid uptake of digital technologies and associated working methods (e.g. data analysis) should be reflected in the national Digital Agenda or in a specific digital government strategy. Specific policy actions should be developed, namely to:

    – map needs across the administration regarding digital skills' development in line with the changing needs associated with the digital transformation of the public sector

    – promote the permanent updating of the digital skills of public officers, bearing in mind the cross-cutting nature of the digital transformation of the public sector

    – encourage leadership skills for the development of digital government across sectors and levels of government, in particular through specific training sessions targeting public sector senior officials.

13. **Consider improving the attractiveness of the profiles of civil servants playing various roles in relation to digital government and with different functions**. This would include better working conditions for more traditional ICT professionals (e.g. ICT architects, programmers) but also for profiles increasingly demanded in a context of digital transformation (e.g. data scientists, or civil servants with horizontal functions), as well as clear communication about the positions requested to address the changing demands of the Norwegian public administration.

14. **Consider the development of a specific policy to attract highly ICT-skilled workers from abroad**, helping the country's economy, particularly its public sector, to address shortages of ICT professionals and to sustain the competitiveness of the Norwegian ICT sector.

15. **As part of an overarching digital government strategy, define a clear vision to better balance the public and private responsibilities for Norway's digital government development**. The vision should clarify the areas and aspects (e.g. general IT maintenance and support, software development, IT prototyping) the government considers fundamental to maintaining its leading role, and those to be outsourced to the private sector. The vision should be reflected in Norway's Digital Agenda - or in a specific national strategy for digital government development. The design process of the vision should benefit from the involvement and engagement of the private sector and civil society, securing a transparent and inclusive approach to better seize the digital transformation of the Norwegian public sector, bringing different perspectives and angles to the table.

16. **Develop a specific strategy for the commissioning of ICT goods and services in the public sector**. Building on the key projects and initiatives already in place, like the Government Procurement Center (Statens innkjøpssenter), the Database for Public Procurement (Doffin) and the State Standard Agreements (SSA), the strategy should leverage the importance of coherent and aligned approaches and processes to commission ICT goods and services , strengthening the government commitment through the following drivers:

    – ***expanding demand aggregation processes to several ICT areas (e.g software development, IT assistance, cloud computing services)***, exploring synergies and increasing the public sector's negotiating capacity with ICT private suppliers

    – ***reinforcing the adoption of existing common standards***, assuming them as clear criteria to guide the public administration's purchasing processes

Proposals for action *(continued)*

– ***strengthening transparency and accountability***, allowing civil society to better track public ICT expenditures, reaping the full benefits of proactive ways to explore the Freedom of Information (FOI) Act.

17. **Consider the development of a public, single digital marketplace in Norway**, learning from other country experiences (e.g. Australia, United Kingdom). This kind of initiative is a strategic policy lever for an intelligent and sustainable ICT public procurement process, which supports the rationalisation of spending, encourages the re-use of solutions, embedding strategic approaches (e.g. open by default), creates space for collaboration and sharing across the administration (e.g. open source and codes sharing). Difi should be responsible for the development and management of this initiative.

From user-focused to user-driven service delivery in Norway

Key assessments

New technological trends like social media, mobile communication and other technology-enabled approaches, such as Open Government Data, allow more simple and direct interactions between citizens/businesses and the public sector. Used to top experiences in terms of usability and friendliness provided by main ICT providers like Google, Facebook, Amazon or Uber, citizens expect public service delivery to be in line with, and up to the level of, these general technological trends.

Citizens and companies expect public services to be designed and delivered in a simple and intuitive way, embedding a user-driven perspective, using life events approaches, re-using information previously provided, and being available in multi-platform alternatives. A proactive public administration is required to serve all users in an efficient, effective, integrated and coherent fashion.

This new digital service delivery culture also raises requisites in terms of security and privacy protection. In a digital world, in which citizens' and companies' data is probably one of the public sector's biggest assets, trust is the key that sustains government legitimacy to manage and take full advantage of this asset. However, a government that embraces new technologies, to be able to operate up to the level of sophistication of a digital economy and society, will have to adjust its approach to risk management. This will imply shifting from the expectation to be able to fully ensure security and privacy to being ready to negotiate an acceptable trade-off with users.

Integrating user preferences into the design of public services

The development of a user-centred public administration is not a new concept. On the contrary, it is a goal and a mindset found in the digital strategies of OECD member countries over the last two decades. However, integrating user preferences into the design of public sector processes requires new ways of reaching out, engaging and involving users in services' design and decision making ("engagement by design").

Moving from a user-centred to a user-driven perspective that places users (and their input) at the centre of public service delivery strategy is required across the whole public service process (e.g. prototyping, delivery-model selection, design, trial, implementation, feedback and redesign)

Several sectors of the Norwegian government have embarked on advanced digital service delivery approaches, aiming to increase user satisfaction. Numerous services available in the Altinn, Norway.no or MyHealth portals are good examples of an ambitious public service delivery commitment. However, there is a significant fragmentation of efforts and models, demonstrating that the public administration perspective is prevailing over a citizen perspective – this, letting aside the adoption of the even more advanced user-driven approach. When questioned about the users' involvement in the design of service delivery processes, most public sector stakeholders assumed that it was not a current practice in Norway. The same applies to the use of life event approaches to facilitate the user experience when interacting with public services.

In Norway, user input and feedback are relevant to measure user satisfaction (e.g. surveys), but not to inform or drive the design of public services. This seems to be leading, in general terms, to a government-centric culture and approach where citizens' needs are inferred and, as a result, not widely met.

A strong consensus was found concerning the need and usefulness to develop, implement and enforce the use of common reference models in terms of online accessibility and usability. Citizens (e.g. including specific population groups, such as the elderly, migrants and the disabled) and businesses would benefit from common design and standardised approaches for public websites. This approach could also be assumed as an opportunity to leapfrog some stages in terms of digital service delivery and to spread citizen-driven approaches across the public and private sectors. This would contribute to the overall and cross-sectoral digital services design policy of the Norwegian government, while decreasing learning curves, significantly increasing the efficiency and effectiveness of services, and improving the overall user experience.

Better integrating digital service delivery

Although countless developments related to improving online service delivery processes are common to OECD member countries, segmented or sector-specific approaches still seem to prevail. Public agencies appear to maintain their own portals, with their own navigation schemes, proper visual identity, specific authentication mechanisms and different usability experiences. A fragmented and, sometimes competitive, agency-specific approach is still more frequent than a citizen-centred or citizen-driven approach; and Norway is not an exception.

In Norway, existing sectoral online one-stop shops can already be considered a significant improvement for citizen interaction with the public sector. In addition, the mechanisms and level of sophistication of these platforms are evidence of Norway's long-time policy to improve public service delivery.

A strategy for a single "look and feel" and integrated channels' management should be further pursued in Norway

Citizens' needs and input could be further placed at the core of public sector priorities for the development of a public services strategy - beyond the citizen-centred policy discourse, thereby letting users drive advances in public service delivery. This integrated strategy, assumed by an existing public sector agency with a clear mandate and enough levers to achieve it (e.g. Difi), would also be an excellent opportunity to explore:

- a coherent use of ICT key enablers (e.g. eID, ePayment), in order to further improve the relationship with users and allow for substantial gains in terms of efficiency and effectiveness (e.g. Difi's ID-porten tool was developed to provide citizens with a co-ordinated/common login solution to public services[7] and reduce the burden that different eID systems impose on them)
- an ambitious and structured mobile digital government approach, reaping the full benefit of one of the highest levels of adoption of smartphones world wide
- an open and engaging approach in terms of public service design and delivery, involving different segments of citizens/service users and integrating their inputs and needs right from the start in the design of services.

Proposals for action

From user-centred to a citizen-driven public administration in Norway

In light of the key assessments exposed above, which draw on the main findings and analysis included in Chapter 4 of this review, the Norwegian government could consider implementing the following policy recommendations:

18. **Establish an integrated service delivery policy** within a new digital government strategy, as a policy instrument to reinforce the coherence, effectiveness and sustainability of the Norwegian public sector's efforts to deliver high-quality services to its economy and society. A Norwegian service delivery standard applicable to all Norwegian public websites, in line with the experience of New Zealand and the United Kingdom, should be developed, highlighting explicitly the following domains:
    - ***one-stop shop*** by default policy (known as "single point of entry"), prioritising the access to services for citizens and businesses through single platforms to increase users' convenience, favouring synergies in the delivery of public services
    - ***life events*** approach, assuring that services are always displayed and provided based on citizens' and businesses' everyday needs and according to life situations (e.g. having a child, losing and finding a job, creating a company)
    - ***multi-channel*** imperative, guaranteeing that services are provided in several digital formats (e.g. online platforms, mobile apps, kiosks, application programming interfaces [APIs]), but also using face-to-face or telephone channels
    - ***once-only principle***, as a mechanism to increase users' convenience and to promote the re-use of data and information across sectors and levels of government
    - ***user engagement and citizen-driven*** approaches, placing the users at the core of service design, development and delivery processes

Proposals for action *(continued)*

- ***common usability and "look and feel"*** standards, increasing the coherence and friendliness of users' interactions with public services.

19. **Establish a leadership and governance model for an integrated public service delivery policy**, reinforcing the mandate of the Ministry of Local Government and Modernisation (KMD) and Difi, and providing them with the necessary financial and human resources to fulfil this cross-government co-ordinating responsibility (see Recommendation 4).

20. **Consider developing Norway's role as promoter of cross-border services among Nordic and Baltic countries**, through the country's active support for the development of a common area for cross-border digital services in the public sector. For this, cross-border delivery should be increasingly assumed by Norwegian public services as a standard requisite in the delivery of new services, and the government should consider assuming a more active leadership of this item as a main priority of its agenda for Nordic-Baltic co-operation, as this could deliver value to Norwegian constituents as well as to citizens and businesses across the region.

Building a data-driven public sector in Norway

Key assessments

The relevance of digital technologies, which are increasingly becoming an integrated part of citizens' everyday lives and private sector's business models, is reinforced by the exponential progress in terms of production, storage, processing and sharing of data. In the digital era context, data has been assumed as a strategic commodity, and the public sector, while permeable, is struggling to react to, leverage, and capitalise on this current trend. Several OECD member countries are today developing data-driven approaches for the public sector and supporting enhanced data management processes to improve the design, delivery and impact of public services policies. The expectation is to be able to create an environment that will fully enable governments to capture the strategic value of government data as core vector for the digital transformation of their public sectors.

The opportunity faced today by governments around the world is to fully reap the benefits of data (i.e. produced, collected or commissioned by government institutions or non-governmental stakeholders) (Ubaldi, 2013) by developing policies and a governance framework for the public sector value chain that can boost data openness, interoperability, processing, exchange and re-use across all policy sectors and levels of government, and actors from the public, private and third sectors. These efforts and commitment can contribute to improving public sector intelligence, allowing for more informed policy making and policy implementation processes, citizen-driven approaches enabled by digital technologies and data, and data-driven economic development and business innovation.

Governing the public sector data value chain in Norway

Given the maturity of the digital environment across the Norwegian public sector, a considerable amount of data is already being collected and stored. A significant conscience seems to exist among public sector stakeholders concerning the potential this reality represents for improving organisational efficiency, foresight capacities to design better policies and services, to deliver public value and to monitor performance. This may lead to developing better service delivery mechanisms and boosting capacity to forecast and predict trends, supporting more proactive initiatives within the public sector.

However, the willingness to develop a data-driven public sector in Norway seems to be mostly more a long-term, forward-looking desire than a reality at the moment, despite the clear achievements of the Norwegian government in this domain (e.g. Difi's Information Governance model, standards and guidelines) and the availability of inter-institutional co-ordination mechanisms. Interesting examples of data exchange and re-use within the public sector can already be found (e.g. Altinn portal, MyHeath portal, Statistics Norway), but efforts are mostly running in parallel, reflecting a lack of system-thinking approaches and a stronger governance framework and leadership at the central level - supported by data stewardship at the institution level - that can reinforce and move forward the implementation of the public sector's digital transformation, as well as the management and governance of the public sector data value chain agenda.

The development of a data-driven public sector in Norway is an untapped opportunity, considering the high level of digitalisation of Norwegian society, economy and the public sector

The Norwegian public sector has developed a mature network of basic data registries, with clear definitions about who is responsible for each of the key tasks associated to the government data management, ownership and value chain.

This data infrastructure is supported by a mature legal and regulatory framework governing the management of the data value chain in the country where only some regulatory challenges prevail. However, the Norwegian government should ensure the availability of an adaptable and sustainable legal and regulatory framework for data governance in the long term.

The existence of clear institutional responsibilities in relation to the management of the registries, of which different public sector institutions, such as the Brønnøysund Register (the entity that manages several public registers) provide good examples, has set the perfect backbone and foundation for a solid governance to develop a data-driven public sector. In this sense, there's an urgent need to further exploit the untapped potential of basic public data registries in Norway and streamline data-sharing processes in order to advance progresses and further develop a data-driven public sector that is supported by automated and cross-sectoral data-sharing organisational models.

The big untapped opportunity: Open government data

Evidence from the OECD peer review mission to Oslo showed that open government data (OGD) as a driver of innovation, economic development, competitiveness and citizens' engagement is untapped in Norway. The need to develop an ambitious, structured and co-ordinated OGD policy is commonly recognised by Norwegian public and private sector stakeholders as a priority that should be better addressed. However, it seems that strategic action has been mainly driven by the implementation of

EU directives and not by clear internal objectives that link OGD to the achievement of national goals.

Despite the adoption of EU directives on public sector information, the availability of a national open government data portal, and numerous good examples of data re-use at the central and local level, an "open by default" data policy is still not being fully assumed as a clear priority by most central level actors. The business case for open government data should be further developed across public sector institutions in order to increase institutional buy-in.

In general terms, the Norwegian public sector remains as the absent player within the data ecosystem, despite its stated willingness to spur data-driven innovation, as included in the Digital Agenda. There is a strong need to reach, collaborate and engage with potential and current OGD users. An open government data ecosystem still needs to be fully developed with the active participation of ministries and agencies to boost data re-use, drawing upon closer collaboration with, and the engagement of, the broader community of data re-users (e.g. businesses, entrepreneurs, civil society organisations [CSOs]).

Some efforts are already in place pushing for a cultural change to encourage more proactive and forward-looking data management and openness in the public sector. Nevertheless, the current and most general commitment still seems to be primarily focused on making data publicly available, sometimes by charging fees. The role and participation of external data users in this context is unclear.

Further public sector efforts are required to respond to data-demand, promote data re-use and engage data users in order to draw upon OGD as an input to foster business innovation, competitiveness and economic development in Norway

More than assuming open government data as an isolated or even autonomous policy issue to be addressed on its own, clearer linkages should be established with ongoing efforts related to data governance and management (e.g. data catalogue for the public sector), as part of the overarching goal to advance the digital transformation of the public sector. Further synergies can be found once an open-by-default policy is fully assumed as a ruling principle in the general management of public sector data and information.

Solid synergies should be established between the open government data efforts underway and the priorities and sense of opportunity identified in the development of a data-driven public sector, capable of leveraging big datasets already managed by the government to create and co-create public value.

Open government data should be assumed, at the political and policy-making level, as part of a broader data-driven public sector policy, a building block of the overall digital transformation of the public sector, and a driver of the digital economy in Norway

Developing data skills for a trustworthy data-driven public sector

There is a clear alignment between the goals of the digital agenda and the willingness of public sector institutions to capitalise on the availability of new technologies (e.g. data analytics, big data) to design data-driven policy solutions and public services, but a stronger skills base should be built for this purpose.

Taking the Norwegian public sector to the next level with regard to the use of new technologies for data management and re-use would also require building the right skills and competencies across public sector institutions

The development of a data-driven public sector in Norway should also focus on the fundamental need to build and maintain citizens' trust. The government should sustain and mobilise its best efforts to demonstrate that citizens' data is, and will remain, securely managed, deeply respecting principles on data protection and personal privacy.

Following several OECD member country experiences, one of the best ways to improve public confidence in this area is to establish mechanisms that can allow citizens to access their personal data held by the public sector, and to know at any time who within the public sector is accessing it and for what purpose. At the same time, there is a need to establish co-shared responsibility mechanisms between government and citizens to ensure that citizens also take ownership of, and control how they share, their data, and with whom.

Proposals for action

Building a data-driven public sector in Norway

In light of the key assessments exposed above, which draw on the main findings and analysis included in Chapter 5 of this review, the Norwegian government could consider implementing the following policy recommendations:

21. **Develop a formal strategy for the management and governance of the public data value chain, placing it at the core of the proposed digital government strategy. This would connect all components of the data value chain, including open government data for the achievement of strategic goals around priority policy areas.** Both strategies should be clear sub-components of the Digital Agenda in order to avoid the propagation of isolated, not connected, and fragmented policy documents. As part of the development of a formal strategy for public data management and governance, the Norwegian government could consider the following actions:
    - The development of an overarching data governance strategy would benefit from using Difi's Information Governance (IG) model as the starting basis. It is necessary to connect the current efforts on information and data management (e.g. Difi's information management model) to open government data and data-driven public sector initiatives under a whole-of-government data governance strategy for the public sector.

Proposals for action *(continued)*

– The data strategy would integrate the development of digital skills among public officials for the construction of a smart government as mid- and long-term policy goals.

– Involving all stakeholders at all levels and using the OGD portal as a consultation mechanism would be beneficial to design an inclusive and comprehensive data strategy, taking into consideration and reflecting the needs of all actors involved in the ecosystem, including actors from the public, private and social sectors.

22. **Strengthen the institutional governance framework to support the implementation of the proposed data strategy and achieve national and supranational goals.** The instrumental and technical support role of Difi, and the contributions of the SKATE and the Norwegian Data Protection Agency (Datatilsynet) have helped to rule, find consensus and co-ordinate the current policy goals defined by the KMD. Yet, while some of the responsibilities of chief data officers (CDOs) across OECD countries are currently part of Difi's mandate, or shared between Difi and the KMD, the specific and dynamic role of a CDO is absent in Norway. It is also not clear if, beyond the strategic use of registries, there is a common vision and leadership for data management and governance in Norway (e.g. including specific policy areas such as open government data). As part of the development of a formal strategy for the management and governance of public data, the Norwegian government could consider the following actions:

– ***Consider the creation of a formal CDO office that co-ordinates with, and responds to, the proposed GCIO's office. The role and mandate of Difi could be strengthened in this regard in order to ensure that the agency evolve to a dynamic driver of data-driven innovation within the Norwegian public sector as an operational way to achieve the objectives set by the digital government strategy, in which case the CDO role could be established within Difi.***

– ***Use the CDO office as a*** **de facto** ***or formal data-driven innovation lab*** and bring in entrepreneurs, academics, and other actors when needed to crowdsource ideas and jointly solve policy challenges in collaboration with public sector institutions, while continuing to build in-house capacities through Difi.

– ***Strengthen the availability of data stewards*** across the public sector: A data-driven public sector requires bringing in or identifying data champions that can help take Norway to a higher level of sophistication of a data-driven public sector and connect overarching policies to technical matters (such as the relevance of data catalogues). Leverage the role of the public sector and attract and retain talent.

23. **Keep investing resources to ensure that the legal and regulatory framework in the country is aligned with the goals of the Digital Agenda, such as open government data, the 2016 Digitalisation Memorandum, and with key digital government principles such as the once-only principle and open by default.** This would contribute to reducing the current limitations for public sector institutions to share and re-use data, thereby contributing to the construction of a data-driven public sector, providing support to the ambitious goals of the Digital Agenda, leveraging regional efforts in the Nordic area, and support the implementation of public sector data and information-related EU directives. To do so:

– ***The creation of an administrative simplification taskforce (led by KMD's relevant bodies) in charge of carrying out or commanding an in-depth assessment of the current legal and regulatory framework affecting data governance and management in the country, and streamlining data-sharing processes within the Norwegian public sector.*** Actions should be taken to perform a regulatory assessment and administrative simplification exercise mapping existing data-sharing practices among government institutions, beyond sectors to break down silos and agency-level solutions, streamline existing practices and enable a more efficient public sector data-

Proposals for action *(continued)*

sharing model. These actions could be gradual: sector-specific measures could be taken to address regulatory and simplification challenges within policy areas in the short run with the long-term objective of developing automated inter-sectoral data-sharing practices whenever possible.

- ***In the long term, the creation of a permanent regulatory oversight body within the KMD could be considered, with the responsibility to monitor and perform ex post regulatory assessments related to data governance, digital government and the digital transformation of the public sector***. Strengthening the governance of digital government in Norway requires the availability of regulatory control bodies and mechanisms that ensure the continuous monitoring of the regulatory environment for digital government, therefore securing the readiness and adaptability of the regulatory framework in relation to digital disruption.

- ***Sustaining the use of sunsetting practices for those primary laws and regulations with an impact on data management and governance, and on digital government overall***, would contribute to ensuring the sustainability of a favourable regulatory environment for the digital transformation of the public sector in Norway.

Specific policy recommendations to improve the governance and management of the public sector data value chain include:

- ***Data security: New risks require new technological responses for risk management.*** The Norwegian government, through the KMD and Difi, could further explore the benefits of these technologies as part of the upcoming digital agendas in the country, highlighting the importance of citizens' awareness and co-responsibility in the responsible management of their own data.

- ***Registries: Connecting open data efforts with other data-sharing efforts across the public sector*** would contribute to breaking down data silos and enable further organisational efficiency inside the public sector as well as data re-use by external actors. These actions should be aligned with the needs of the actors for quality data. Therefore it is necessary to ensure that data is discoverable, understandable and interoperable. This would require: 1) running a centralised and one-stop data access portal (e.g. leveraging the OGD portal, data.norge.no) as the default indirect access portal connected to the institutional and/or sectoral access portals for the registries; 2) making the registries available as open data whenever feasible; and 3) ensuring the provision of the necessary metadata, standardised semantics and APIs by default.

Moving open government data policies and initiatives forward in Norway

24. **Defining and co-creating a formal open data strategy (part of the data governance and management strategy) in collaboration with private, public and third-sector actors** is necessary to take open data to the next level and achieve specific policy goals of the Norwegian Digital Agenda related to economic development and business innovation. Yet open data should be understood as an inter-connected and not isolated element of the whole data governance strategy. Further:

    - ***The strategy requires defining a clear roadmap for open data and key delivery milestones beyond the responsibilities defined in the 2016 Digitalisation Memorandum***. Ensuring the participation of Difi as the instrumental arm of the policy, and involving other leading public sector actors, such as the Norwegian Mapping registry, in the early policy development stages is crucial to ensure the alignment of the strategy with current and future policy goals.

    - ***Use organisational efficiency as the main driver supporting the development of OGD initiatives at the agency level.*** Open data is not a priority for public sector institutions because the benefits are not clear. It is necessary to strengthen the business case for open data among ministries and agencies in order to build a common vision under the leadership of the CDO. Open government data should

Proposals for action *(continued)*

be understood as a tool to contribute to organisational efficiency at the agency level in order to increase buy-in among agencies for the development of open data initiatives. Scaling up initiatives such as the "hack4no" initiative in order to build greater take-up and involvement by other public sector actors would contribute in this respect.

- ***Develop a formal open data infrastructure for the country, drawing upon the current data categories identified by the Norwegian government as a priority for publication*** (government spending, geodata (in line with EU directives), transport, research, and culture data. However, the development of the open data infrastructure should take into consideration the inputs of current and potential data users; therefore, the infrastructure should be developed as the result of a consultation process.
- ***Move from the current reactive approach to data publication - such the use of FOI requests to inform and prioritise the publication of OGD - to a more dynamic, proactive and user-driven publication***. The implementation of consultation exercises at the sectoral level is necessary to ensure the sustainability and impact of open data efforts in Norway. It is necessary to exploit the potential of the OGD portal as a consultation and collaboration platform.
- ***Link the open data policy to broader policy areas, such as public procurement, to support the use of open data as a driver of more accountable and transparent public procurement processes***. The publication of open contracting data in a standardised fashion and across the whole public procurement process would also contribute to using data to strengthen institutional and social knowledge in relation to public procurement processes. Ensuring that the data available on Norway's public procurement portal, doffin.no, is published as open data would ease the access and analysis of open data pools of public contractors and the analysis of procurement results by auditing bodies, by public entities to spot opportunities for more strategic approaches to the commissioning of ICT services across the administration., and by social actors for public accountability purposes.

Setting the basics: Skills and competencies for a data-driven public sector

25. **Define a roadmap for the development of a data-driven public sector as a core element of the digital government strategy and as a backbone for the overall public data governance and management strategy in Norway**. To do so:
    - ***capitalise on the synergies resulting from the willingness of the central government to explore the use of data science and big data as drivers of public sector efficiency and the opportunities that public sector institutions see for the development of data-driven services and foresight activities, and explore the contribution of the private sector in this respect*** (e.g. procurement and private provision of cloud-based or data analytics services)
    - ***formalise strategic partnerships with universities and other actors in order to develop skills inside public sector institutions for open data and a data-driven public sector, and link these initiatives with the overall strategic actions to attract skilled human resources for digital government*** (see Chapter 3).

Notes

1. In the 2016 edition of the *eGovernment Benchmark*, Norway integrates the Mature Cluster, side by side with Denmark, Finland, Iceland, Netherlands and Sweden. This group of countries has the "highest level of penetration and a high level of digitisation, displaying a successful process of innovation, making it possible to exploit the opportunities offered by ICT. The Mature Cluster also achieves quite a high level of satisfaction, showing a market-oriented approach that succeeds in meeting users' needs. Use of eGovernment services and online interaction with governments in these countries might be the most mature in Europe, but are not close to 100%. Similarly, there is still more that can be done to digitise the internal processes and harmonise both between government tiers as well as across borders." (European Commission, 2016)
2. In the 2016 edition of the *United Nations E-Government Survey*, Norway ranks 18th world wide (United Nations, 2016).
3. For more information, see www.difi.no/fagomrader-og-tjenester/digitalisering-og-samordning/digitaliseringsradet.
4. For more information, see www.difi.no/fagomrader-og-tjenester/digitalisering-og-samordning/medfinansiering-av-digitaliseringsprosjekt.
5. For more information, see www.regjeringen.no/no/dokumenter/digitaliseringsrundskrivet/id2522147/.
6. For more information, see www.regjeringen.no/no/dokumenter/digitaliseringsrundskrivet/id2462793/#kap3.1.
7. For more information, see http://eid.difi.no/en/id-porten.

References

European Commission (2017), "Digital Economy and Society Index 2017: Norway", Digital Single Market, https://ec.europa.eu/digital-single-market/en/scoreboard/norway.

European Commission (2016), *eGovernment Benchmark 2016*, European Commission, Brussels, http://ec.europa.eu/newsroom/dae/document.cfm?action=display&doc_id=17855.

KMD (Ministry of Local Government and Modernisation) (2016), "Digital Agenda for Norway in brief: ICT for a simpler everyday life and increased productivity", English version, KMD, www.regjeringen.no/en/dokumenter/digital-agenda-for-norway-in-brief/id2499897/sec1.

Mickoleit, A. (2014) "Social media use by governments: A policy primer to discuss trends, identify policy opportunities and guide decision makers", *OECD Working Papers on Public Governance*, No. 26, OECD Publishing, Paris, http://dx.doi.org/10.1787/5jxrcmghmk0s-en.

OECD (2017), *Government at a Glance 2017*, OECD Publishing, Paris, http://dx.doi.org/10.1787/gov_glance-2017-en.

OECD (2016), "Executive Summary", in *OECD Economic Surveys: Norway 2016*, OECD Publishing, Paris, http://dx.doi.org/10.1787/eco_surveys-nor-2016-3-en.

OECD (2014), "Recommendation of the Council on Digital Government Strategies", OECD, Paris, www.oecd.org/gov/digital-government/recommendation-on-digital-government-strategies.htm.

Ubaldi, B. (2013), "Open government data: Towards empirical analysis of open government data initiatives", *OECD Working Papers on Public Governance*, No. 22, OECD Publishing, Paris, http://dx.doi.org/10.1787/5k46bj4f03s7-en.

United Nations (2016), *United Nations E-Government Survey 2016*, UN, New York, https://publicadministration.un.org/egovkb/Portals/egovkb/Documents/un/2016-Survey/Executive%20Summary.pdf.

Further reading

OECD (2016), *Digital Government in Chile: Strengthening the Institutional and Governance Framework*, OECD Digital Government Studies, OECD Publishing, Paris, http://dx.doi.org/10.1787/9789264258013-en.

OECD (2016), *Open Government Data Review of Mexico: Data Reuse for Public Sector Impact and Innovation*, OECD Digital Government Studies, OECD Publishing, Paris, http://dx.doi.org/10.1787/9789264259270-en.

OECD (2016), "OECD Digital Government Toolkit", www.oecd.org/governance/digital-government/toolkit/.

OECD (2015), *Open Government Data Review of Poland: Unlocking the Value of Government Data*, OECD Digital Government Studies, OECD Publishing, Paris, http://dx.doi.org/10.1787/9789264241787-en.

OECD (2005), *OECD e-Government Studies: Norway 2005*, OECD Publishing, Paris, http://dx.doi.org/10.1787/9789264010680-en.

Chapter 1

On the path to digital transformation in Norway

This chapter discusses the evolution from e-government to digital government in Norway since 2005, when the OECD published the OECD e-Government study of Norway. It highlights the path the Norwegian government has followed in terms of the governance for digital government in the country. It also underlines the main social, economic and policy context driving the digital transformation of the public sector in Norway, and the potential contribution of digital technologies for the achievement of national and supranational policy goals.

Background: The 2005 e-Government study of Norway

In 2005, at the request of the former Norwegian Ministry of Modernisation, the OECD launched the e-Government study of Norway (OECD, 2005a). Among other topics, the study focused on assessing the governance, policy, technical and legal environment related to e-government in the country. It drew upon specific policy goals that, at the time, were a priority for Norway, such as fully reaping the potential benefits of information and communication technologies (ICTs) for public sector modernisation leading to greater organisational efficiency, and improved delivery of public services.

The review stated that, by 2005, the strong interest of the Norwegian government to develop an information society played a catalyst that underpinned e-government in the country. The Norwegian e-government policy was the government's response to an increasingly inter-connected society and high levels of Internet penetration. By 2005, roughly 67.5% of individuals in Norway had home-based Internet access, above the OECD average at the time (40.95%) (OECD, 2005b). The implementation of modernisation strategies was the *sine qua non* of the Norwegian government's actions to leverage ICTs as tools for economic and social development. Public sector reform and decentralisation policies drove e-government initiatives in the country.

When published, the 2005 review highlighted Norway's key achievements on e-government at the time (OECD, 2005a):

- Forward-looking e-government strategies, which were influenced by European directives, were the result of the visionary work of the central government in regard to the strategic use of ICTs within public sector institutions. In addition, the development of a favourable regulatory environment was a lever for the implementation of e-government initiatives (e.g. Norway's strong organisational culture for public sector efficiency favoured the implementation of administrative and legislative simplification measures).
- The use of the Internet for government modernisation focused on using ICTs as a driver of organisational efficiency and inter-institutional data-sharing activities. The advancements on the use on ICTs for back-office activities set precursory building blocks to draw upon these achievements as the counter stone to further improve front- and back-office services and processes, and design online solutions for service delivery (e.g. citizens and businesses one-stop shop portals) (see Chapter 4).
- Strategies to develop ICT-related skills among citizens and public officials triggered the availability of an "information technology (IT) qualified workforce" within public sector institutions, improved "business skills and competences", and promoted "IT education in schools".

The 2005 review also identified systemic challenges and opportunities which, after 12 years (2017) and in some instances, are still relevant:

- Increasing the use of Norway's basic registries by ministries and agencies was needed to design more efficient services for citizens and spur inter-institutional collaboration. Scaling-up existent inter-agency data standardisation and interoperability efforts were highlighted as necessary to define and implement overarching e-government initiatives, but this lack of interoperability was also a barrier to, indeed, spur this collaboration.

- Vertical governance models called for the need to strengthen inter-institutional co-ordination. The quick adoption of ICTs by some agencies resulted in dispersed and unbalanced levels of technological capacities across the public sector, particularly among agencies. The latter led to a silo approach where "more or less autonomous agencies have used ICTs to support their own internal organisational efficiency." The exchange within the public sector of knowledge on e-government took a bottom-up approach were ICT-capable, strong and independent agencies shared such knowledge with ministries, and not the opposite.
- There was an asymmetry between the central systemic vision and/or understanding about e-government, and the agency-specific translation of such a vision "into concrete plans". This scenario drove change among some agencies, but in some cases ministries and agencies struggled to fully discern how central e-government strategies had to be translated within the context of their institutional goals.
- While IT-skill development programmes supported the availability of an IT-qualified workforce (e.g. capable of using computational software), project management skills were needed inside agencies. Competencies for ICT projects' management were "unevenly diffused" across public bodies, in particular among agencies. Public sector institutions also lacked the experience to develop business cases for ICT projects.
- A government-wide framework to monitor and assess the impact of e-government initiatives was not available. Inter-institutional sharing and mutual learning (e.g. from best practices and failure) was needed to build systemic knowledge of measurement frameworks (e.g. return on investment and cost-benefit analysis).
- The potential of ICT-driven citizen engagement and consultation activities (e-engagement) was not fully exploited. Efforts to engage citizens were limited, thereby affecting a more citizen-centred design of public services, and the better understanding of citizens' needs and demands. When implemented, engagement efforts focused on getting input from individuals, but the needs and demands of businesses were rarely taken into account. Public-private partnerships were not yet fully exploited by ministries and agencies.

The scenario above was framed within the context of a decentralised and consensus-based public sector where the "central government had played a limited role in developing its ICT use" (OECD, 2005a). The guiding role of key ministries and/or agencies was needed to align efforts across the public sector. A more active approach by the central government was also required in order to overcome and go beyond its limited regulatory and policy-making role.

As a result of the assessment above, the OECD Secretariat provided a set of key policy recommendations to help the Norwegian government advance its e-government agenda over the course of the following years (see Box 1.1).

Box 1.1. 2005 OECD e-Government study of Norway: Key policy recommendations

The following recommendations from the 2005 e-Government study of Norway centred on the following three key areas:[1]

Governance and leadership

- Clarifying policy co-ordination and decision-making responsibilities was necessary to increase institutional awareness and institutional support and buy-in for the implementation of a government-wide, consensus-based and non-partisan approach to e-government.
- Definition and dissemination of clear and measurable goals and implementation guidance under a clear institutional leadership was necessary to help ministries and agencies to implement and translate government-wide goals into specific actions.
- The role of the Norwegian Ministry of Finance was perceived of particular strategic relevance in order to 1) use the budget cycle as a lever to spur the development of aligned e-government strategies at the agency level; and 2) help agencies to better understand the benefits of developing business cases for ICT investments.

Public sector intelligence

- Knowledge-sharing was necessary to tackle silos and address isolated intra-agency innovation clusters through the implementation of knowledge-sharing instruments. This, in order to enable the government-wide construction of public sector intelligence.
- Spurring horizontal co-operation and inter-institutional collaboration was needed to guide and prioritise the investments on skills' development activities for e-government, drawing upon the knowledge and capacities already available among specific Norwegian trend-setter agencies.

Public service delivery and user satisfaction

- Improving citizens' experience (as end users of public services) required further consulting and engaging them by default (proactively) and by design (as a core element of e-government strategies' design). These activities had the objective of better identifying citizens' demands *a priori* in order to design (or re-engineer) public services with a more user-focused approach.
- It was equally necessary to "better align and integrate back-office operations and systems (e.g. data sharing and interoperability) with front-office delivery" in order to build a more efficient public service delivery, spur user satisfaction, and improve users' experience.

1. For further information, see OECD (2005c), "Assessment and Proposals for Action", in *OECD e-Government Studies: Norway 2005*, OECD Publishing, Paris, http://dx.doi.org/10.1787/9789264010680-2-en.

Source: OECD (2005a), *OECD e-Government Studies: Norway 2005*, OECD Publishing, Paris, http://dx.doi.org/10.1787/9789264010680-en.

Driving the digital transformation of the Norwegian public sector

Technology has evolved since the above-mentioned study was carried out and its recommendations were published. The fast-paced development of digital technologies has brought new opportunities for governments, businesses and citizens around the globe. In 12 years (2005-17), technological development triggered social media networking and the availability of smart mobile telephony. Facebook and Twitter were launched in 2004 and 2006 respectively. Apple's iPhone was first introduced in 2007 - disrupting traditional mobile technology, giving birth to the app market, permanently affecting the interaction between humans and mobile devices, and having a permanent impact on people's lives.

The so called "digital era" underpinned and democratised the use of inter-connected online services, drawing upon the availability of new web-based technologies such as cloud computing, artificial intelligence, block chain and the Internet of Things (IoT). This has all taken place within the context of an increasingly networked society - a society that places knowledge building and sharing at the core of social and economic development (OECD, forthcoming).

Numeracy and literacy have been, are, and will remain, basic requirements to ensure social inclusiveness and economic development. Yet, in line with the principles of the OECD Recommendation on Digital Government Strategies (OECD, 2014a), digital skills and competencies are needed to ensure that all segments of the population such as the elderly, migrants and students can benefit from technological evolution and digital public services. Fighting the expansion of technology-driven digital exclusion and social inequality is needed to reduce capacity gaps among population groups.

The technological evolution is also a force driving the sustainable and continuous digital transformation of the public sector (see Figure 1.1). Public sector institutions' achievements in e-government - mainly focused on improving public sector efficiency and productivity drawing upon the opportunities brought by the Internet to back-office processes, and one-way service delivery. This laid the foundations for digital government. Nevertheless, evolving from e-government to digital government will require a complete paradigm shift in the way technology is understood by politicians, policy makers, public managers and public officials.

Figure 1.1. **The digital transformation of the public sector**

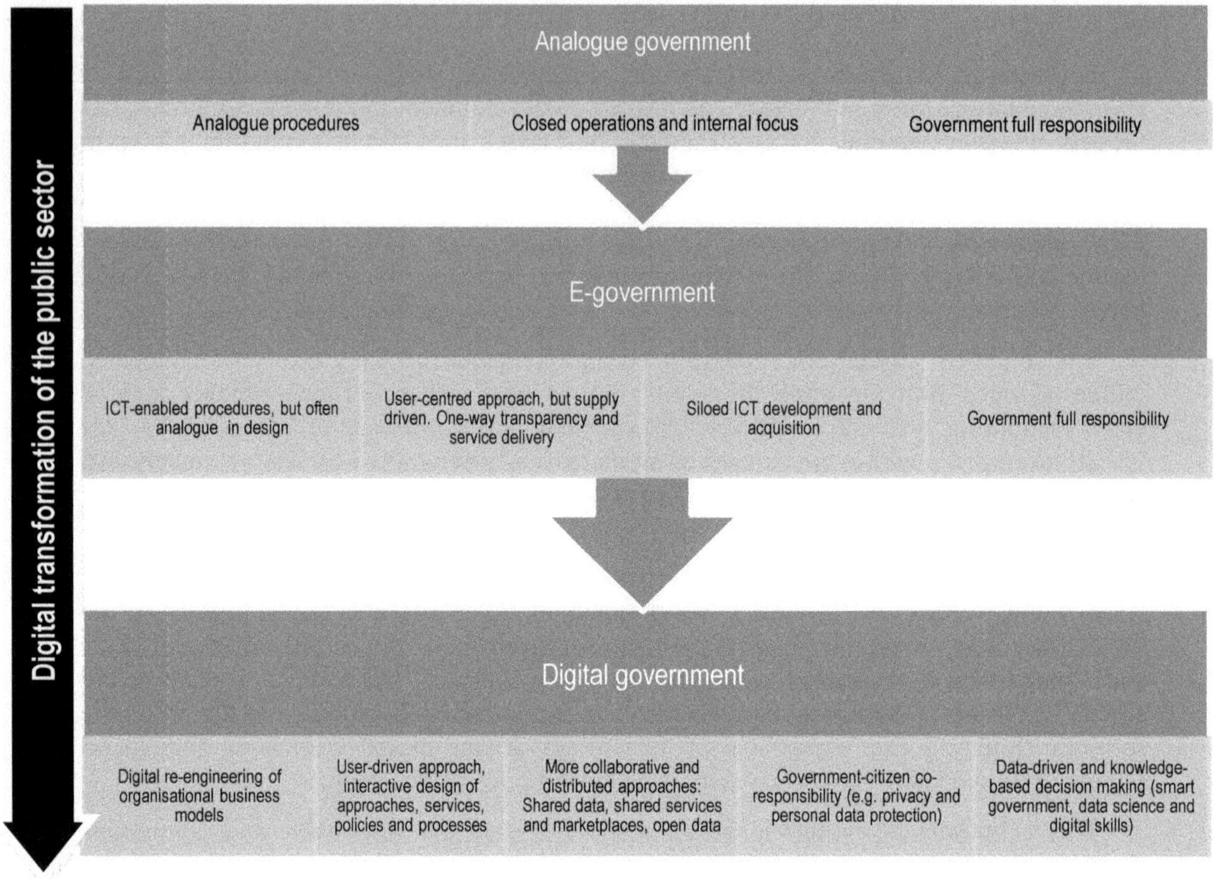

Source: OECD (forthcoming), "The digital transformation of the public sector: Helping governments respond to the needs of networked societies", *OECD Working Papers on Public Governance*, OECD Publishing, Paris.

Digital government goes beyond citizen-centred public services, back-office improvements and one-stop-shop portals. It calls for the design of dynamic, open and inclusive services and processes, enabled by technology, that supports a digital two-way communication and engagement with all actors of the digital government ecosystem (e.g. citizens and businesses).

Given the context described above, the Norwegian government faces the challenge of reacting to fast-paced technological changes, while drawing upon earlier achievements on e-government development. Moreover, digitalising the Norwegian public sector, in a structured and system-based fashion, is necessary to better respond to the needs of Norwegian citizens and businesses that are emerging in a context of a rapid digital transformation of the economy and society.

The Norwegian government should remain open to changes occurring in the broader economic and social environments from different perspectives. On the one hand, it should be open in order to reach, consult and engage citizens and businesses and crowdsource ideas and input from these external actors, which might influence the shaping of citizen-driven public services and policies. This openness spurs transparency, accountability and inclusiveness of public services and policies.

On the other hand, the Norwegian public sector should also remain open to technological developments in order to spot opportunities that can drive change, public sector innovation and the continuous digital transformation of the public sector. For instance, public bodies in countries like Argentina, Mexico, Singapore and the United States are already using "chatbots" to better respond to citizens' enquiries or to better communicate with public sector officials. These practices result from the work of skilled, visionary and engaging public sector institutions that embrace technology and use it for their benefit. Norway has put in place a good set of key enablers for digital government (i.e. an electronic identification system [eID], basic registries, one-stop portals) that create an ideal context to help Norway advance its developments as a leader in digital transformation among OECD countries.

The broad Norwegian context for digital government – including the overall governance framework, as well as the policy, social and economic environments - has evolved since 2005. However, as previously mentioned, evidence from the OECD mission to Oslo in 2016 indicates and corroborates that some of the long-term challenges identified in 2005 are still present within the public sector. These challenges (e.g. siloed approach, lack of horizontal co-operation between policy sectors) are somehow the result of a traditional and well-established organisational model of the public sector (see Chapter 2) - a model that, in general terms, is largely based on decentralisation, sector-oriented strategies, and the strong independence of agencies. Whereas this model did not impede important advances on e-government, more emphasis on co-ordination and collaborative models, sharing and integration, as well as system-based approaches appear pivotal for an efficient evolution towards a digital government era. As a result of the current situation, in some specific cases (e.g. open government data) the Norwegian government has not participated as an active actor within the open data ecosystem, missing out on the opportunity to make the most of collaborations with digitalised society and economy to respond to the needs of its businesses and citizens.

There is an urgent need to go beyond the mere adoption of emerging technologies by ministries and agencies (e-government approach). This requires the reform and transformation of organisational business models within the Norwegian public sector, therefore confronting inherited legacy systems (from a technical and an organisational perspective) that may obstruct this evolution. Balancing the well-established agency and sectoral-oriented organisational culture with system-oriented and citizen-driven organisational thinking is imperative to establish a governance environment that favours the design and implementation of a digital agenda that supports the digital transformation of the public sector. In this line, it would be necessary to overhaul systems and structures within the public sector apparatus (digital government approach), thereby defining a stronger basis to drive the digital transformation of public sector institutions.

Making the most of a privileged context: The business case for strategic action in Norway

The Norwegian government faces the challenge of triggering change within a wealthy and stable national context. Crises (e.g. economic, social, natural and political) are, in some instances, the ultimate driver of change. Yet, despite the occurrence of some major national safety issues in past years in Norway, these events have not affected its overall stability. They have, however, contributed to the availability of risk-adverse institutions that, in some cases, may resist experimenting and exploring new collaborative and innovative alternatives to improve well-established organisational models, therefore hindering the digital transformation of the public sector. Taking Norway's public sector to the next level in regard to digitalisation will imply overcoming such risk aversion and embracing technological change.

In Norway, a sense of urgency to transform the public sector should come from within the government apparatus. Such proactive change should be, however, perceived as an opportunity to better serve Norwegian citizens and businesses (the outcome), and not as a mere mechanism to improve long-time established organisational models (the processes). It should not come as a threat, either, to the positive traits of the status quo, i.e. an efficient and productive public sector.

Norway has a vibrant economy and an equalitarian, skilled and inter-connected society. On the one hand, Norway's fixed broadband penetration rates have remained above the OECD average since first measured by the OECD in 2003. Alongside this scenario, the expansion of the penetration and use of Internet-connected mobile devices opened a window of opportunity for the Norwegian government to make public services accessible to citizens and businesses anywhere and anytime (see Figure 1.2). On the other hand, Norway has one of the highest shares of adults among OECD countries with moderate ICT-related and problem-solving skills (OECD, 2015a), which illustrates medium-to-high levels of digital literacy in the country (see Figure 1.3).

Figure 1.2. **Fixed and mobile broadband penetration rates in Norway, 2003-16**

Subscriptions per 100 inhabitants

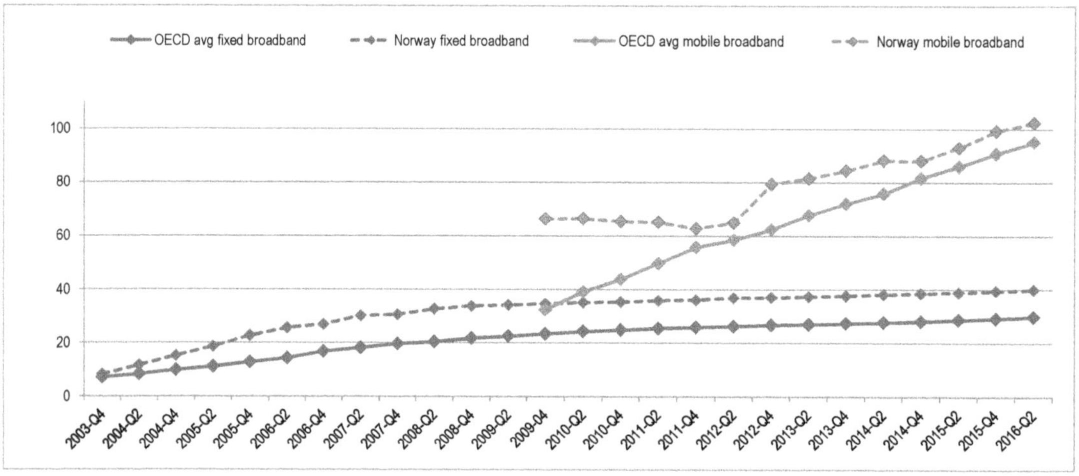

Note: Data for mobile broadband penetration rates only available from 2009.

Source: OECD (2017a), "Fixed and wireless broadband subscriptions per 100 inhabitants", *OECD Broadband Portal* (database), www.oecd.org/sti/broadband/oecdbroadbandportal.htm.

Figure 1.3. **Adults with good ICT-related and problem-solving skills, by educational attainment in Norway and selected countries, 2012**

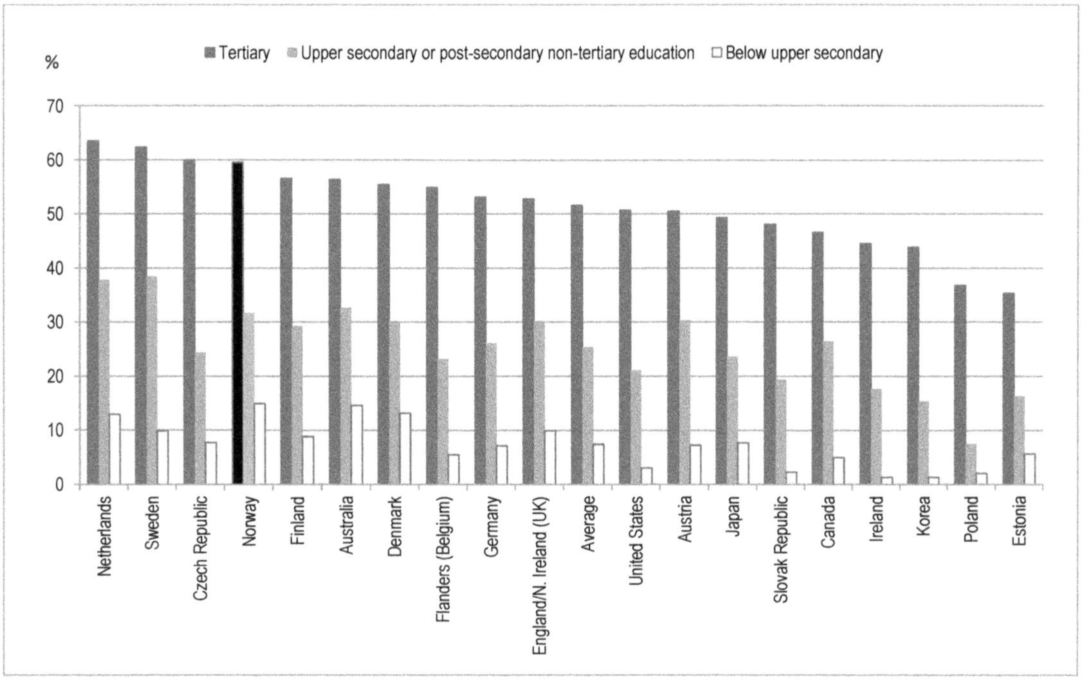

Source: OECD (2015b), *Education at a Glance 2015: OECD Indicators*, OECD Publishing, Paris, http://dx.doi.org/10.1787/eag-2015-en.

Given the above-mentioned indicators, Norway is partial to an inter-connected and ICT-skilled ecosystem ideal to spur business innovation and civic tech. Such a context is not common to all OECD countries and Norway should capitalise and leverage it to advance the digital transformation of its public sector.

Norway leads the OECD Better Life Index, which benchmarks 24 well-being indicators aggregated into 11 composite measures (e.g. housing, income, work-life balance) that reflect the 11 dimensions used by the OECD to measure well-being (OECD, 2015c) (see Figure 1.4). Employment rates for Norwegian citizens aged 15-64 years (73.9% by 2017) and workers aged 55-64 (72.2% by 2015) are also well above the OECD average (OECD, 2015d) (see Figure 1.5). Pension reforms and the good management and use of oil revenues have also ensured the well-being of the elderly (OECD, 2014b). These indicators illustrate the relatively high levels of social well-being, but also support the business case for sustaining current government efforts to implement digital inclusion policies for the elderly (see Chapter 2).

Figure 1.4. **OECD Better Life Index, 2016**

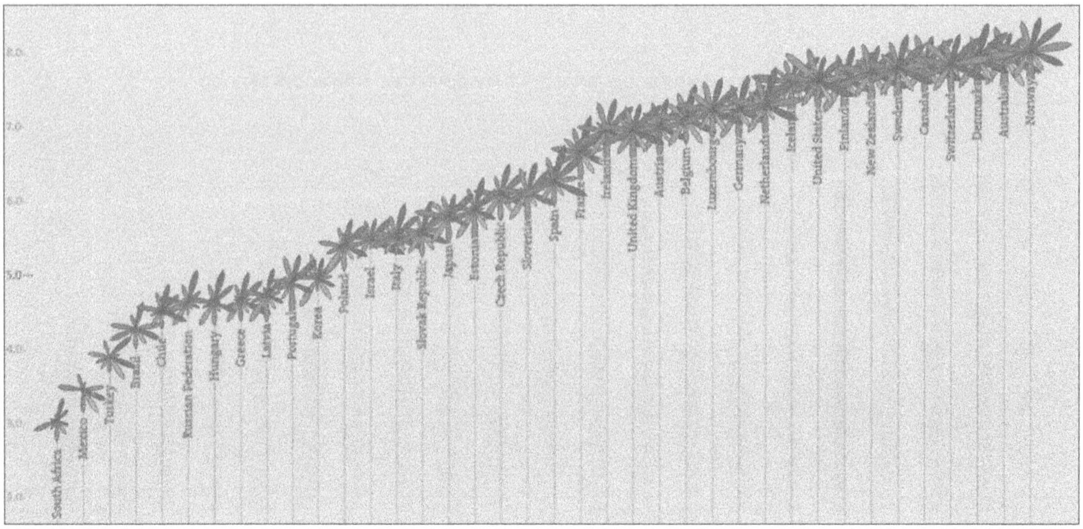

Source: OECD (2016a), OECD Better Life Index, www.oecdbetterlifeindex.org.

Figure 1.5. **Employment rates in Norway**

A. Population aged 15-64 years in % of working-age population, 2014-16

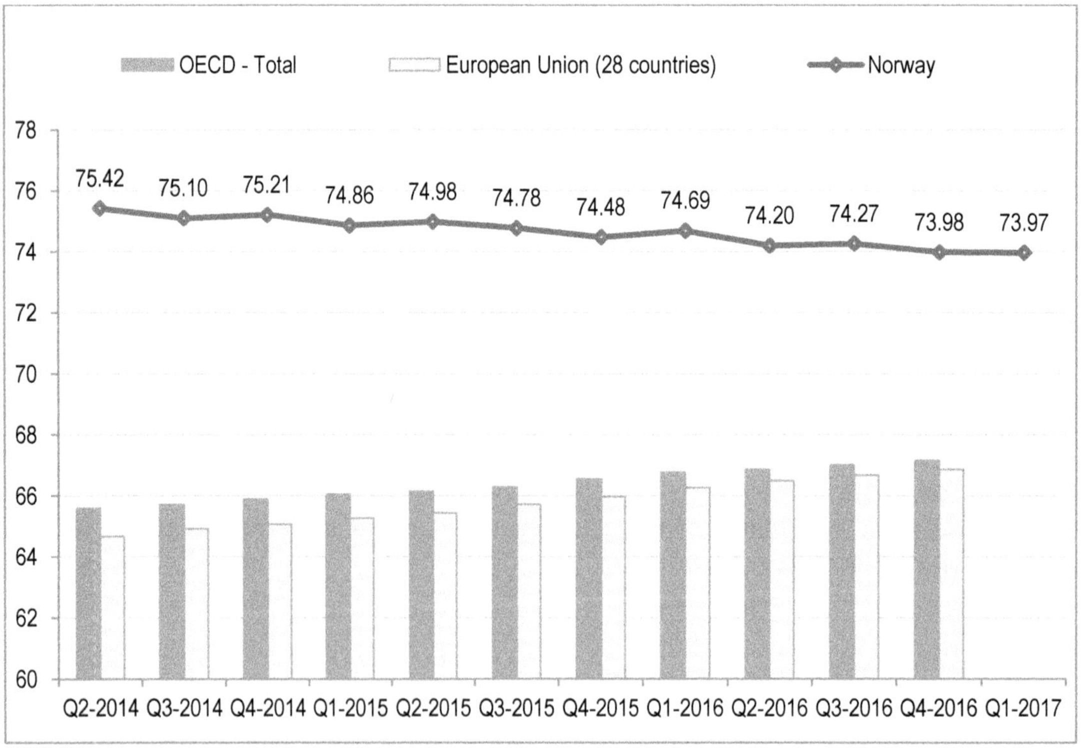

Source: OECD (2017b), "Short-Term Labour Market Statistics", *OECD.Stat* (database), http://stats.oecd.org/index.aspx?r=149175.

Figure 1.5. **Employment rates in Norway** *(continued)*

B. Population aged 55-64 and 65-69 years in % of the age group, 2005-15

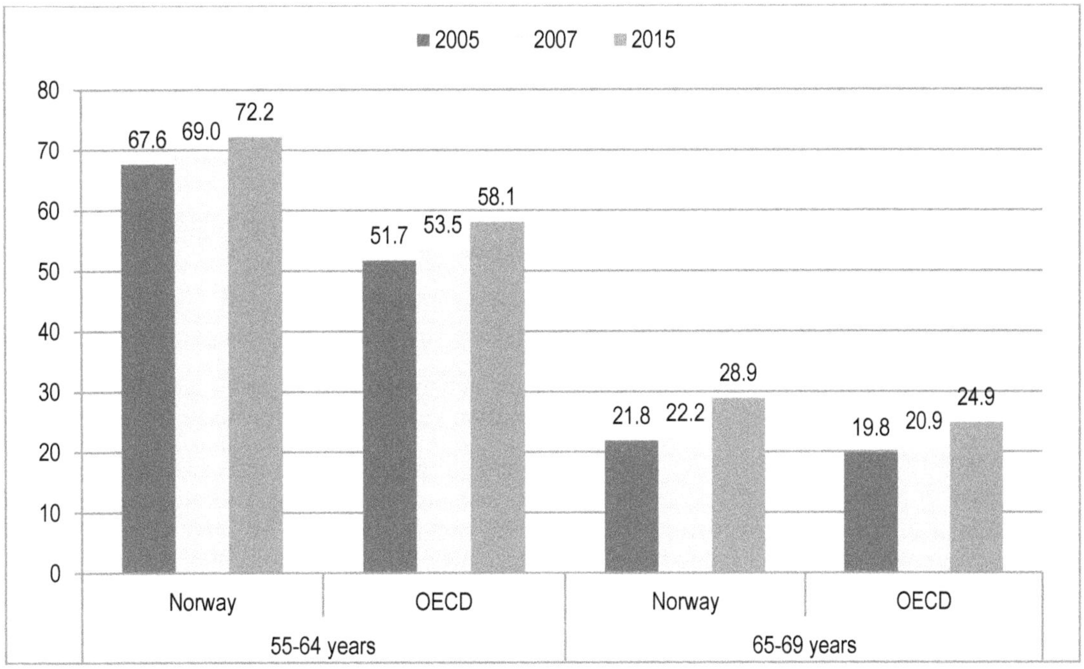

Source: OECD estimations based on data from the *OECD Employment Database*, the *OECD Earnings Distribution Database*, the *OECD Education Database* and the *OECD Survey of Adult Skills (PIAAC)*. Data available at www.oecd.org/employment/ageingandemploymentpolicies.htm.

The richness of the country, due to the availability of natural resources like oil, has enabled Norway to cope with the global economic crisis in a relatively stable fashion. However, the strong dependence of the Norwegian economy on oil revenues, and the reduction of oil prices since 2014 may give rise to the need to further develop and incentivise the mainland economy (OECD, 2016b). At the same time, the current approach of the Norwegian government to leveraging the green economy (e.g. by incrementally implementing policies focusing on reducing the pressure on natural resources for economic growth) should be taken an as opportunity to draw upon digitalisation as a tool to achieve Norway's goals in this domain.

In Norway, the digital transformation of the public sector should be understood by politicians and policy makers as a key element of long-term policies aiming to boost national and public sector productivity, civic tech (e.g. ICT-driven citizens' participation in public service design and decision making), business innovation, and sustainable green growth (see Box 1.2). It would be the government's awaited response to the needs and demands of a skilled society and a demanding private sector, just as e-government policies were to Internet penetration 12 years ago.

Box 1.2. *OECD Economic Survey of Norway 2016*: Highlights

- Norway has very high material living standards and scores well on other aspects of well-being, thanks to a mix of natural resources wealth, good policy making and inclusive and egalitarian social values, including active efforts to break down barriers to women's careers. However, the substantial oil-price falls since 2014 have been a reminder of Norway's exposure to external risks and consequently the importance of a flexible and competitive mainland economy.
- Norway lost some competitive edge in the past 10-15 years and trend productivity growth has been slowing. Improving the framework conditions to address these issues is key.
- Given the wide range of public services assigned to counties and municipalities in Norway, it is important that sub-national governments are assisted and encouraged to improve efficiency and quality.
- Reforms that enhance skills are also important for economic success and social well-being. Further improvements to both compulsory and tertiary education in terms of quality and efficiency are essential.
- Past OECD Economic Surveys have underscored that Norway has room for greater private provision in the supply of public services (for instance through outsourcing) including in areas such as health and education and through larger private contributions to the financing of such services. Systems for increasing private provision need to be carefully designed, for instance to control the quality of services provided.
- Going forward, the structure of Norwegian economic activity will most likely shift away from petroleum-related activities. Domestic oil production is already declining and opportunities for exploration activity (both domestically and globally) will trend downwards as the number of likely locations for new economically viable reserves diminishes.
- There are already long-established non-oil sectors, such as shipping and energy-intensive activities that tap into Norway's substantial sources of hydropower (for instance, aluminium smelting and fertiliser production). However, given the diversity of activities, and risks predicting which sectors will flourish in the future, ensuring supportive conditions and competitive environments for all forms of business activity needs to be a core theme of policy.

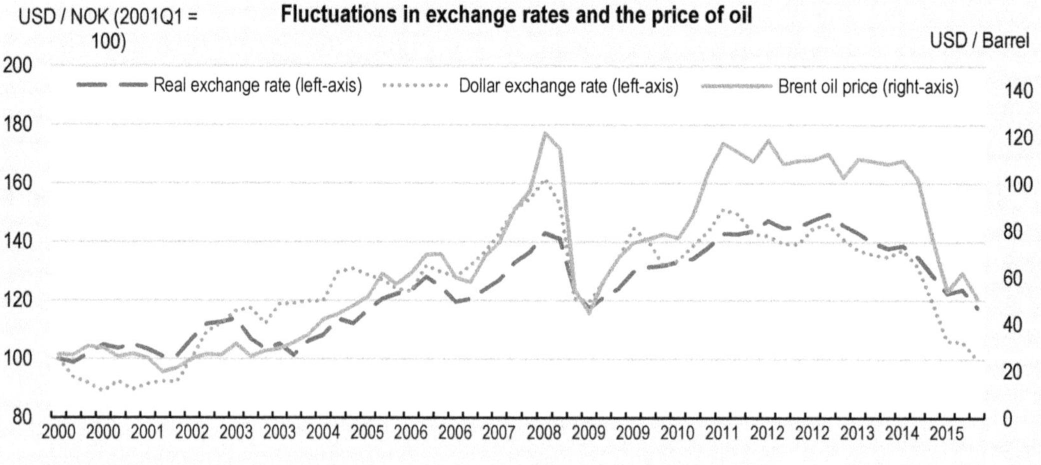

Source: Text and data from OECD (2016b), "Executive Summary", in *OECD Economic Surveys: Norway 2016*, OECD Publishing, Paris, http://dx.doi.org/10.1787/eco_surveys-nor-2016-3-en.

Cross-national co-operation: The Nordic regional agenda for digitalisation

Encouraging international co-operation in the context of digital government is in line with Principle 8 of the OECD Recommendation of the Council on Digital Government Strategies, which highlights the importance of strengthening international collaboration to better serve citizens and businesses across different borders, drawing upon the contribution of digital technologies for such a purpose (OECD, 2014a).

In line with the above, the urgency of transforming the public sector in Norway is also driven by supranational agreements and cross-national policy goals. The strong and close collaboration and common agenda between Norway and other Nordic and Baltic countries (Åland, Denmark, Estonia, Finland, Faroe Islands, Greenland, Iceland Latvia, Lithuania and Sweden) exert influence on Norway's policy ambitions at the national level. Cross-border collaboration fora such as the Nordic Council and the Nordic Council of Ministers have been put in place between Nordic countries precisely to facilitate and underpin co-operation between these countries around common policy objectives and shared challenges.

The Nordic-Baltic Ministerial Conference on Digitalisation held in Oslo (24-25 April 2017) provided evidence on how digitalisation matters have become a priority for Nordic and Baltic governments - therefore reaching the political sphere. Ministers from these countries agreed on the urgency to further invest efforts to spur digitalisation as a mechanism to better serve their constituencies. The joint Ministerial Declaration, which resulted from such cross-national compromise, mirrors these priorities. It provides a set of specific measures that should be implemented by central governments in order to contribute to the full digitalisation of the society, business activity and government operations. These measures centre on three specific areas (Ministry of Local Government and Modernisation [KMD], 2017):

- The digital transformation of Nordic and Baltic governments and societies, which would contribute to the design of cross-border digital services (e.g. through cross-national and shared eID services, and free cross-national data flows). The potential to further enable cross-national shared services and processes such as electronic identification and cross-border business registers was underlined by some Norwegian ministries and agencies through the OECD survey. This approach is in line with previous bi-national work of the OECD in the region that explored the potential for cross-border services in Estonia and Finland (OECD, 2015e).
- Strengthening business competitiveness (e.g. implementation of ICT-skill building programmes in co-operation with academic institutions, the development of a versatile regulatory framework that supports business innovation and entrepreneurship).
- Enhancing the digital single market in the region (e.g. exchange of best practices in areas relevant to digitalisation such as the sharing economy and data-driven innovation).

The Ministerial Declaration scaled up the goals of other parallel Nordic programmes already in place. For instance:

1. The Nordic Co-operation Programme for Regional Development and Planning 2017-20 highlights three areas of co-operation between Nordic countries (Nordic Council of Ministers [NCM], 2017): sustainable rural development; innovative

and resilient regions; and sustainable cities and urban development. The inclusion of key domains related to digital transformation in the programme (e.g. skills development, social innovation and smart cities) stresses the business case for the digitalisation of the public sector in Norway.

2. The 2014-17 Nordic Co-operation Programme for Innovation and Business Policy addresses public sector digitalisation issues. The programme, which centres on four subjects, includes five specific initiatives (called "lighting house projects") that aim to contribute to the achievement of the goals of each cross-national co-operation subject (see Figure 1.6). Each Nordic country has the responsibility of leading at least one lighting house project. For instance, Norway and Sweden are responsible for exploring the development of multi-stakeholder innovative welfare solutions (see Box 1.3) and the contribution of public procurement for such a purpose (NCM, 2014).

Figure 1.6. **Nordic Co-operation Programme for Innovation and Business Policy 2014-17: Areas of work and lighting projects**

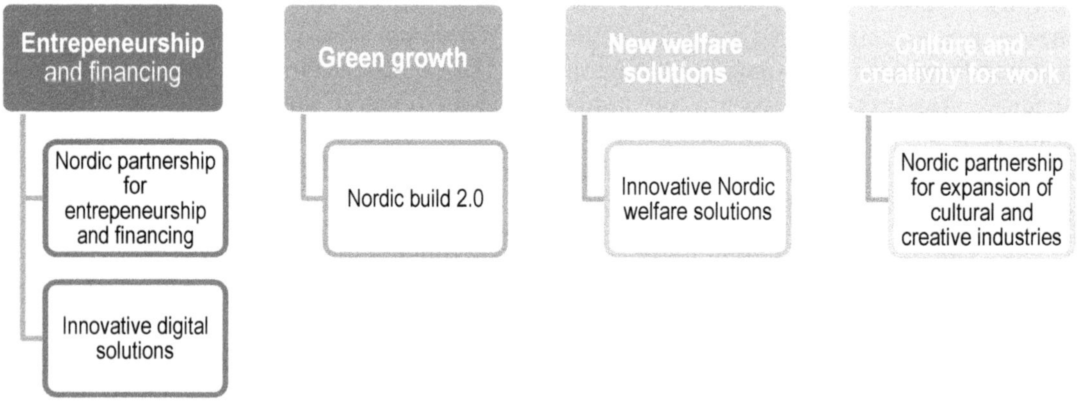

Source: Author, based on information from NCM (Nordic Council of Ministers) (2014), "Nordic Co-operation Programme for Innovation and Business Policy 2014-17", NCM, http://norden.diva-portal.org/smash/get/diva2:740766/FULLTEXT01.pdf.

Box 1.3. **Using digital technologies to transform public services in welfare areas**

Today, only a modest number of OECD member countries have digital government strategies that cover large welfare areas, education, healthcare, and social care and protection. Many factors account for this relatively low number of digital government strategies to date, including the limited role of the public sector in the actual delivery of services in some countries, and the division of responsibilities horizontally, across sectors, or vertically, across levels of government in all countries. However, as seen in those Nordic countries in which the state has a strong co-ordinating role, it is important to establish adequate co-ordination across policy sector areas to align digital transformation of public welfare services.

This alignment implies increasing use of public and private collaboration, and an increased focus on the growth of ecosystems to extend the public value chain beyond the limits of the public sector. Encouraged, for example by actors such as the European Union, some countries with open economies are seeing that cross-border services can help them reduce labour market rigidities, and they are analysing and prioritising the cross-border services that add the most value. This development also includes directly improving public welfare services, for example, by sharing services across countries and re-using existing public sector developed digital solutions, such as the joint "education cloud" applied in a cross-border collaboration between Estonia and Finland.

Closely related to the challenge of achieving alignment across the whole of government is the issue of pooling supply and demand. Where Nordic societies remain very well-connected by international standards, reliable high-speed connectivity can still be a barrier for some real-time data consuming digital welfare, even though most services can be developed and implemented within existing broadband limits. Maintaining strong links between supply and demand across the whole of government can help encourage the development of more fair business cases related to infrastructure investments, for example in high-speed broadband. Infrastructure investments require particular attention in the development of the underlying business cases.

As more services can and are being shared as digital offerings across the public sector, such joint solutions help reduce costs and redundancy across the government. Achieving these benefits, however, requires clear national leadership to, for instance, clarify the organisational parts of business cases, such as how joint services are developed, operated, financed, etc. This cross-governmental institutional need is clearly emerging, partly as a centralisation of existing tasks, and partly as a joint development of new emerging services, transforming public administration, service production and service delivery.

Source: Text from OECD (2016c), *OECD Comparative Study Digital Government Strategies for Transforming Public Services in the Welfare Areas*, OECD, www.oecd.org/gov/digital-government/Digital-Government-Strategies-Welfare-Service.pdf.

Analogue organisational models can't respond to a digitalised society in the same fashion a digitalised public sector would (OECD, forthcoming). While the main focus of the Nordic Co-operation Programme for Innovation is private sector and not public sector innovation, the role of Nordic public sectors is clear due to their responsibility to develop and implement digitalisation policies that would respond to businesses and societal demands in a collaborative and regional fashion. By doing so, Nordic countries, including Norway, would contribute to spurring Nordic innovation and competitiveness across the overall economy and society. For instance, by making public services more efficient through private-public co-operation agreements (as explored by Norway and Sweden), and contributing to business entrepreneurship and developing innovative solutions to address public, social and private sector challenges by sharing government data in machine-readable and open formats.

The Nordic Council of Ministers created Nordic Innovation (NI) as the body in charge of supporting and advising the implementation of the Nordic Co-operation Programme for Innovation and Business Policy 2014-17. As a result, Nordic Innovation[1] has centred its work on three streams (NI, 2017):

- **Electronic identification (Nordic eId)**: This stream is led by Norway's Agency for Public Management and eGovernment (Difi) and it explores and assesses the challenges of cross-border use of national electronic identification tools in the Nordic region (see Chapter 4).,
- **Smart government**: This stream, led by Danish Business Authority and Nordic Innovation, explores the improvement of cross-national and inter-institutional data sharing and data collection practices between and by public sector institutions in the Nordic region. The overall goal is to improve the innovation and business climate across Nordic countries. Automated data collection practices (e.g. through improved IT infrastructure and the use of innovative technologies) are explored as part of this stream's work in order to reduce data provision burdens on businesses.
- **Data-driven innovation**: Centring on data re-use by non-governmental actors and multi-stakeholder collaboration, this stream aims to spur business and social innovative solutions and co-create public value. The re-use and mash-up of data from multiple national open databases in the Nordic region, and the development of tools that can be used to address common regional challenges are key elements of this stream (NI, 2016) (see Chapter 5).

Co-operation with other regions, such as Europe (e.g. within the framework of the European Economic Area, EEA) and the Baltic countries will remain highly relevant to fully reap the benefits of digitalisation for the public sector and the Norwegian and Nordic populations. This would contribute to address common policy challenges. At the same time, it would contribute to lever Nordic countries' current efforts in areas such as open government data resulting from the implementation of the revised European Directive on the re-use of public sector information, thereby building a stronger basis in light of new European data protection regulations impacting areas such as cross-border data sharing and personal data protection,2 and the current European efforts to spur the Electronic Exchange of Social Security Information (EESSI project).

Understanding the evolution of the governance for digital government in Norway: 2005-17

Governance arrangements around digital government policies have changed in Norway since 2005. In 2004, the creation of the now extinct Ministry of Modernisation (MOD) contributed to addressing ICT and e-government policy co-ordination and leadership issues, as signalled by the OECD Secretariat at the time (OECD, 2005a). These governance issues were the result of overlapping policy co-ordination roles between the former Ministry of Labour and Government Administration (AAD) and the former Ministry of Trade and Industry (NHD). By centralising policy co-ordination and e-government responsibilities under the responsibilities of the former MOD, the central government succeeded in addressing leadership and policy co-ordination issues and fragmented responsibilities between these ministries, as highlighted by the OECD in 2005. The MOD itself went through different stages, becoming the Ministry of Government Administration and Reform in 2006, and then the Ministry of Government Administration, Reform and Church Affairs (FAD) in 2010.

In 2014, the Norwegian government decided to integrate the former FAD with the former Ministry of Local Government and Regional Development (KRD). This decision gave birth to the current governance for digital government in Norway, led by the Ministry of Local Government and Modernisation (KMD) (See Chapter 2).

Currently (2017), the KMD and its subordinate agency, the Agency for Public Management and eGovernment (Difi), play a key role in the definition, co-ordination and implementation of the Digital Agenda in Norway:

- **The Ministry of Local Government and Modernisation (KMD)** has the role and responsibility to modernise the Norwegian public sector, and define and implement the national ICT policy,[2] centring, for instance, on public sector reform and the increased use of ICTs by society. KMD defines policy guidelines within the framework set by the Norwegian government.
- **The Agency for Public Management and eGovernment (Difi)**: KMD oversees the functions and activities of Difi, which plays a key advisory, audit and technical role regarding public sector modernisation and digital government in Norway.

The advisory role of the government: From Statskonsult to Difi

Difi itself has gone through different stages of its governance arrangements, which was the result of changes in political decisions and policy priorities over time. Understanding the evolution of this body is useful to better comprehend the current governance context for digital government in Norway.

The creation of Difi in 2007 set this agency's responsibilities in the domain of ICT and digital government. Difi is the result of the fusion of three public sector agencies:

- the former Statskonsult (which for a brief period of time functioned as a stated-owned limited liability company), a public sector body which had the role of providing strategic guidance to ministries and agencies on matters of public management, including the strategic use of ICTs
- Norway.no (the still-functioning Norwegian citizens' portal, created in 2000)
- the Norwegian eProcurement Secretariat.

Of the above-mentioned bodies, the case of Statskonsult (in particular, its evolution from a public sector institution to a state-owned company in 2004) was widely discussed throughout the 2005 OECD e-Government study of Norway .

In 2005, the OECD Secretariat concluded that while morphing Statskonsult into a state-owned company was in line with the central government's market-oriented policies, this reform also diluted the advisory role of the agency, and represented a loss of institutional memory for the government (OECD, 2005a). This rose concerns about the overall impact that such a reform would have on the government's capacity to provide strategic guidance to ministries and agencies, identify technological trends, and foresee the strategic use of these opportunities with a government-wide approach. For a brief period of time (2005-07), public sector institutions had the option of seeking - and paying for - advice either from Statskonsult or private sector firms.

The institutional reform that took place in 2007 (which included the creation of Difi as a subordinated agency of the KMD) returned the above-mentioned advisory capacities to the central government. By doing so, the Norwegian government aimed to address issues related to the government's capacity to guide and support ministries and agencies during the definition and implementation of ICT projects. This helped set government-wide building blocks for the digital transformation of the public sector in a more structured fashion, in line with the objectives of the e-government policy at the time.

This being said, challenges remain at the policy implementation level, in particular, due to Difi's lack of levers to ensure – or enforce - a more structured policy implementation approach within a consensus-based, decentralised and highly vertical public sector. This public sector context often creates implementation silos and sector-oriented actions, slows down the adoption of co-ordinated decisions, and hinders the use of central standards and guidelines by public sector institutions and local governments.

As discussed in depth in Chapter 2, the Norwegian government faces the challenge of finding an effective governance model in order to increase Difi's empowerment to achieve its goals and mandate within a consensus-based and sector-oriented government apparatus, particularly as the government wishes to advance its digital transformation agenda. This is of strategic relevance in light of decision-making processes that appear to be in some cases slower than necessary – affecting in particular joint decision making with local governments (e.g. development of common standards), as mentioned by Norwegian public officials during the OECD mission to Oslo.

From the previous eNorway plans to the current Norwegian Digital Agenda

Norway has been forward-looking for over a decade as the government has constantly prioritised the development and implementation of policies oriented towards the achievement of goals related to digital government. Earlier e-government strategies such as the former eNorway plans aimed to leverage the potential technology for greater public sector efficiency to bring the government closer to citizens. The eNorway plans recognised the benefits of technology beyond the public sector, e.g. underlining the need to ensure greater public access to ICTs, develop digital skills and literacy among different segments of the population, increase digital inclusion, and spur economic development and business innovation.

Despite changing political priorities, the above-mentioned key policy goals have remained practically unchanged, therefore ensuring the continuity and resilience of ICT-related policy goals and political commitment through different government administrations. With time these goals have evolved into broader *de facto* principles that govern the design and implementation of digital government strategies. Results from the OECD survey confirm that according to most ministries and agencies, there is relatively stable political support dating 10-12 years back in time, when earlier digital strategies (e.g. eNorway plans) were first put in place (2005-17).

Norway's current central administration (in power since 2013) is not the exception. Norway's coalition government has also paid particular attention to technology and the opportunities it offers to achieve the key objectives included in the political agenda (Politisk plattform) (see Figure 1.7). By highlighting the potential of ICTs for business competitiveness, 24-hour public sector and the availability of good quality, accessible and inclusive welfare, health and safety public services, the central government granted political support to the ICT and digital government agenda, making it a priority in the short and medium terms.

Figure 1.7. **Norway's political agenda 2013 (Politisk plattform): Key priorities**

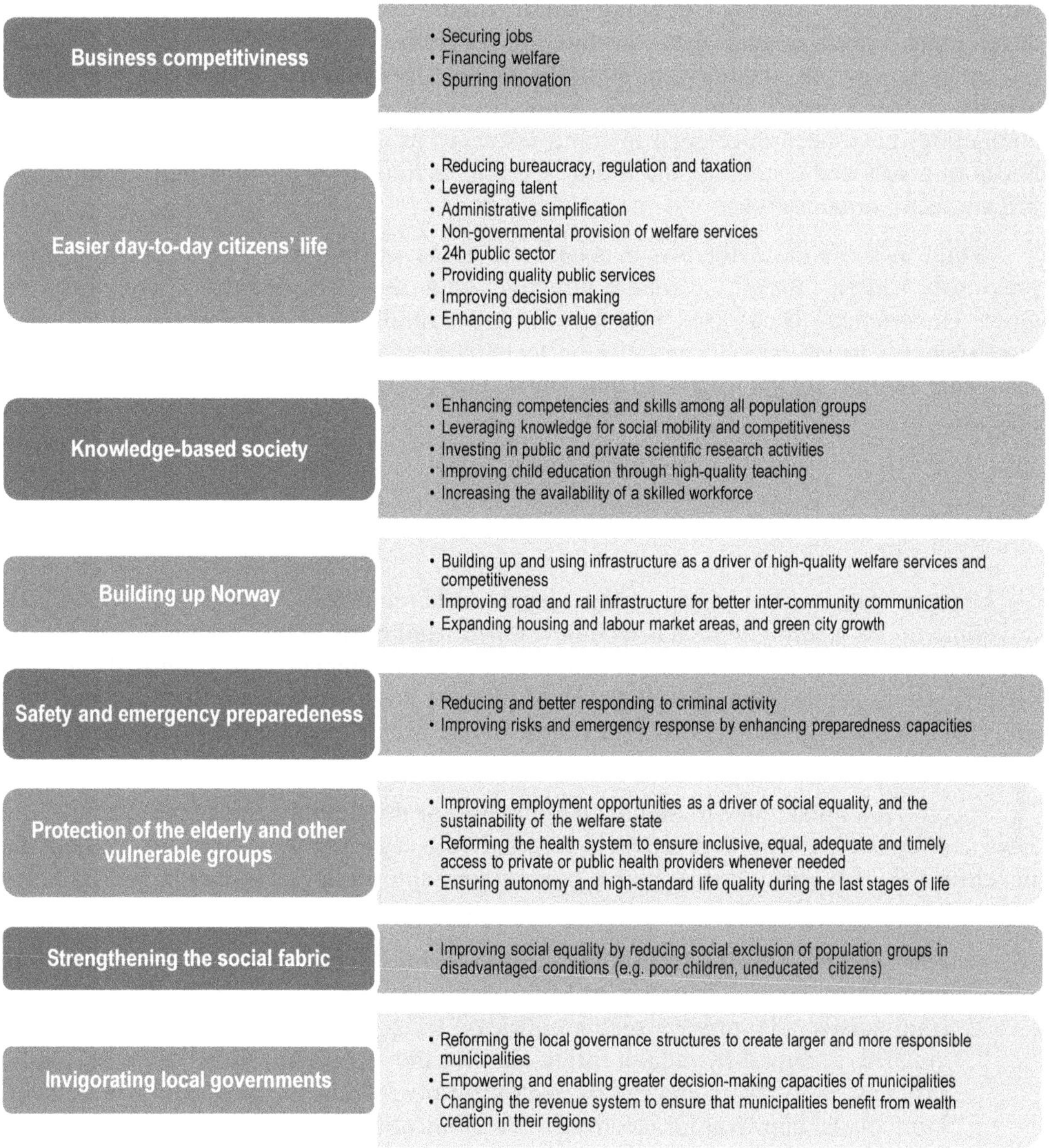

Source: Author, with information from Norway's 2013 Politisk plattform, available at www.regjeringen.no/no/dokumenter/politisk-plattform/id743014//.

The current government's Digital Agenda for Norway (also known as the "White Paper") reflects the government's political priorities and is expected to contribute to their achievement, and grounds the overall mission and objectives on digital government of the current central administration. The agenda has the Parliament's support, thereby contributing to it sustainability and resilience across changes of government.

The White Paper, published in 2016, established a set of five policy priorities for the upcoming years (KMD, 2016) including the strategic goals such as the digitisation (digitalisation) of the public sector, economic development, and digital inclusion (see Chapter 2). The objectives of the White Paper manifest KMD's openness to transform the public sector in Norway, drawing upon digital evolution. Global technological developments such as open data, the Internet of Things, block chain, mobile and smart government, and the data-driven digital economy have clearly influenced the digital agenda of the country. Topic-specific strategies with cross-sectoral impact (e.g. cloud computing) have been developed in some instances as a result of the willingness of the KMD to assess and encourage the use of specific technologies by Norwegian public and private sector organisations.

While in some cases there is a need to leverage institutional efforts drawing upon previously and/or currently available directives (e.g. the 2012 and 2017 Guidelines on Open Government Data) (see Chapter 5), the overall challenge for the Norwegian government is to effectively capitalise on technological development in order to achieve the goals of the Digital Agenda, and avoid the fragmentation of efforts during this process.

The progression of the legal and regulatory framework for digital government in Norway

Norway can count on a mature legal and regulatory framework for digital government. As a result of such a well-developed legal basis, it has been possible for the Norwegian government to define and implement e-government and, eventually, digital government initiatives since the 1990s. Most of these laws have been influenced by a vast array of European Directives in areas such as electronic signature, the publication of public sector information, and intelligent transport systems.

Specific laws that relate to digital government - or the amendments applied to specific laws and regulations that rendered them relevant with regard to the digital era – reflect the development of Norway concerning e-government and digital government policies (see Figure 1.8), namely:

- **1967 Public Administration Act (Forvaltningsloven)**: Regulates administrative procedures in and between public sector institutions and with private actors (individuals and private sector entities). In 2013, an amendment to the law enabled a digital-by-default principle for the communication between public officials, individuals and public sector entities.[3] As a result of this amendment, individuals' approval for electronic communication is no longer required. Instead, individuals (if desired) can opt out from electronic communication with public sector entities. As confirmed by public sector officials during the OECD mission to Oslo in 2016, this approach draws upon a similar model implemented by the Danish Government ("digital first" approach).
- **1999 Public Procurement Act (Anskaffelsesloven)** (superseded): Defined the relevance of public procurement as a mean to build public trust in public sector institutions. With a focus on accountability and efficient expenditure, the act also mandated the Ministry of Fisheries and Industry to publish regulations on e-

Invoicing. The 1999 act was superseded by the **2016 Public Procurement Act (Anskaffelsesloven)**.

- **2000 Act on Personal Data (Personopplysningsloven)**: Legislates the protection of privacy and citizens' personal data by Norwegian authorities. Among other mandates, it defines citizens' rights to be informed on requests to access their private information held by government authorities and sets legal mandates on cross-border personal data transfers. Additional legal mandates and penalties related to privacy protection and confidentiality breaches are also available in the **2005 Norwegian Penal Code (Straffeloven)**.
- **2001 Electronic Signature Act (eSignaturloven)**: This act established a set of rules for the development of e-signature systems and its use by individuals, granting equal legal value to electronic signatures in relation to traditional signatures.
- **2003 Electronic Communications Act (eSignaturloven)**: With a focus on the provision of - and citizens' rights to - access quality ICTs services, it aims to set a fair competitive environment for private sector provision of services, which can contribute to spurring business and social innovation. It aims to ensure equal access to affordable services, thereby contributing to digital inclusion in Norway.
- **2006 Freedom of Information Act (Offentleglova):** This act sets mandates on citizens' rights to request, access and re-use public sector information, and the obligation of public sector institutions to publish the latter on digital formats that can be processed through electronic means (e.g. open government data).

Figure 1.8. **Main legal framework for digital government in Norway, 2017**

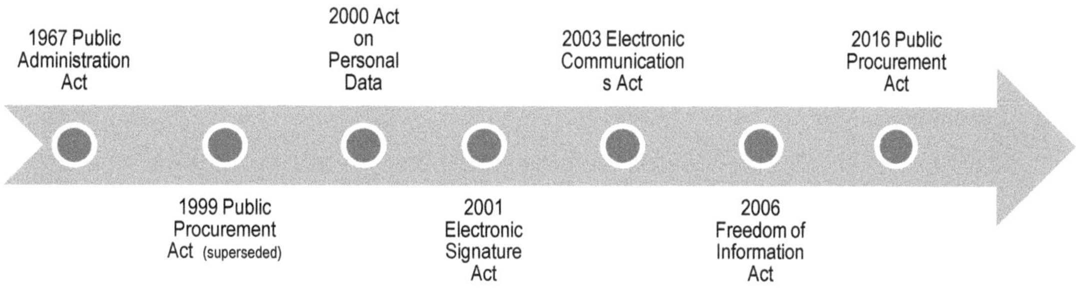

Source: Author, based on available legislation.

Other sector or domain-specific legislation with direct links to digital transformation include the **2015 Intelligent Transport Systems (ITS) Act**. The 2015 ITS Act draws upon the potential of digital technologies for the development of coherent and interoperable intelligent transport services and platforms (e.g. mobile applications). The ITS Act reflects on the European Directive for the Deployment of Intelligent Transport Systems (2010/40/EU) and responds to the well-known fast-paced developments on citizens' urban mobility that have disrupted the industry in recent years.

As a result of the above-mentioned legal evolution, ministries and agencies have published overarching or sector-specific legal instruments that complement the overall regulatory context for digital government in Norway. These include legal instruments regulating the basic registries and geospatial data (the latter, in line with European standards) (see Chapter 5), and other regulations such as the:

- 2003 Regulations on the Use of Information and Communication Technologies
- 2004 Regulations on Electronic Communication with and within the Public Administration (eForaltningsforskriften)
- 2013 Regulations on IT Standards within the Public Administration
- 2013 Regulations on Universal Design (see Box 1.4)
- 2014 Regulations on the Loan Fund's Access to Public Sector Information
- 2015 Regulations on ICT Standards in Health Care.

Box 1.4. **Universal design: Norway's approach to inclusive services in the digital era**

In 2013, the former Ministry of Government Administration, Reform and Church Affairs (FAD) (a now extinct ministry that, together with the former Ministry of Local Government and Regional Development [KRD], preceded the KMD) published the Regulations on the Universal Design of Information and Communication Technology Solutions (UDRs). The UDRs centred on the premise that universal design, in the context of ICTs, requires designing or adapting [transforming] ICT-based solutions to democratise its use by as many people as possible, and contribute to the overall regulatory framework for universal design developed, based on the 2013 Discrimination and Accessibility Act's legal mandates (Government of Norway, 2013a).

These regulations are focused on the inclusive delivery of public services through digital means. Therefore, acting as a regulatory mechanism that sets an accessible-by-default principle for the public sector (accessibility for everyone is the rule) in order to:

1. transform the conception of new ICT-based public services, making them **accessible by design**.
2. re-engineer the business models for those public services already in place in order to ensure the above-mentioned ruling principle.

The UDRs are coherent with the overarching goals of Norway's 2015-19 Government Action Plan for Universal Design. The action plan includes a set of measures that should be taken by different ministries and agencies in Norway (e.g. the KMD, Difi, the Ministry of Children, Equality and Social Inclusion, the Ministry of Labour and Social Affairs, and the Ministry of Culture) in order to ensure, for instance, social inclusiveness, the democratised accessibility of public services and physical government premises, and the development of skills and competencies among all population groups to ensure they can benefit from such policies.

Difi acts as the authority for universal design regarding ICT-based solutions, and are thus in charge of developing and monitoring the observance of universal design standards and guidelines, and of putting in place learning spaces to help public sector institutions implement them.

Source: Author, with information from Government of Norway (2013b), "Regulations on the Universal Design of Information and Communication Technology Solutions", https://lovdata.no/dokument/SF/forskrift/2013-06-21-732?q=20130621732 and Ministry of Children, Equality and Social Inclusion (2016), "The Government's Action Plan for Universal Design 2015–19", www.regjeringen.no/en/dokumenter/regjeringens-handlingsplan-for-universell-utforming/id2473299/.

In broad terms, there are no major legal barriers to digital government in Norway. This draws upon the aforementioned long-established efforts of the Norwegian government to develop a legal framework that favours and motivates the adoption of technology by ministries and agencies. The latter is in line with the goals of Norway's former e-government agendas and the current digital agenda, which have pushed for the efficient use of ICTs as a driver of public sector modernisation.

Yet, despite the availability of such a mature legal framework, advancing the digital agenda would still require overcoming some regulatory challenges hindering the digital transformation of the public sector. These challenges are mainly related to the lack of consistency between policy goals (e.g. the construction of a data-driven public sector and cloud-based solutions), and the burdens brought by some regulations still in place that act as barriers to achieve such policy goals that are in line with key digital government principles, e.g. digital by design, open by default and the once-only principle.

Results from the OECD mission to Oslo and the OECD survey show evidence of issues related to regulatory adaptability and readiness in regard to data governance (e.g. producing, collecting, processing, storing, accessing, sharing, and re-using data). For instance, data sharing within the public sector, the publication of open government data to be re-used by external actors (e.g. to support the digital economy, business innovation and civic technology), and the potential re-use by public sector institutions of external data (e.g. data produced by businesses and citizens).

Advancing the digital agenda in Norway will require the government to address these regulatory challenges, so as to create a coherent, up-to-date and adaptable regulatory environment that favours the achievement of policy goals in the short and medium terms (see Chapter 5), and supports a full shift towards the implementation of digital government and a data driven public sector.

Notes

1. For further information, see www.nordicinnovation.org/.
2. Information provided by the Norwegian government.
3. Public Administration Act, Article 15a. For more information, see https://lovdata.no/artikkel/statsrad_14_juni_2013/1222.

References

Government of Norway (2016), "Public Procurement Act", https://lovdata.no/dokument/NL/lov/2016-06-17-73.

Government of Norway (2015), "Intelligent Transport Systems Act", https://lovdata.no/dokument/NL/lov/2015-12-11-101.

Government of Norway (2014), "Regulations on the Norwegian State Educational Loan Fund's Access to Public Sector Information", https://lovdata.no/dokument/SF/forskrift/2014-08-28-1123.

Government of Norway (2013a), "Discrimination and Accessibility Act", https://lovdata.no/dokument/NL/lov/2013-06-21-61/KAPITTEL_3.

Government of Norway (2013b), "Regulations on the Universal Design of Information and Communication Technology Solutions", https://lovdata.no/dokument/SF/forskrift/2013-06-21-732?q=20130621732.

Government of Norway (2006), "Freedom of Information Act", https://lovdata.no/dokument/NL/lov/2006-05-19-16?q=offentleg.

Government of Norway (2005), "Penal Code (Straffeloven)", https://lovdata.no/dokument/NL/lov/2005-05-20-28.

Government of Norway (2003), "Electronic Communications Act", https://lovdata.no/dokument/NL/lov/2003-07-04-83/KAPITTEL_5.

Government of Norway (2001), "Electronic Signature Act", https://lovdata.no/dokument/NL/lov/2001-06-15-81.

Government of Norway (1967), "Public Administration Act", https://lovdata.no/dokument/NL/lov/1967-02-10.

KMD (Ministry of Local Government and Administration) (2017), "Nordic-Baltic Ministerial Conference on Digitalisation: Ministerial Declaration", 24-25 April 2017, www.regjeringen.no/contentassets/5ed83530b83c4e4ba85338c29eb50c63/ministerial-declaration.pdf.

KMD (2016), "Digital Agenda for Norway in brief: ICT for a simpler everyday life and increased productivity", English version, KMD, www.regjeringen.no/en/dokumenter/digital-agenda-for-norway-in-brief/id2499897/sec1.

Ministry of Children, Equality and Social Inclusion (2016), "The Government's Action Plan for Universal Design 2015–19", www.regjeringen.no/en/dokumenter/regjeringens-handlingsplan-for-universell-utforming/id2473299/.

NCM (Nordic Council of Ministers) (2017), "Nordic Co-operation Programme for Regional Development and Planning 2017–20", NCM, http://dx.doi.org/10.6027/ANP2017-723.

NCM (2014), "Nordic Co-operation Programme for Innovation and Business Policy 2014-17", NCM, http://norden.diva-portal.org/smash/get/diva2:740766/FULLTEXT01.pdf.

NI (Nordic Innovation) (2017), "Innovative Nordic digital solutions", webpage, http://enternordic.info/index.html (accessed 12 August 2017).

NI (2016), "Announcing Hack4Norden: Nordic data driven innovation challenge", http://nordicinnovation.org/en-GB/projects/datainnovation/.

OECD (forthcoming), "The digital transformation of the public sector: Helping governments respond to the needs of networked societies", *OECD Working Papers on Public Governance*, OECD Publishing, Paris.

OECD (2017a), "Fixed and wireless broadband subscriptions per 100 inhabitants", *OECD Broadband Portal* (database), www.oecd.org/sti/broadband/oecdbroadbandportal.htm.

OECD (2017b), "Short-Term Labour Market Statistics", *OECD.Stat* (database), http://stats.oecd.org/index.aspx?r=149175.

OECD (2016a), OECD Better Life Index, www.oecdbetterlifeindex.org.

OECD (2016b), "Executive summary", in *OECD Economic Surveys: Norway 2016*, OECD Publishing, Paris, http://dx.doi.org/10.1787/eco_surveys-nor-2016-3-en.

OECD (2016c), *OECD Comparative Study Digital Government Strategies for Transforming Public Services in the Welfare Areas*, OECD, www.oecd.org/gov/digital-government/Digital-Government-Strategies-Welfare-Service.pdf.

OECD (2015a), "Norway", in *Education at a Glance 2015: OECD Indicators*, OECD Publishing, Paris, http://dx.doi.org/10.1787/eag-2015-73-en.

OECD (2015b), *Education at a Glance 2015: OECD Indicators*, OECD Publishing, Paris, http://dx.doi.org/10.1787/eag-2015-en.

OECD (2015c), *How's Life? 2015: Measuring Well-being*, OECD Publishing, Paris, http://dx.doi.org/10.1787/how_life-2015-en.

OECD (2015d), *OECD Employment Outlook 2015*, OECD Publishing, Paris, http://dx.doi.org/10.1787/empl_outlook-2015-en.

OECD (2015e), *OECD Public Governance Reviews: Estonia and Finland: Fostering Strategic Capacity across Governments and Digital Services across Borders*, OECD Public Governance Reviews, OECD Publishing, Paris, http://dx.doi.org/10.1787/9789264229334-en.

OECD (2014a), "Recommendation of the Council on Digital Government Strategies", OECD, Paris, www.oecd.org/gov/digital-government/recommendation-on-digital-government-strategies.htm.

OECD (2014b), "Working Better with Age: Norway - Assessment and recommendations, OECD, January, www.oecd.org/els/emp/NORWAY_Assessment%20and%20recommendations%20WEBPAGE.pdf.

OECD (2005a), *OECD e-Government Studies: Norway 2005*, OECD Publishing, Paris, http://dx.doi.org/10.1787/9789264010680-en.

OECD (2005b), "ICT access and usage by individuals", *OECD.Stat* (database), ICT Access and Usage by Households and Individuals, http://stats.oecd.org/index.aspx?queryid=72702.

OECD (2005c), "Assessment and Proposals for Action", in *OECD e-Government Studies: Norway 2005*, OECD Publishing, Paris, http://dx.doi.org/10.1787/9789264010680-2-en.

Further reading

Difi (Agency for Public Management and eGovernment) (2015), *Forprosjektrapport: Evaluering Av Prosjektet "Fjerne tidstyver"*, December, Difi, www.difi.no/sites/difino/files/forprosjektrapport_evaluering_av_prosjektet_fjerne_tidstyver.pdf.

European Parliament (2016), "Regulation (EU) 2016/679 of the European Parliament and of the Council of 27 April 2016 on the protection of natural persons with regard to the processing of personal data and on the free movement of such data, and repealing Directive 95/46/EC (General Data Protection Regulation)", *Official Journal of the European Union*, 4 May 2016, http://ec.europa.eu/justice/data-protection/reform/files/regulation_oj_en.pdf.

Government of Norway (2017), "Department of ICT Policy and Public Sector Reform", institutional website, www.regjeringen.no/en/dep/kmd/organisation/departments/department-of-ict-policy-and-public-sect/id1589/ (accessed 12 August 2017).

Government of Norway (2014), "Act on the Management of Health Records and Data", https://lovdata.no/dokument/NL/lov/2014-06-20-43?q=helseregisterloven.

Government of Norway (2010), "Geodata Act", https://lovdata.no/dokument/NL/lov/2010-09-03-56?q=geodataloven.

Government of Norway (2005), "Cadastre Act", https://lovdata.no/dokument/NL/lov/2005-06-17-101?q=Matrikkellova.

Government of Norway (2004), "Regulations on e-Administration and Management", https://lovdata.no/dokument/SF/forskrift/2004-06-25-988.

Government of Norway (2000), "Personal Data Act", www.datatilsynet.no/English/Regulations/Personal-Data-Act-/.

Government of Norway (1994), "Act on Legal Entities", https://lovdata.no/dokument/NL/lov/1994-06-03-15?q=enhetsregister.

Government of Norway (1970), "Census Act", https://lovdata.no/dokument/NL/lov/1970-01-16-1.

KMD (Ministry of Local Government and Administration) (2016), "2016 Digitalisation Memorandum", KMD, www.regjeringen.no/no/dokumenter/digitaliseringsrundskrivet/id2522147/.

KMD (2016), "Cloud Computing Strategy for Norway", English version, KMD, www.regjeringen.no/en/dokumenter/cloud-computing-strategy-for-norway/id2484403/.

KMPG (2014), "Barriers to digitizatioen", Executive summary in *KPMG report to the Norwegian Ministry of Local Government and Modernisation*, www.regjeringen.no/globalassets/upload/kmd/aif/dokumenter/barriers_to_digitizatioen.pdf.

OECD (2015), *OECD Regulatory Policy Outlook 2015*, OECD Publishing, Paris, http://dx.doi.org/10.1787/9789264238770-en.

OECD (2012), "Recommendation of the Council on Regulatory Policy and Governance", OECD, www.oecd.org/gov/regulatory-policy/49990817.pdf.

Chapter 2

Governing the digital transformation of the Norwegian public sector

This chapter analyses and discusses the governance of the digital transformation of the public sector in Norway, based on the OECD Recommendation on Digital Government Strategies and the analytical work conducted on the governance of digital government in a number of OECD member countries and partner economies. The chapter starts by considering the Norwegian Digital Agenda and the digital government priorities assumed by the public sector. It then assesses the governance and co-ordination framework in place and the institutional arrangements that support digital government development in the country. It concludes by exploring the challenges and opportunities for the development of a more robust system-thinking culture in the public sector, to improve the public administration's performance in delivering value to its citizens and businesses.

Introduction

The digital transformation of the public sector can have a cross-cutting impact on all sectors and levels of government. In order to address its challenges, governments need a clear mandate and the proper institutional arrangements to promote the use of technologies in a coherent and effective way. Suitable institutional frameworks are needed to guarantee that digital government policies are properly designed and ensure effective co-ordination between relevant stakeholders, and sustainable delivery of results. It also requires a clear connection with other public sector reform agendas, contributing to countries' broader national policy goals.

There is not a one-size-fits-all approach that can be adopted in all contexts; OECD countries' diverse experiences demonstrate the different paths that can be taken. In line with the OECD Recommendation on Digital Government Strategies (2014a), Figure 2.1 illustrates in a non-exhaustive way several dimensions that contribute to the analytical framework underlying this review. From the institutional framework that supports the digital government strategy to the stakeholders' involvement, passing through the co-ordinating mechanisms in place or the policy levers available, the ability of each country to lead the digital transformation of the public sector will substantially depend on its governance ecosystem.

Figure 2.1. **Governing the digital transformation of the public sector: Dimensions of analysis**

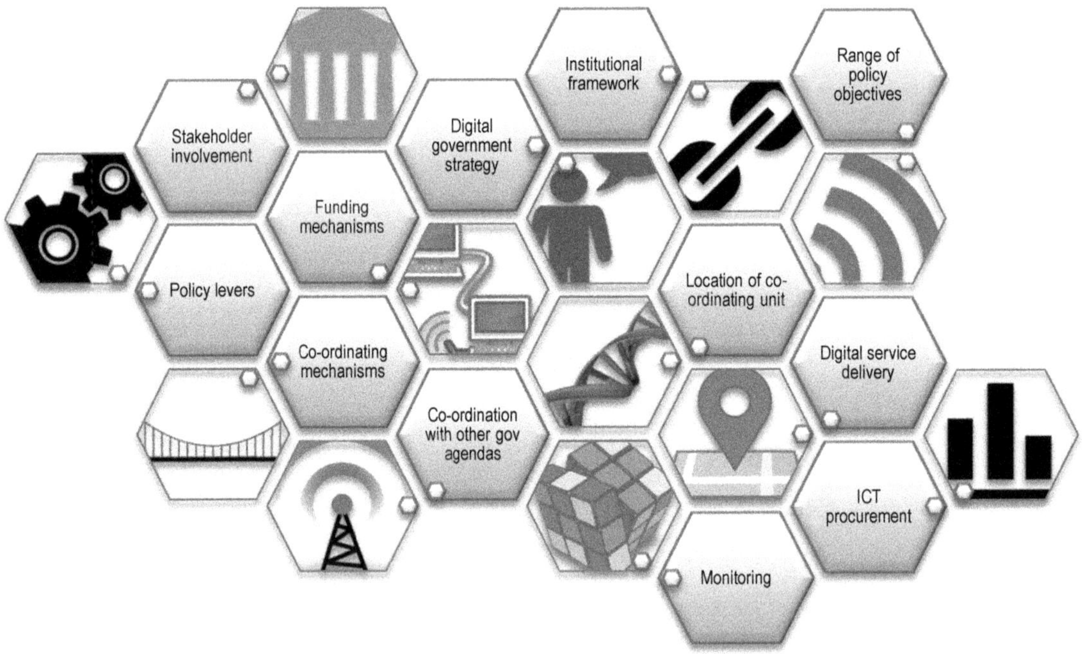

Source: Author, based on OECD (2016a), *Digital Government in Chile: Strengthening the Institutional and Governance Framework*, OECD Digital Government Studies, OECD Publishing, Paris, http://dx.doi.org/10.1787/9789264258013-en.

This chapter analyses the governance of the digital transformation of the public sector in Norway. The analysis will start by examining the digital government strategy in place, its goals, priorities and alignment with the OECD Recommendation on Digital Government Strategies. A second section will focus on the governance framework in place, namely the institutional set-up and the practices that structure the leadership and co-ordination mechanisms for digital government development. The last section will analyse the context supporting system-thinking approaches across the Norwegian public sector, particularly as they relate to the digital government landscape, highlighting mechanisms that can help overcome the silo-based and vertical-thinking approaches found in the public sector.

Setting goals: Leading the digital government agenda

The existence of a digital government strategy is a fundamental element to consider when analysing countries' institutional approaches. According to the OECD Digital Government Performance Survey (2014b), all OECD countries stated having a national digital government strategy. However, the institutional frameworks to implement the strategy vary from country to country. The co-ordination instruments foreseen, the policy levers available and the funding mechanisms to support a strategy's implementation are some of the elements to be considered when analysing different countries' approaches to the governance of digital government.

A digital government strategy is an essential tool to align policy objectives across policy sectors and levels of government, but its design and development are also crucial moments to bring the relevant stakeholders together, enabling the proper discussion about the objectives to be achieved and the institutional tools to be mobilised. The government has at these stages the unique opportunity to build precious consensus, as well as a sense of shared ownership and accountability for its success or failures. The support for the implementation of each of the priorities foreseen in the strategy will benefit from the level of engagement the government is able to stimulate among the stakeholders during the formulation stage.

Similarly to other OECD countries, Norway adopted several information society and/or digital government agendas in recent years. Each of them builds upon each other, reflecting continuity but also showing the evolution of the government's priorities and assumed diverse targeted goals to be achieved (see Chapter 1). The current (2017) strategy is the Digital Agenda for Norway (also known as the "White Paper"). It covers several policy areas, from digital economy to digital inclusion or general information and communications technology (ICT) policy. One of the policy areas covered is digital government, underlining the need to use digital technologies to modernise, simplify and improve the public sector's processes and external outputs.

To make the lives of citizens and businesses easier and enhance their productivity, the Digital Agenda identifies the following government priorities (Ministry of Local Government and Modernisation [KMD], 2016a: 6) (see Figure 2.2):

1. **User-centric focus**: Use technologies to support a user-centric public administration that provides seamless and integrated public services to its constituents.

2. **ICT as a significant input for innovation and productivity**: Digitise public operations in ways that support the productivity of economic agents and overall digital innovation.
3. **Strengthened digital competence and inclusion**: Continuous improvement of digital competence throughout all life phases.
4. **Effective digitisation of the public sector**: Embed digital technologies in public sector reform efforts to reduce the complexity of the administration and deliver user-friendly digital services. Develop common solutions and foster their use in the central and local government and facilitate interoperability with European solutions.
5. **Sound data protection and information security**: Data protection and security conceived as integrated elements of ICT development and use. Citizens should, as far as possible, have control over their own data. Ensuring ICT security to maintain trust in digital solutions.

Figure 2.2. **Digital Agenda for Norway**

Source: KMD (2016a), "Digital Agenda for Norway in brief: ICT for a simpler everyday life and increased productivity", English version, Ministry of Local Government and Modernisation, www.regjeringen.no/en/dokumenter/digital-agenda-for-norway-in-brief/id2499897/sec1.

The Digital Agenda recognises Norway's positive performance in several international indexes (see Chapter 1). However, it underlines that permanent efforts are fundamental to maintain the performance reflected in the indexes, continuously improving ICT integration in several policy sectors (see Box 2.1).

Box 2.1. **The Digital Agenda for Norway: From positive performance to the recognition of permanent improvement**

"Norway is a digitally mature market. A substantial proportion of the population has access to the Internet, and a large proportion of these use the Internet on a daily basis. Several service industries, such as banking, finance and tourism, have come a long way in digitising their business processes and have achieved huge efficiency gains as a result. Norway has also succeeded in many areas in its efforts to digitise public services. Government agencies and municipalities increasingly offer digital services, and the use of these services is growing dramatically. Norway generally scores high in international rankings of ICT development.

Nonetheless, the rapid pace of development means that we must constantly improve in order to keep up with the best and to take even more advantage of the potential that lies in digitisation for restructuring and increasing productivity."

Source: KMD (2016a), "Digital Agenda for Norway in brief: ICT for a simpler everyday life and increased productivity", English version, Ministry of Local Government and Modernisation, p. 23, www.regjeringen.no/en/dokumenter/digital-agenda-for-norway-in-brief/id2499897/sec1.

The Digital Agenda for Norway applies to all levels of government: central and local (i.e. counties and municipalities). This gives the government a wide mandate to articulate priorities not only at central level, but also with regard to the 19 counties and the 426 Norwegian municipalities (per 1 January 2017).

The scope of the Norwegian strategy is wide in terms of policy areas, illustrating the government's commitment to leading the digital transformation in the public sector. The strategy covers from public services to economic development, from open government data to ICT policy and infrastructure (e.g. broadband access) and education (e.g. skills and competencies).

The alignment of the Digital Agenda for Norway with the OECD Recommendation on Digital Government Strategies is very significant. The Agenda sets objectives in several areas commonly considered priorities by OECD member countries when the Recommendation was approved. Figure 2.3 presents some examples of clear alignment in the areas of openness and engagement; governance and co-ordination; and capacities to support implementation.

Figure 2.3. **Examples of strategic alignment between the OECD Recommendation for Digital Government Strategies and the Digital Agenda for Norway**

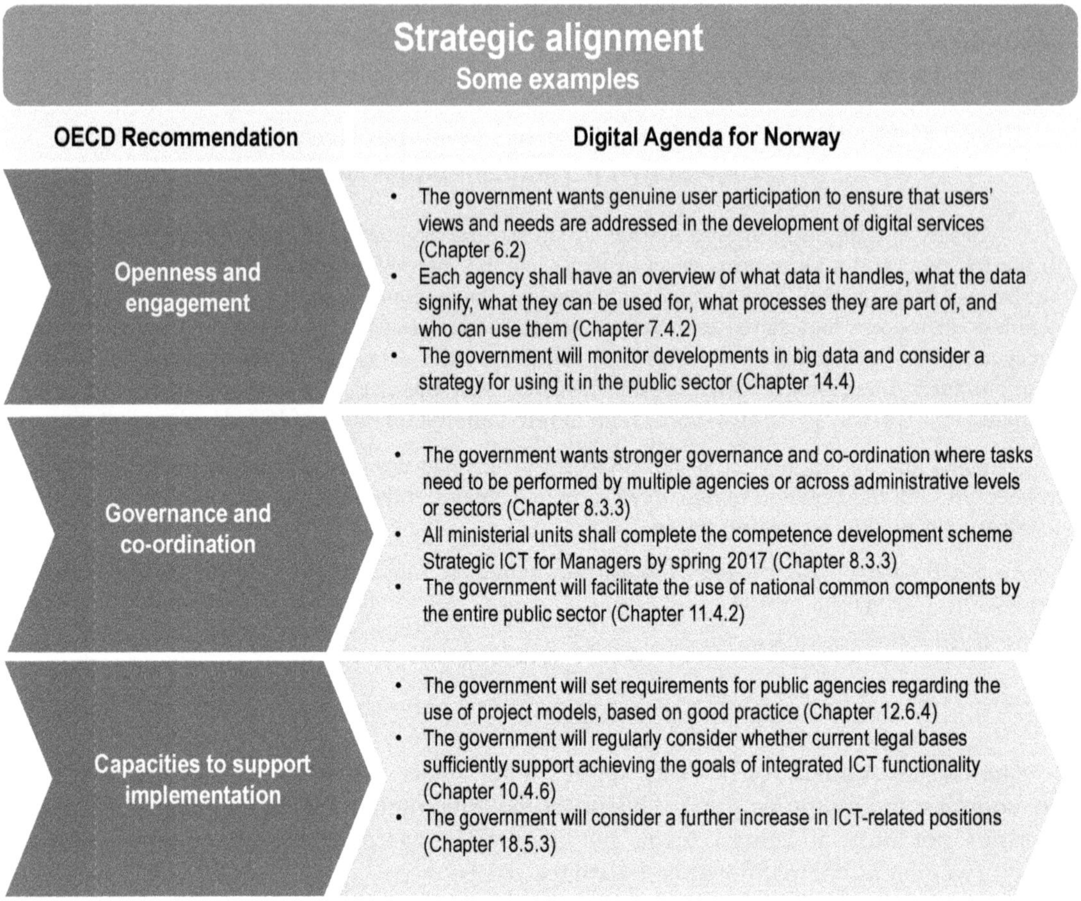

Source: Author, based on OECD (2014a), "Recommendation of the Council on Digital Government Strategies", OECD, Paris, www.oecd.org/gov/digital-government/recommendation-on-digital-government-strategies.htm and KMD (2016a), "Digital Agenda for Norway in brief: ICT for a simpler everyday life and increased productivity", English version, Ministry of Local Government and Modernisation, www.regjeringen.no/en/dokumenter/digital-agenda-for-norway-in-brief/id2499897/sec1.

As previously mentioned, the priorities embedded in the Digital Agenda for Norway cover a broad range of topics, in different areas and sectors, as also common in other OECD member countries' strategic programmatic documents. Based on the survey directed to the Norwegian entity that co-ordinates digital government development (OECD, 2017a), the Department of ICT Policy and Public Sector Reform (AIF) from the Norwegian Ministry of Local Government and Modernisation (KMD), Figure 2.4 raises interesting questions worth mentioning.

Figure 2.4. **Perceived levels of priority of digital government themes in the Norwegian public sector**

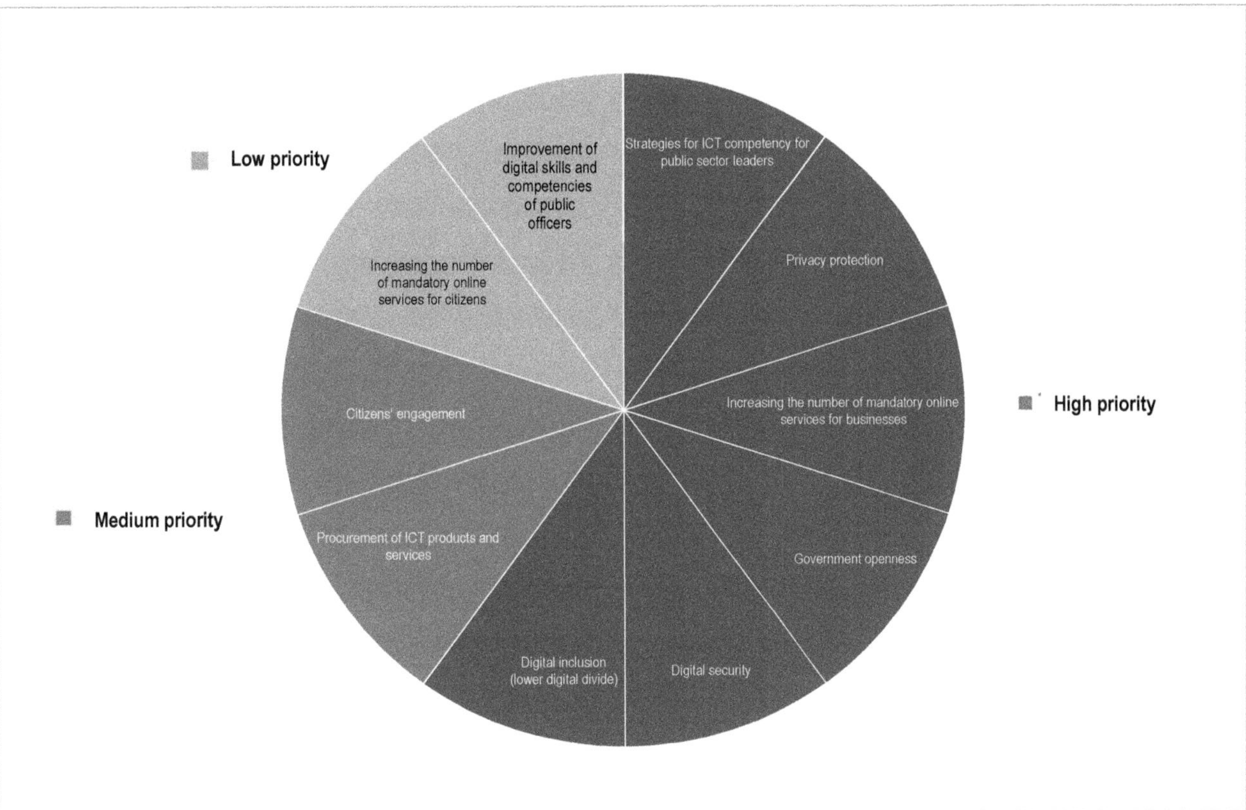

Source: OECD (2017a), "Digital Government Survey of Norway", central version, OECD, Paris. Based on the question, "Please indicate the level of priority in your digital government strategy for each of the following topics".

For example, it is significant that government openness is considered a high priority in the national digital government strategy, but effective citizens' engagement is considered a medium priority (Figure 2.4). This seems to indicate that the Norwegian government sees digital technologies primarily as a useful mechanism to improve the transparency of its processes and less as a means to involve and collaborate with citizens and businesses for policy making and delivery.

It is also paradoxical that the improvement of digital skills of public officers is perceived as a low priority in the Norwegian Digital Agenda. Evidence from the OECD survey shows that, according to ministries and agencies, there is a need to further develop (or bring in) strategic capacities and digital skills among public managers and more operational staff in order to fully reap the benefits of digital technologies at the institutional level and within the overall Norwegian public sector – which is a necessity recognised in the White Paper and in the programme targeting managers in the public sector. The deficit or lack of capacities at the managerial and strategic level (e.g. lack of strategic foresight or the absence of institutional Chief Information Officers [CIOs] was perceived as the third most important barrier limiting the strategic use of digital technologies in the Norwegian public sector (see Figure 2.5).

Figure 2.5. **Main barriers to fully reap the benefits of digital technologies in the Norwegian public sector**

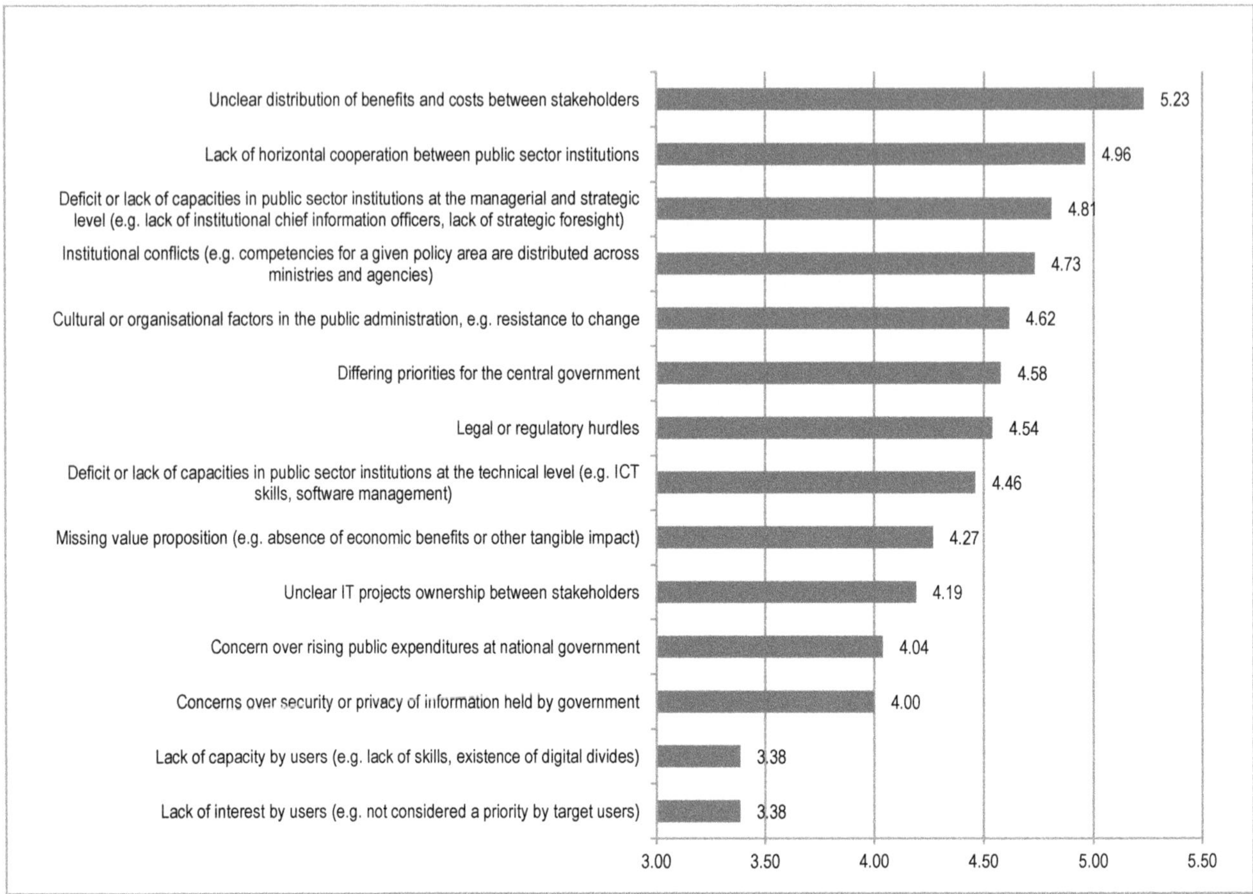

Note: Based on information provided by 27 Norwegian public sector institutions to the question "How strong are the following barriers to fully reap the benefits of ICTs in the Norwegian public sector?" Rank 1: Not relevant, 7: Highly relevant.

Source: OECD (2017b), "Digital Government Survey of Norway", public sector institutions version, OECD, Paris, Question 24.

The level of priority attributed by the Norwegian government to some generic principles for digital government development also provides some interesting insights. The relevance accorded to issues such as a digital-by-default approach, the once-only principle adoption and the trustworthiness and security principle demonstrates the country's alignment with the priorities agreed in the framework of the European Union (European Commission, 2016) (see Figure 2.6).

Figure 2.6. **Perceived levels of priority of digital-by-design principles in the Norwegian public sector**

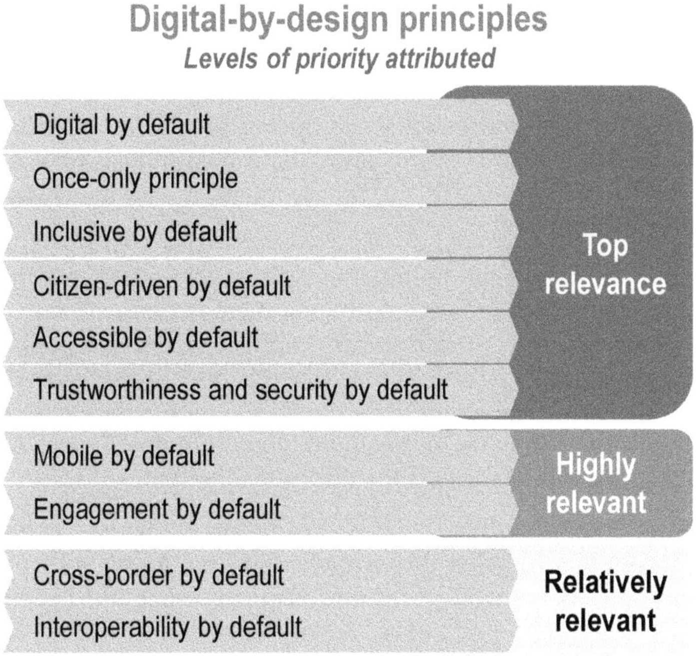

Source: OECD (2017a), "Digital Government Survey of Norway", central version, OECD, Paris. Based on the question, "To what extent are the following overarching principles of digital transformation considered in Norway's Digital Government Strategy?"

However, despite the overall alignment of the Norwegian priorities with the European Union's in terms of digital government, it is surprising to observe that questions of cross-border services development were not perceived by the respondents to the survey administered for this review as a top priority in the Norwegian strategy. Principle 8 of the OECD Recommendation on Digital Government Strategies (2014a) stresses the importance of international co-operation for digital government development. Given the level of international integration of the Norwegian economy, it would be expected that cross-border services to citizens and businesses would assume a higher relevance in the country's strategy.

The development of cross-borders services, supported by cross-border exchange of data, is an opportunity that could be further explored in the region considering the generally consolidated stage of development of digital government, and key basic registries, in Nordic and Baltic countries. The benefits for Nordic and Baltic citizens and businesses would be significant; the Norwegian government should thus prioritise playing a continuous leading role for the further development of this co-operation (see Chapter 4).

Citizens' expectations regarding the public administration are increasing in terms of convenience, efficiency and effectiveness. The ability of the public sector to connect its platforms and to exchange data between different sectors and levels of government is a basic requisite of the digital transformation of the public sector. Public services and internal processes need to be interoperable to respond to this imperative, allowing the public sector to reap the full benefit of data exchange to serve citizens and businesses with more integrated and seamless digital services (OECD, forthcoming). Interoperability is not considered by the respondents of the OECD survey as a top or highly relevant priority in the national Digital Agenda (Figure 2.6), which is quite telling if we take into account that it is recognised as a priority by the national authorities in charge of digital government, as evidenced through the work on ID-porten, eID (electronic identification system), eIDAS (electronic identification, authentication and trust services) and their active involvement in the international co-operation at the Nordic and EU levels. Considering the country's context in this area, interoperability is one of the key enablers that should be better prioritised for further development in the future (this aspect is further explored in Chapter 4).

The dependency or not on the political cycle is a relevant dimension of analysis for the development of digital government. Although there is no quantitative data to evaluate the correlation between the sustainability and coherency across time of digital government strategies and the political cycle (e.g. changes in government) among OECD member countries, most senior officials tend to recognise that changes in their governments frequently affect in a negative way the development of projects and initiatives (e.g. lack of continuity of efforts due to changing priorities).

The above mentioned influence can be negative when governments change, determining an abrupt modification of priorities and abandonment of projects underway. However, changes in the political cycle can also represent the launching of new and updated priorities, goals and initiatives, often with the intention to complement or upgrade the work carried out by previous governments. In Norway, 70% of those public institutions that provided a response to the survey agreed that a correlation could be established between the digital government strategy in Norway and the political cycle (see Figure 2.7). Nevertheless, as discussed in Chapter 1, the evolution from the previous eNorway agenda to the Digital Agenda has ensured the continuity and evolution of key policy goals.

Figure 2.7. **The influence of political cycles in the Norwegian digital government strategy**

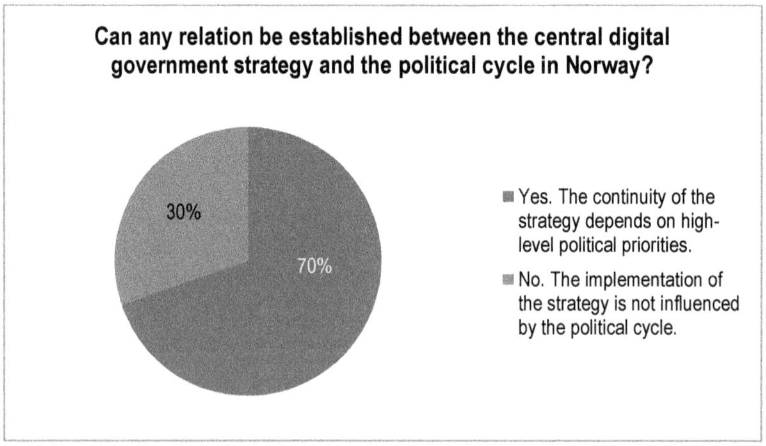

Source: OECD (2017b), "Digital Government Survey of Norway", public sector institutions version, OECD, Paris.

The policy relevance attributed to digital government issues over the past decade in Norway is unquestionable and the current Digital Agenda, which builds upon the previous strategies, represents the government's commitment to this policy area. Nonetheless, the relevance of having an autonomous digital government strategy, as a stand-alone policy instrument that can be clearly identified and used by all stakeholders, can bring several advantages in terms of co-ordination and monitoring. A dedicated strategy can also be useful to establish the necessary bridges and synergies with other public sector reform agendas, such as public sector innovation, administrative simplification, open government or public service delivery.

Improving governance

Like several other cross-cutting policy areas, digital government policies require horizontal management and development across the public sector to be able to generate the expected outputs, outcomes and impacts efficiently and effectively. The OECD Recommendation on Digital Government Strategies (2014a) highlights the need to set clear institutional roles as one of the basic preconditions for sound governance of digital government and to sustainably support the digital transformation of the public sector.

Considering the complexity of the task to be undertaken, roles and responsibilities should be clear to all stakeholders involved in the digital transformation process. Appropriate mechanisms for co-ordination are also necessary to ensure multi-stakeholder engagement and the co-creation of value through new forms of collaboration and partnership between public, private and civil actors. A sound governance framework facilitates decision-making processes, the establishment of agreements, the joint definition of guidelines and of mechanisms to secure enforcement for observance in relation to digital government (OECD, forthcoming). A proper governance framework is a decisive variable for efficient policy implementation and coherent investments in the public sector, avoiding overlaps in projects and initiatives and boost opportunities for cross-sectoral synergies. Adequate governance frameworks are also fundamental to set up mechanisms to follow up and monitor alignment of investments across sectors and levels of government with digital government overarching priorities. The sections below address all the different aspects relevant to the existing governance framework in Norway.

The institutional setting for policy decision and implementation

According to the data collected across OECD countries, 96.3% of OECD member countries report having units, bodies or agencies responsible for co-ordinating digital government policies (OECD, 2014b). The institutional framework may vary, depending on several factors, like the administrative culture of the country or the historical legacy of the government's organisation and division of policy areas.

The institutional location of the co-ordinating unit is also a key aspect to consider. Governments of OECD member countries employ different practises regarding this aspect of the analysis. Depending on the institutional legacy or the political priorities, the public authority responsible for designing the digital government strategy and co-ordinating its implementation is commonly located in:

- centre of government (e.g. head of state or head of government)
- co-ordinating ministry responsible for public administration or internal affairs, or the Ministry of Finance

- line ministry (e.g. Ministry of Communications, Ministry of Economy or Ministry of Science and Innovation).

In Norway, the co-ordination of digital government policies and public sector reform is the responsibility of the Ministry of Local Government and Modernisation (KMD). KMD is also in charge of housing policy, the Planning and Building Act, local government finances and local administration, rural and regional policy, the conduct of elections, government employment policy, minority affairs, national mapping and geodata policy (Government of Norway, 2017).

The KMD exerts its digital government co-ordination role through different mechanisms, including a Digitalisation Memorandum (Digitaliseringsrundskrivet), which is distributed among all ministries in Norway (including the Office of the Prime Minister). The memorandum provides a set of strategic actions to be implemented by ministries in line with the objectives of the national digital government policy. Once published, it is the responsibility of ministries to ensure the implementation of these directives within the policy area under their responsibility (see Box 2.2).

Box 2.2. **The 2016 Digitalisation Memorandum (Digitaliseringsrundskrivet)**

The Digitalisation Memorandum comprises the Norwegian government's requirements and recommendations related to the digitalisation of the public sector, and the role that ministries and, in particular, agencies have in this regard. The Digitalisation Memorandum has been distributed by the KMD since 2009 on a yearly basis. Previous versions of the Memorandum have included, for instance, guidelines on architecture principles, standardisation and common solutions (2011), the adoption of the Digital Mailbox by agencies (2013, 2014), and the definition, objectives, implementation and financing of digitalisation projects (2015).[1]

In 2016, KMD's Digitalisation Memorandum defined a set of actions in key areas to be prioritised by public sector organisations with regard to digitalisation and includes (among other things) specific requirements within the following areas:

- **Digital by default**: Ministries should assess opportunities in regard to the digitalisation of public services and organisational processes, and the definition of user-centred services.
- **Digital mailbox**: In order to reduce the burden on citizens created as a result of multiple communication channels, agencies should use the Digital Mailbox[2] as the default option to communicate with citizens. Agencies using the Altinn platform's mailbox[3] (business-oriented) should migrate to the Digital Mailbox in order to contribute to this transition.
- **Electronic invoicing**: It is the responsibility of agencies to ensure contractors' use of electronic invoicing. The latter should be included as a prerequisite for new public procurement contracts. Agencies should also produce electronic invoices.
- **Open government data (OGD)**: Public sector organisations should invest further efforts to open up government data in machine-readable formats, under an open licence (e.g. the Norwegian open data license), and following the guidelines on the publication of open government data developed by the Agency for Public Management and eGovernment (Difi). Agencies are encouraged to avoid developing services that might duplicate similar OGD-based private sector products.

Box 2.2. **The 2016 Digitalisation Memorandum (Digitaliseringsrundskrivet)** *(continued)*

- **Information security**: Agencies should implement actions in line with the 2004 Regulations on Electronic Communications with and within the Public Administration, and the 2015-17 Action Plan for Information Security in the Public Administration. Agencies are expected to create internal areas in charge of information management, control and security.

The memorandum also highlights the importance of providing **support and guidance to citizens** in order improve their **user experience** when using public services, and the relevance of **using central architecture principles and common components** (e.g. ID port, Digital Mailbox) as building blocks for the design of ICT-based solutions. The **private provision of ICT solutions and services** and the use of **cloud-based solutions** are encouraged.

Ministries and agencies are required to **use a best practice project management model** for projects with a total cost of more than NOK 10 million in order to ensure the cost-efficiency of ICT projects. In this line, the memorandum recommends the use of **Difi's "Project Wizard" project management platform,** www.prosjektveiviseren.no. The Agency for Financial Management **(DFØ)'s guidelines for cost-benefit analysis and benefits realisation** have been embedded within the framework of Difi's platform. The memorandum also recommends seeking advice from the **Digitalisation Council** in order to improve the benefits and reduce the costs for ICT projects with a total cost equal to or higher than NOK 10 million.

The relevance of financial levers to build a systemic ICT project quality management culture are also included in the 2016 Memorandum:

- The yearly central budgeting process and budget allocation from the Ministry of Finance to other ministries, and KMD's assessment of ministries' ICT-related project proposals are underlined as ICT projects' quality control mechanisms. The involvement of the KMD in the budgeting process aims to ensure ICT projects emphasis on the "simplification and improvement of public services, and the overall improvement public sector's efficiency".
- **Difi's co-financing mechanism**:[4] This mechanism aims to reinforce Difi's capacity to better pursue a systemic quality management approach for ICT projects by providing additional budget (up to 50%) for ICT projects with a total cost ranging from NOK 5 million to NOK 50 million. Difi's co-funding is limited to a maximum financial contribution of NOK 15 million.

1. Prior to 2012, the Digitalisation Memorandum was distributed as the "Memorandum on the co-ordination and management of ICT-related investments in the State".

2. See www.norge.no/en/choose-digital-mailbox.

3. See www.altinn.no/en/.

4. See www.difi.no/fagomrader-og-tjenester/digitalisering-og-samordning/medfinansiering-av-digitaliseringsprosjekt.

Source: Author, with information from KMD (2016b*)*, "2016 Digitalisation Memorandum", KMD, www.regjeringen.no/no/dokumenter/digitaliseringsrundskrivet/id2522147/.

Within the KMD, the Department of ICT Policy and Public Sector Reform (AIF) is in charge of "the administration and modernisation of the public sector as well as national ICT policy, including the supervision of the Agency for Public Management and eGovernment (Difi)" (Government of Norway, 2017) (see Chapter 1). AIF's work focuses on four key areas:

1. **Public sector reform and e-government**: Modernisation and reform of the public sector through the definition of "principles for ICT solutions (ICT architecture) and common ICT components in government administration", and co-ordination of government-wide efforts to lever administrative and regulatory simplification, user-centred services, user participation, and inter-institutional standards.
2. **Society's use of ICTs**: Underpinning the use of ICTs in all sectors of society through the implementation of: a) efficient infrastructures that support the development of ICT-based services (e.g. identity management and electronic identification tools); b) social inclusion, digital participation and privacy protection policies; and, c) measures to increase awareness of the social and economic costs of technology, "including realisation of profits of ICT investments in the private and public sector."
3. **Administration policy**: Analysis and definition of efficient government administration structures towards the achievement of organisational goals (including international co-operation in this area).
4. **Economic analysis** mainly focused on assessing the economic benefits of public sector investments, including assessments carried out by third-party actors. Ensuring the efficient use of public sector resources (including ICT-related expenditures) is growing in relevance in light of the substantial oil-price falls since 2014 (OECD, 2016b) (see Chapter 3), which may have a negative impact on, among others, the availability of resources to finance the welfare and employment state in Norway.

Expanding on the general background presented in Chapter 1, Difi (under the supervision of AIF) is the Norwegian public sector agency responsible for the executive management and implementation of digital government policies. Created in January 2008 and with about 260 staff members in Oslo and Leikanger (Difi, 2017), Difi's primary audiences are central government and the municipalities. Co-operation with local government is substantial in areas that include procurement, ICT management and innovation (OECD, 2017a) (see Table 2.1).

Table 2.1. **Difi's main goals and areas of focus**

Main goals	Areas of focus
Contribute to increased co-ordination in the public sector Build and document knowledge Contribute to capacity building in the public sector Develop and manage joint solutions for the management Supervise regulations on the universal design of ICT solutions	Management development, organisation, management, innovation and skills development Digitisation of public services and work processes Development and management of common solutions Public procurement Preventive ICT security Universal design of ICT solutions

Source: Author, based on Difi (Agency for Public Management and eGovernment) (2017), www.difi.no, official agency website (accessed 1 April 2017).

Difi chairs the Digitalisation Council (Digitaliseringsrådet), a collective body involving stakeholders from all sectors and levels of the government, and also from the private and third sectors (see Chapter 3). The council is responsible for evaluating ICT projects between NOK 10 million and NOK 750 million, providing advice and supporting agencies in the definition, development and implementation of cost-efficient and sustainable ICT projects.

Difi's agenda (as for most agencies in the Norwegian public sector) is governed by an annual letter of allocation issued by KMD. For 2017, the letter of allocation to Difi included strategic items instructing the agency to implement specific co-ordinated actions towards the accomplishment of government-wide goals. Among others, the letter:

- highlights and stresses the policy co-ordination and advisory role of the Agency in line with the objectives of the Norwegian government to spur innovation and modernisation within a user-centred public sector
- clearly identifies Difi as a driver of change in Norway
- defines Difi's responsibilities to develop a digitalisation strategy for the public sector in Norway, and underlines the key role of the Agency within the framework of electronic procurement
- sets the budget for the Agency (one-year period), in line with Difi's ongoing activities and mandate and/or any new responsibilities that result from the letter.

Difi's mandate, and the yearly definition of objectives and priorities set through KMD's allocation letter, places this agency at the core of the digital government institutional governance, and as a key player within the overall digital transformation of the Norwegian public sector.

There is general consensus among different stakeholders about the central policy co-ordination role of the Ministry of Local Government and Modernisation (KMD) and the strategic instrumental role of Difi in boosting the Digital Agenda for Norway (OECD, 2017b). All the Norwegian public sector institutions consulted through the OECD survey recognised the role of KMD and Difi as charged to co-ordinate the strategic use of digital technologies within the central government.

However, in line with the perceptions collected from different stakeholders during the peer review mission, the OECD survey (2017b) confirms that the specific responsibilities of KMD and Difi for the development of digital government are not clear or recognised by several public sector institutions. Even when asked about central responsibilities, like the "Development of technical guidelines for the development of ICT architecture" or "Ensuring horizontal co-ordination between public sector institutions at central level", less than 65% of the institutions that responded to the survey were able to attribute them to KMD and Difi (see Figure 2.8).

Figure 2.8. **Responsibilities attributed to KMD and Difi: Norwegian stakeholders' perceptions**

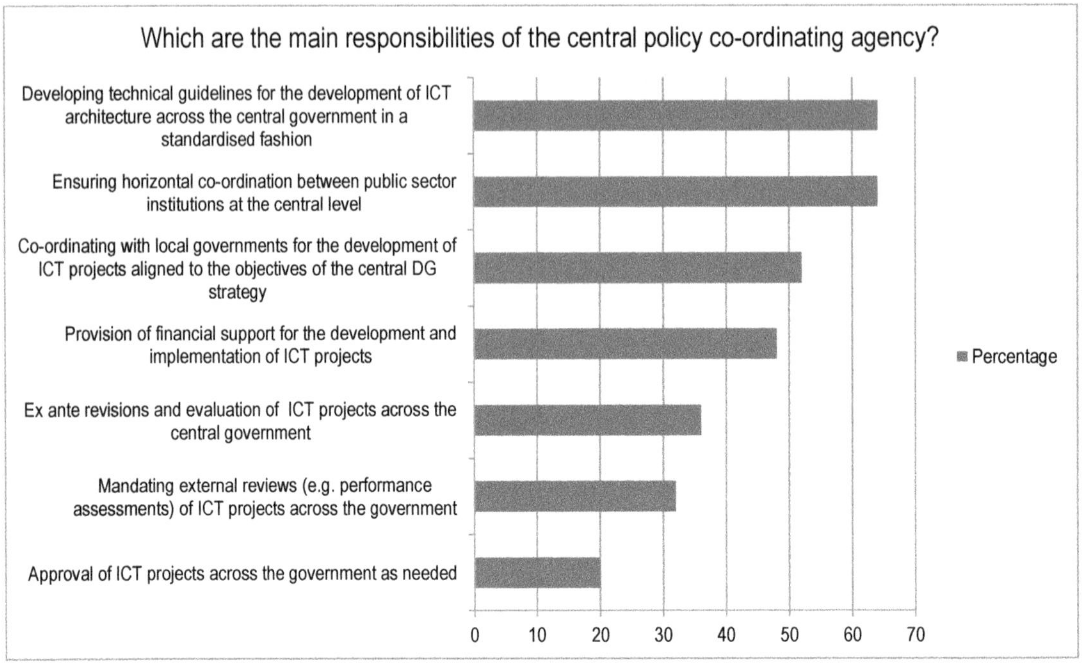

Source: OECD (2017b), "Digital Government Survey of Norway", public sector institutions version, OECD, Paris.

Difi's responsibilities and competences assume a central place in the discussion about the Norwegian government framework. Although the Agency role is recognised in setting priorities, formulating guidelines and monitoring the implementation of the Digital Agenda, several doubts were raised about its current capacity to fulfil its mandate. The role and potential of Difi are perceived as not totally fulfilled in co-ordinating the implementation of digital government policies across sectors of government, due to the lack of adequate human and financial resources, the proper political support and a clear mandate within in the Norwegian digital government institutional setting.

There is also room for improvement in the co-ordination between central and local government. Although the Digital Agenda for Norway applies to counties and municipalities, the synergies across levels of government still seem below the potential identified by the OECD peer review team and the demand expressed by the country's stakeholders. The reinforcement of the mandate and resources of Difi for cross-level co-operation would favour a more integrated and inclusive development of digital government across Norway.

The formal identification of a Government Chief Information Officer (GCIO) (or a position with equivalent responsibilities, such as the Chief Digital Transformation Officer in some countries) contributes to strengthening the effectiveness of the institutional set-up and related responsibilities within the governance framework (OECD, 2016a) (see Box 2.3). The establishment of the position equivalent to the one of a Government Chief Information Officer, with a clear mandate and formally recognised as a public "champion" leading the digital transformation of the country's public sector in a cross-cutting way would help strengthen and clarify the governance for digital government.

Box. 2.3. **Chief Information Officer (CIO): Role and responsibilities**

The figure of the central/federal government CIO or equivalent position has become the most common form of co-ordinating unit or body for digital government activities. In some cases, the CIO's role is complemented by more experimental institutions or units depending on governments' priorities and efforts.

The traditional role of the CIO has been focused on supporting the strategic use of technology by government in order to achieve its goals, frequently driven by efficiency gains and the administration's own priorities. However, following recent trends, these governing bodies have increasingly moved towards more user-centred and, in fewer instances, user-driven approaches. CIO structures across the OECD have developed units with the mission to improve user engagement, service design and delivery and, in many cases, data management as governments seek to improve public sector intelligence.

Levers of ICT governance in OECD countries

In percentage

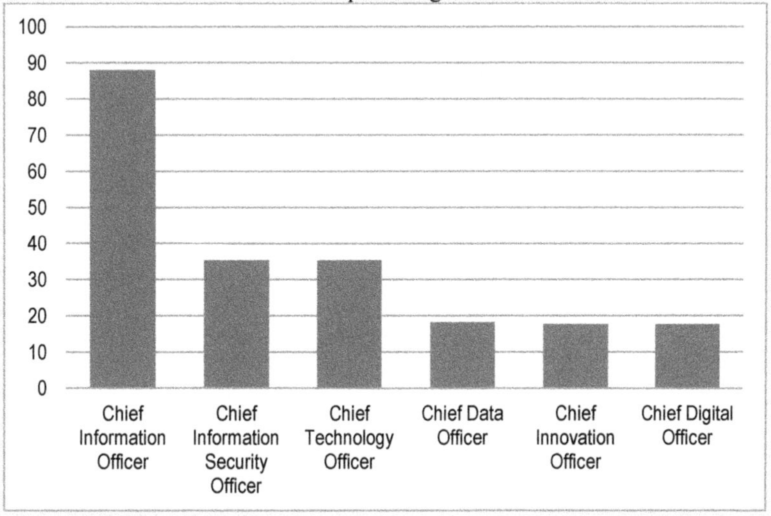

Source: OECD (2016a), *Digital Government in Chile: Strengthening the Institutional and Governance Framework*, OECD Digital Government Studies, OECD Publishing, Paris, http://dx.doi.org/10.1787/9789264258013-en.

Co-ordination for policy coherence across sectors of government

As previously mentioned, co-ordinating mechanisms among sectors and levels of government are fundamental to secure an effective, coherent and sustainable digital government development. Countries' experiences, like those of Denmark and the Netherlands, show that high-level co-ordination is needed, bringing together ministers or senior officials from each ministry, so as to ensure broad co-ordination of the strategy. Side by side with this high-level co-ordination, an operational and technical co-ordination mechanism is also required to deal with implementation challenges and to overcome bottlenecks (Box 2.4). The existence of these two levels of co-ordination can be particularly useful to assure the coherence and sustainability of the decisions supporting implementation.

Box 2.4. Co-ordination mechanisms in Denmark and the Netherlands

Denmark

Denmark has found an original and sustainable mechanism for achieving co-ordination and commitment to the national strategy across the public sector. The Steering Committee for Cross Government Co-operation (Styregruppen for Tværoffentlige Samarbejder [STS]) was set up to create a common ground in the work on digital government. The STS consists of high-level representatives (at the level of permanent secretaries/managing directors) from the five most important ministries for digital government implementation from the central government and the associations representing the municipalities and the regions. The committee is responsible for determining overarching principles and coherent framework conditions for digital government, co-ordinating initiatives across the public resources in order to better use resources, deciding on resource allocation, and determining models for digital government operations and maintenance of projects.

At the operational level, the inter-ministerial project office sits at the Agency for Digitalisation that serves as the secretariat for the Danish Council of IT Projects. It also develops and maintains information technology (IT) project models, business cases and programme models. It serves as the Consultancy Secretariat for IT operations assisting the central government with the management and procurement of outsourced IT operations. Members of the council are ICT managers: half from the public sector, half from the private sector. The focus is on ensuring the presence of really experienced managers in the council.

Netherlands

To tackle the problems of co-ordination and funding, a National Commissioner for Digital Government (digi-commissioner) was appointed by the Dutch Cabinet in 2014. The National Commissioner for Digital Government or Digi-commissioner is responsible to a Ministerial Commission, consisting of the Prime-Minister, the Vice-Premier, the Minister of Internal Affairs and Kingdom Relations, the Minister of Economic Affairs, the Minister for Housing and the Central Government Sector and the Minister of Finance, a representative of the local governments and a representative of the major execution-organisations.

The governance structure consists of four aspects: Politics, Strategic, Tactic and Operational. The Political and Strategic level steers the vision, the multi-annual Digi-programme and the multi-annual funding of the complete Generic Digital Infrastructure. These levels are steered from the National Council for Digital Government. The digi-commissioner presides the National Council for Digital Government. This Council is responsible for the Generic Digital Infrastructure as a whole and consists of Director-Generals of the departments (each responsible for its domain), directors of the associations of Municipalities, Provinces and Water Boards, and directors of major executive organisations.

The Tactical and Operational level manages continuity, development, innovation and implementation/use of the Generic Digital Infrastructure in the four clusters. These clusters in which the Generic Digital Infrastructure is organised are: authentication and identification; service provisioning; data management; and interconnectivity. These levels are governed by four Directing Boards and four Customer Boards (each separately per cluster). The Directing Boards are presided by the director of the Bureau for Digital Government and the exact formation can differ per cluster.

Source: OECD (2016c), "OECD Questionnaire on Governance of Digital Government" (unpublished dataset), OECD, Paris; OECD (2010), *Denmark: Efficient e-Government for Smarter Public Service Delivery*, OECD Publishing, Paris, http://dx.doi.org/10.1787/9789264087118-en. Digi-commissioner (2015), "The Netherlands - National Commissioner for Digital Government (Digi-commissioner)", www.digicommissaris.nl/english (accessed 4 May 2017).

When asked about regular co-ordination with KMD/Difi, only 32% of the Norwegian institutions responded positively, against 56% stating that they do not co-ordinate regularly (Figure 2.9). Data show in a clear way that the Norwegian public sector can improve its internal co-ordination. Although recognised for leading the implementation of the country's digital agenda, the effective co-ordination of central public bodies with KMD and Difi seems scarce.

Figure 2.9. **Co-ordination with KMD/Difi: Norwegian public sector institutions' perceptions**

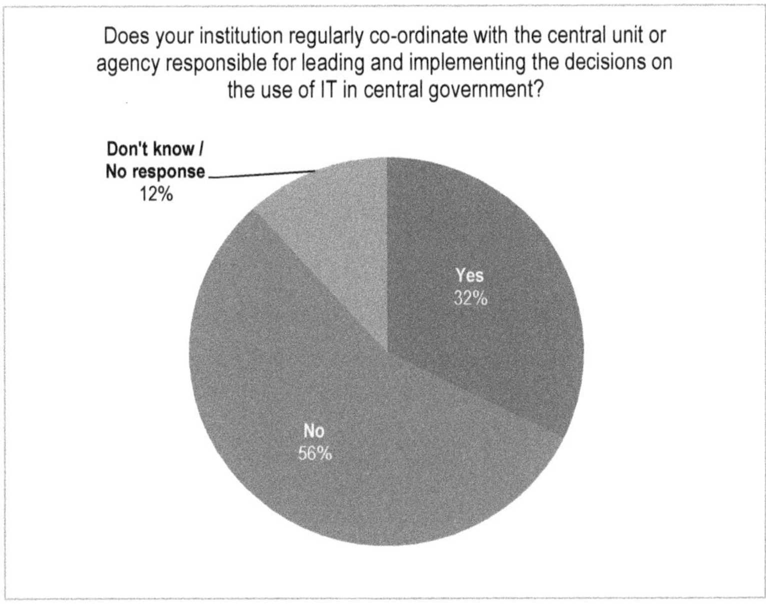

Source: OECD (2017b), "Digital Government Survey of Norway", public sector institutions version, OECD, Paris.

Regarding formal mechanisms for co-ordination at the central level of government in Norway, the SKATE (Strategic Cooperation Council for Management and Coordination of eGovernment Services) is a strategic collaborative council and advisory body meant to ensure co-ordination of the digitalisation of the public sector to benefit the citizens, businesses and the management of the public administration (Difi, 2017). Established in 2012, SKATE is considered a "key policy advisor concerning which ICT measures ought to be implemented and how to finance them." SKATE also "advise on future development policy and on administration of the common components in the central ICT infrastructure" (Ministry of Government, Administration, Reform and Church Affairs, 2013). The SKATE is a strategic co-ordination forum for the government directorates and agencies responsible for the common components/enablers, with a general mandate to assist in "coordinating the digitisation of the public sector, giving benefits to citizens, businesses and government" (Difi, 2017). As such, it brings together heads/directors from key Norwegian public institutions from various policy sectors: from education to justice, from taxes to health. The local government is also represented through the Association of Local and Regional Authorities (KS) (see Box 2.5). Other countries, such as Denmark and Uruguay, have bodies similar to the SKATE, with a stronger mandate (e.g. some decision-making power) and more representative inclusion of a broad range of relevant stakeholders, such as from the private sector and civil society.

Box 2.5. **Mandate and composition of SKATE**

SKATE discusses topics related to the digitisation of the public sector and addresses issues that are pertinent and important to all participants. Skate advises on measures and investments in the ICT area and issues comments on measures that apply to several of the members, including funding, management and organisation of common solutions.

SKATE has the following priorities:

- ensure public stakeholders' involvement in the digitalisation policy and developing national ICT common components
- assess the needs and suggestions for changes in common public ICT standards and architecture
- establish a forum for exchange of experiences and advice
- discuss investment needs and plans related to the digitalisation of the public sector
- develop recommendations
- assess the management performance of ICT common cross-sectoral components.

SKATE brings together senior managers from 12 public sector agencies and from several sectors of government:

- Difi (Chair)
- Brønnøysund Register Centre
- Tax Administration
- Norwegian Labour and Welfare Service
- Mapping Authority
- Directorate of Health
- Directorate of e-Health
- National Police Directorate
- State Educational Loan Fund
- Statistics Norway
- National Archives
- KS/KommIT.

Note: SKATE's mandate was approved in October 2012 by the Ministry of Government Administration, Reform and Chair Affairs (FAD) (parts of this defunct ministry were later incorporated into KMD).

Source: Ministry of Government, Administration, Reform and Church Affairs (2013), "Digital Agenda for Norway, ICT for Growth and Value Creation", FAD; Difi (2017), www.difi.no, official agency website (accessed 1 April 2017).

Even though, given its current mandate, the SKATE does not require the engagement of private sector, academia and civil society representatives in digital government development policies (e.g. advisory council), their involvement, particularly when discussing specific items, would contribute to the positive integration of more heterogeneous and pluralistic views in the leadership of the digital transformation of the public sector, taking a diverse and comprehensive set of needs into account. The involvement of non-governmental stakeholders would indeed allow for a higher responsiveness of the digital government strategy to citizen and business needs, contributing to the necessary shift from a citizen-centred to a more citizen-driven digital transformation of the public sector (OECD, forthcoming: 10).

Given the cross-cutting nature of the functional role of the SKATE, its advisory task in relation to the institutional co-ordination of ICT policies for the public sector should be broadly acknowledged across the administration. However, when asked about a formal mechanism in place to enable the co-ordination among central government agencies for public IT projects, only 35% of the institutions answered positively (Figure 2.10).

Figure 2.10. **Acknowledgement of institutional co-ordination between ministries/agencies: Norwegian public sector institutions' perceptions**

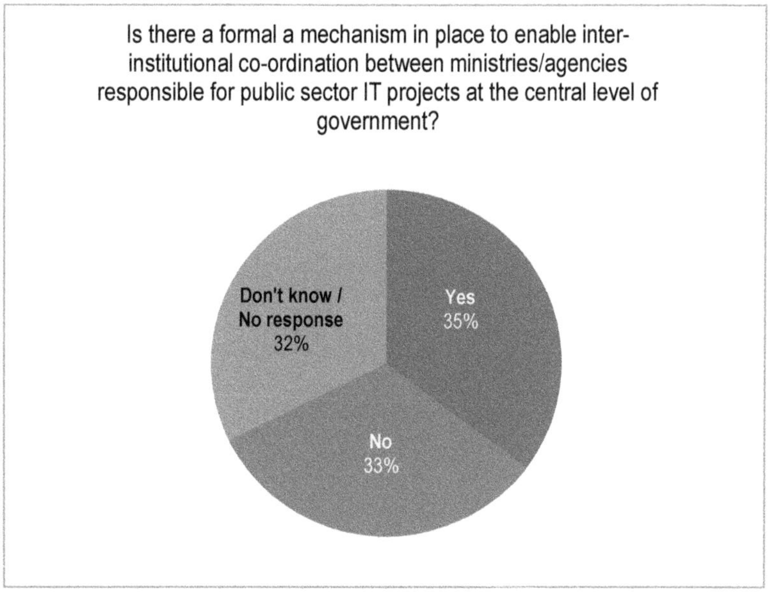

Source: OECD (2017b), "Digital Government Survey of Norway", public sector institutions version, OECD, Paris.

A general consensus seems to exist among the interviewed stakeholders about the necessity to reinforce institutional co-ordination for digital government development in the Norwegian public sector. To fulfil this need, the advisory role of SKATE, and its composition, is considered insufficient to support an efficient, effective and inclusive digital transformation of the public sector, which increasingly requires the collaboration and engagement of a high number of stakeholders. According to some of its members interviewed in the peer review mission, the spaced regularity of the meetings and its consensus-based nature makes it a very useful forum for information sharing, but with limited co-ordinating powers.

Policy levers for reinforced policy implementation

Besides co-ordination mechanisms, the governance framework for digital government should also incorporate policy levers that can support the coherent implementation of digital government across policy sectors and levels of government. These policy levers range from soft ones - such as the availability of common guidelines and system of incentives, to more coercive policy instruments - like regulations or funding mechanisms. Some OECD countries, like New Zealand and Portugal, adopted more coercive levers to boost digital government development, ensuring more intense co-ordination. Other countries, such as Sweden, rely on soft levers (OECD, 2016a) (see Figure 2.11).

Figure 2.11. **Levers of ICT governance in OECD countries**

What are the main responsibilities of the unit/function leading and co-ordinating ICT deployment in the central government?

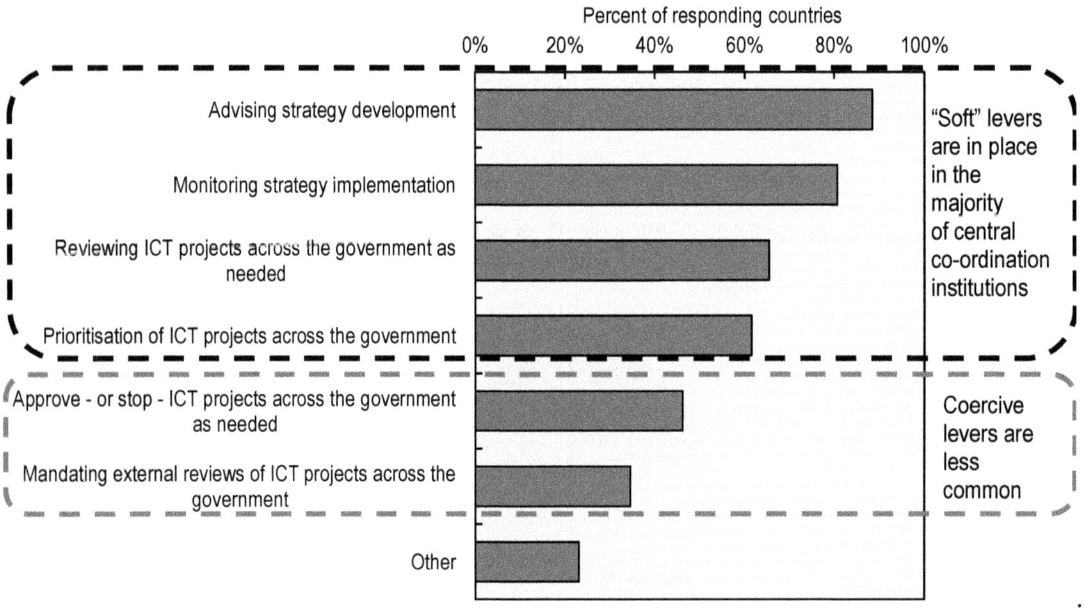

Source: OECD (2014b), "OECD Survey on Digital Government Performance" (dataset), OECD, Paris, http://qdd.oecd.org/subject.aspx?Subject=6C3F11AF-875E-4469-9C9E-AF93EE384796.

There isn't a one-size-fits-all model that can be recommended to all countries. The adoption of more coercive or softer policy levers should be adapted to the governance ecosystem in place, ensuring its synchronisation with dimensions like the existing political support, the legal and regulatory framework or the dominant institutional culture of the country.

When it comes to Norway, Difi appears to lack adequate policy levers to steer a co-ordinated and coherent digital transformation of the public sector. While the 2016 Digitalisation Memorandum aims to address this issue through the creation of Difi's co-financing mechanism, the agency's ability to enforce the structured implementation of central guidelines and policies is still limited.

In order to reinforce Difi's mandate, some strategic policy levers may need adopting. Based on several OECD countries' experience, the following should be considered:

1. **Evaluation of ICT projects**: Following examples from other countries, such as Denmark, Mexico, Portugal and Spain, the responsibility of the authority in charge of digital government to evaluate ICT projects can reinforce the digital government policy coherence across the public sector as well as the alignment of decisions and investments with the guidelines and overarching strategic objectives, thus helping to avoid overlaps and promote a share and re-use culture among public entities. The reinforcement of the mandate of the Digitisation Council (Digitaliseringsrådet) chaired by Difi, would strengthen the Difi's capacity to positively influence digital government development across different sectors and levels of government (see Chapter 3).

2. **Funding capacities**: The reinforcement of Difi's funding capacities, whether through the direct co-ordination of funding programmes or assuming a central role in the funding decision-making processes is also a solution to be considered to strengthen Difi's role as a cross-cutting promoter of the digital government potential. At the time of this review, Difi was looking at its capabilities and how to best harness them through its strategic goals and work.

3. **Digital service delivery**: Across OECD member countries, the digital government co-ordinating units frequently lead the government's digital service strategy. Since government CIOs are often in charge of rethinking government processes, service delivery policies emerge as a key area for a sound digital transformation of the public sector. Moving from government-centred to citizen-centred approaches, and evolving to citizen-driven practices, is a shift happening across OECD countries world wide (see Chapter 4). The Government Digital Service of the United Kingdom, the 18F Agency of the United States, the recent establishment of the Centre for Digital Services in Canada and the Digital Transformation Agency of Australia are good examples of public bodies that co-ordinate digital government and digital service delivery policies, as described further in Chapter 4 (OECD, 2016a).

4. **ICT procurement**: The co-ordination of ICT procurement can also be a useful policy lever to reinforce the role of the digital government co-ordinating units. The establishment of the Government Procurement Center (Statens innkjøpssenter) in Difi was an important step to better streamline decisions in this domain in Norway. Integrated ICT procurement policies and strategies are recognised today as a central instrument to secure efficiency, coherence and sustainability of digital government investments and results (see Chapter 3). Co-ordinated procurement processes in the public sector can facilitate economies of scale when buying products or services and can greatly foster interoperability of the public sector, by foreseeing the use of common standards, for example. It is important to stress that the identification of common - and strategic - procurement needs, and more recent approaches to the procurement of digital services, like cloud computing, have been at the origin of the establishment of shared services units, or specific public entities responsible for ICT procurement across the public sector. These are usually established with the mandate to provide support for the deployment of software, hardware, or for the provision of consultancy services. Estonia, Spain and New Zealand are among the countries that provide shared IT services under the office of the CIO (OECD, 2016a). In several other countries,

like Portugal, an autonomous public body co-ordinates the decisions on ICT procurement with the national CIO. In Denmark, Statens IT (the Agency for Governmental IT Services) is a separate agency from the one responsible for digital government even though they are both attached to the Ministry of Finance.

5. **Monitoring**: Mechanisms and tools to constantly and consistently monitor the implementation of the digital government agenda are an essential component of a governance framework. According to the overall analysis on ten OECD countries,[1] most of them concentrate the responsibility to monitor the developments of the digital transformation in the public sector under the digital government co-ordinating unit (OECD, 2016a). In Portugal, a Project Management Office closely follows each ministry's developments on digital government, based on several sectoral action plans elaborated to implement the national strategy. In Denmark, a budget threshold mechanism and a mandatory ICT project management instrument also guarantees considerable monitoring responsibilities to the central co-ordinating body.

The development of the cross-cutting responsibilities of Difi would not only help to assure a more coherent policy implementation of digital government initiatives in the Norwegian context, but could also bring value to central planning and monitoring activities in the sector. Broader supervision and co-ordination responsibilities for Difi would help avoid siloed and fragmented initiatives that respond in an inadequate way to citizen and business needs.

Developing a strategic system-thinking approach

A siloed approach to decision and policy making is a critical challenge commonly found in public administrations world wide. The different focus of public policies, political influence and competition for limited resources are some of the reasons that might explain this common trend across OECD countries across all levels of government. Beyond the missed opportunities for synergies and economies of scale, as an example, due to fragmented and non-articulated approaches, citizens and businesses are the most affected by this vertical approach, e.g. they hinder the delivery of integrated services that are more easily accessed and more convenient for users. Instead of a public sector that is able to act in an efficient, coherent and holistic way, citizens have to deal with an administration where agency-thinking approaches seem to prevail.

The high level of digitalisation of the Norwegian economy and society is complemented by a widespread penetration of digital technologies in all areas of the public sector (see Chapter 1). Stakeholders representing the Norwegian economy, society and public sector interviewed during the peer review mission unanimously recognised the importance of leveraging digital technologies to improve internal processes and transform the delivery of services to citizens and businesses. However, system-thinking practices are considered to be an exception across the Norwegian public sector according to the majority of the stakeholders met, since most public bodies appear to be focusing on overcoming specific institutional challenges and seizing opportunities.

1. Australia, Canada, Denmark, Estonia, New Zealand, Portugal, Spain, United Kingdom, United States and Uruguay.

For instance, during the peer review mission, both the Ministry of Health and Care Services (HOD) and the Ministry of Education and Research presented mature examples of sectoral digital service delivery platforms. However, some reluctance was found with regard to the adoption of central ICT key enablers. The common argument underlying the reluctance is the lack of adaptability of the mentioned enablers to the specific requisites and needs of a sectoral area. The Department of eHealth of the HOD, for example, does not use the Altinn platform (see Chapter 4) with the argument that it doesn't respond to the health sector's needs.

Even though the use of common solutions requires investments within each policy sector, these costs are normally compensated by the associated benefits, in terms of easier services' use and access for citizens and businesses, and improved efficiency and effectiveness for the entire public sector.

By embracing a more holistic approach aimed to reinforce a system-thinking culture when dealing with digital government related matters, the Norwegian government would more easily find integrated solutions to cross-cutting problems, increase its capacity to align efforts and enable synergies among public stakeholders. This could very well end up improving the coherence, effectiveness and sustainability of digital government policies management across the public sector (see Box 2.6).

Box 2.6. **System thinking for better policy making**

Complexity is a core feature of most policy issues today, yet governments are ill-equipped to deal with complex problems. Governments are confronted by uncertain and complex challenges whose scale and nature call for new approaches to problem solving. Some of them have started to use systems approaches in policy making and service delivery to tackle complex or "wicked" problems in areas ranging from education to ageing, healthcare and mobility.

Traditionally, policy makers have addressed social problems through discrete interventions that are layered on top of one another. However, these may shift consequences from one part of the system to another, or address symptoms while ignoring causes.

In a context of complexity and uncertainty, traditional analytical tools and problem-solving methods no longer work nor produce their intended purpose. Since the recognition of this complexity gap (the gap between the problems faced by institutions and their capacity to tackle them) systems thinking, and other systems approaches such as design thinking, have gained traction. Looking at the whole system rather than the parts allows one to focus on where change can have the greatest impact.

Source: OECD (2017c), *Systems Approaches to Public Sector Challenges: Working with Change*, OECD Publishing, Paris, http://dx.doi.org/10.1787/9789264279865-en.

The development of a system-thinking culture could also represent a strategic opportunity to involve the different agents of the digital government ecosystem in policy processes. The first and second principles of the OECD Recommendation on Digital Government Strategies (2014a) underline how the engagement of citizens, businesses and civil society in the design of digital government strategies and related policies can bring value by crowdsourcing and collecting perspectives, expectations and needs. But it is also a strategic way to secure the commitment and co-responsibility of stakeholders sharing successes and failures of a given policy implementation. Inclusive policy design processes are able to secure that the policy output is rooted and grounded in the ecosystem.

The development of the Digital Agenda for Norway provides a good example of the approach described in previous paragraphs, as it was designed through an open and inclusive process involving several key stakeholders, i.e. central level public sector institutions, regional or local level public sector institutions, civil servants, as well as representatives from the private sector and the academia. KMD organised a series of public meetings, bilateral meetings and seminars with the purpose of engaging key stakeholders and interest groups. Clear effort was put in place to acknowledge, understand and integrate the views of a broad range of sectors (OECD, 2017a).

When asked about the level of openness in the elaboration of the digital government strategy, almost 80% of the Norwegian institutions confirmed that it was developed through a co-ordinated process (Figure 2.12). This practice was fundamental to guarantee that different views, needs and perspectives were reflected in the digital strategy, favouring a system-thinking approach in the policy design process that will increase the likelihood of an effective and sustainable implementation of the Digital Agenda.

Figure 2.12. **Co-development of the Digital Agenda for Norway: Norwegian public sector institutions' perceptions**

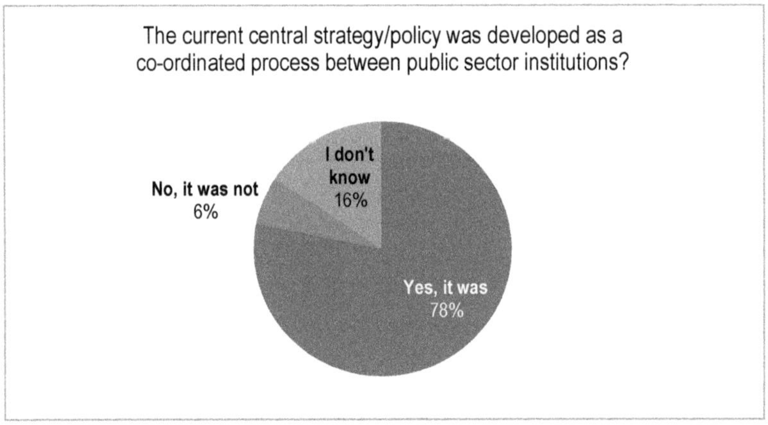

Source: OECD (2017b), "Digital Government Survey of Norway", public sector institutions version, OECD, Paris.

Inclusive policy-making processes are not a guarantee that a system-thinking approach will be followed in the implementation or management stages of a policy. Nevertheless, the ability to listen and integrate the views of the stakeholders allows for the development of a culture prone to holistic practices that better address complex challenges. Two practices can contribute in a decisive way to this process (OECD, 2017c: 37-39):

1. **Dwelling**: Investing substantial efforts and time to understand and connect the problem and the objective, in order to avoid biases or excessive reliance on tacit knowledge. Engagement practices where officials involve different stakeholders to better understand a complex problem is a way to foster this approach in the public sector.
2. **Connecting**: Using co-creation processes for the strong engagement of civil society can help promote a sense of commitment and ownership grounded in outcomes, and get close to citizens in a meaningful, constructive and respectful way.

Although the policy design phase of the Digital Agenda was conducted in a participatory and co-ordinated way, the policy implementation that followed did not maintain the initial level of inclusiveness and engagement with stakeholders. As mentioned previously, the institutional mechanisms in place are not able to assure the proper co-ordination among the Norwegian public sector to implement Norway's Digital Agenda.

The co-ordination of public bodies in the design and development of digital government strategies is also a practice that can help overcome and/or avoid siloed approaches that risk leading to public sector inefficiency in general terms. When probed on the existence of a "formal institutional digital strategy in place drawing upon the potential of ICTs to support your institution's operations and broader policy and service delivery objectives", almost 75% of the Norwegian institutions answered in a positive way (OECD, 2017b). However, when asked about the co-ordination of the mentioned strategies with other public bodies/ministries, only 32% replied positively (Figure 2.13).

Figure 2.13. **Co-ordination of the development of ICT strategies among public bodies: Norwegian public sector institutions' perceptions**

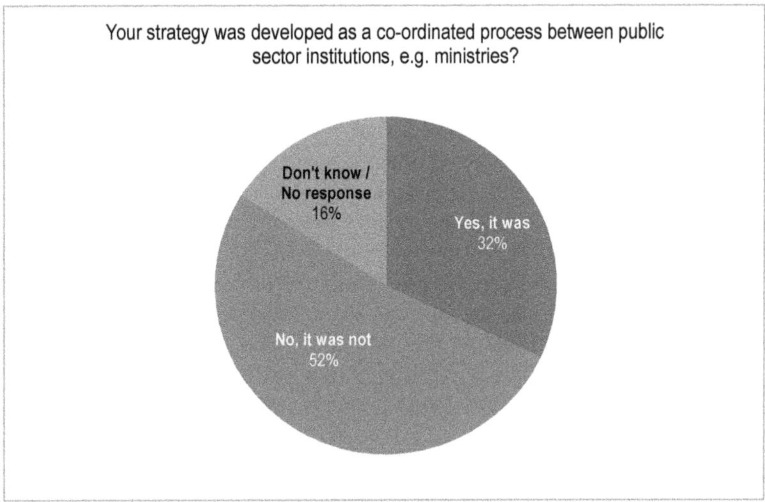

Source: OECD (2017b), "Digital Government Survey of Norway", public sector institutions version, OECD, Paris.

Today, the Norwegian government faces the challenge of responding to civil servants' expectations of a stronger system-thinking culture across the public sector, which could happen should the governance framework be clarified and the co-ordination policy tools for digital government be strengthened. As mentioned above, a sound governance framework, with clear leadership and distributed responsibilities, is crucial for better co-ordination across the public sector and to support more coherent and holistic policies for the development of digital government in Norway (see Box 2.7 for some examples of system approaches in the public sector). The development of a system-thinking culture in the Norwegian public sector should, in this context, be assumed as a deeply correlated and inter-connected objective.

Box 2.7. System approaches in the public sector: Examples from Canada and Finland

Regulating the sharing economy public transportation system in Canada

In Canada, different types of policies connected to the emerging fields of the sharing economy (housing and transportation bylaws, insurance, taxation, etc.) are regulated at different levels of government. This creates a problem of policy ownership. Confronted with Uber starting to operate in Toronto in 2014 without specific regulatory oversight, the city had to move quickly to regulate an unusual company and appease an alarmed incumbent industry. To tackle the regulatory challenge while simultaneously ensuring that the beneficial aspects of a sharing economy could be preserved, an independent arbiter, MaRS Solutions Lab, facilitated productive dialogue between different stakeholders. Utilising systems thinking and design methodologies, they proposed a user-centric vision and sharing economy city strategy for Toronto (and by extension, cities across Ontario) and contributed to a new form of legislation that enables the city and its citizens to both regulate and benefit from new entrants disrupting old businesses.

The experimental policy design in Finland

In 2015, Finland started to develop a new framework for experimental policy design. Together with Demos Helsinki, a Nordic ThinkThank, the Prime Minister's Office (PMO) of Finland employed a combined systems and design-thinking approach to develop a new policy framework to carry out experiments in government. As a result, experimentation was included in the strategic Government Programme ('Finland, a Land of Solutions') in May 2015 and an experimental policy-design programme was set up. The new approach to policy design allowed both broader "strategic experiments" (formalised policy trials) – for example, the ongoing basic income experiment – and grassroots experiments designed to build up the "experimental culture" in the public sector in Finland. There are by now over 20 experiments in process by the central government and many more conducted on the municipal level. In 2017, the Finnish government is launching a digital platform called Kokeilun Paikka (Place to Experiment) to support the government's key goal: find innovative ways to develop public services.

Source: OECD (2017c), *Systems Approaches to Public Sector Challenges: Working with Change*, OECD Publishing, Paris, http://dx.doi.org/10.1787/9789264279865-en.

References

Difi (Agency for Public Management and eGovernment) (2017), www.difi.no, official agency website (accessed 1 April 2017).

Digi-commissioner (2015), "The Netherlands - National Commissioner for Digital Government (Digi-commissioner)", www.digicommissaris.nl/english (accessed 4 May 2017).

European Commission (2016), "EU eGovernment Action Plan 2016-2020, Accelerating the digital transformation of government", http://eur-lex.europa.eu/legal-content/EN/TXT/PDF/?uri=CELEX:52016DC0179&from=EN.

Government of Norway (2017), "Government.no", official government website, www.regjeringen.no/en/ (accessed 31 March 2017).

KMD (Ministry of Local Government and Modernisation) (2016), "Digital Agenda for Norway in brief: ICT for a simpler everyday life and increased productivity", English version, KMD, www.regjeringen.no/en/dokumenter/digital-agenda-for-norway-in-brief/id2499897/sec1.

KMD (2016b), "2016 Digitalisation Memorandum", KMD, www.regjeringen.no/no/dokumenter/digitaliseringsrundskrivet/id2522147/.

Ministry of Government, Administration, Reform and Church Affairs (FAD) (2013), "Digital Agenda for Norway, ICT for Growth and Value Creation", FAD.

OECD (forthcoming), "The digital transformation of the public sector: Helping governments respond to the needs of networked societies", *OECD Working Papers on Public Governance*, OECD Publishing, Paris.

OECD (2017a), "Digital Government Survey of Norway", central version, OECD, Paris.

OECD (2017b), "Digital Government Survey of Norway", public sector institutions version, OECD, Paris.

OECD (2017c), *Systems Approaches to Public Sector Challenges: Working with Change*, OECD Publishing, Paris, http://dx.doi.org/10.1787/9789264279865-en.

OECD (2016a), *Digital Government in Chile: Strengthening the Institutional and Governance Framework*, OECD Digital Government Studies, OECD Publishing, Paris, http://dx.doi.org/10.1787/9789264258013-en.

OECD (2016b), "Executive Summary", in *OECD Economic Surveys: Norway 2016*, OECD Publishing, Paris, http://dx.doi.org/10.1787/eco_surveys-nor-2016-3-en.

OECD (2016c), "OECD Questionnaire on Governance of Digital Government" (unpublished dataset), OECD, Paris.

OECD (2014a), "Recommendation of the Council on Digital Government Strategies", OECD, Paris, www.oecd.org/gov/digital-government/recommendation-on-digital-government-strategies.htm

OECD (2014b), "OECD Survey on Digital Government Performance" (dataset), OECD, Paris, http://qdd.oecd.org/subject.aspx?Subject=6C3F11AF-875E-4469-9C9E-AF93EE384796.

OECD (2010), *Denmark: Efficient e-Government for Smarter Public Service Delivery*, OECD Publishing, Paris, http://dx.doi.org/10.1787/9789264087118-en.

Further reading

European Commission (2017), "Digital Skills and Jobs Coalition", webpage, https://ec.europa.eu/digital-single-market/en/digital-skills-jobs-coalition (accessed 8 April 2017).

European Commission (2016), "eGovernment Factsheets: Norway", https://joinup.ec.europa.eu/community/nifo/og_page/egovernment-factsheets#eGov2016

OECD (2015), *OECD Public Governance Reviews: Estonia and Finland: Fostering Strategic Capacity across Governments and Digital Services across Borders*, OECD Public Governance Reviews, OECD Publishing, Paris, http://dx.doi.org/10.1787/9789264229334-en.

OECD (2015), *OECD Digital Economy Outlook 2015*, OECD Publishing, Paris, http://dx.doi.org/10.1787/9789264232440-en.

OECD (2015), *Government at a Glance 2015*, OECD Publishing, Paris, http://dx.doi.org/10.1787/gov_glance-2015-en.

Chapter 3

Improving ICT management and strategic planning in Norway

This chapter focuses on the existing capacities across the Norwegian public sector to support an efficient, coherent and sustainable digital transformation. Starting with an overview of the information and communications technology (ICT) expenditures in the Norwegian public administration, the analysis will assess the cost-benefit practices in use, namely business-case methodologies to guide ICT investments. The existence of standardised models for ICT project management in the public sector will also be explored as a relevant policy lever to increase co-ordination, synergies, knowledge sharing and sound monitoring of digital government development. The chapter will discuss the landscape of digital skills in the Norwegian public sector and the strategic selection of responsibilities between the public and private sector with regard to core functions and tasks, e.g. related to ICT projects management. The analysis will close with an assessment of the Norwegian public sector's experience and practices in the procurement of ICT.

Introduction

The progressive digitalisation of all public administration activities and the rising presence and uptake of digital technologies require governments' sound approaches for information and communications technology (ICT) deployment and maintenance. Strategic planning is necessary to structure ICT investments across sectors and levels of government, but also to secure the availability of appropriate skills in the public sector workforce. Digital technologies are increasingly diverse and come with progressive levels of complexity, demanding different cost structures (e.g. specialised human resources, specific hardware, development of tailored software, security tests, usability tests, load tests, legal consulting services) to face dependencies from numerous variables (e.g. economic or social sector to be applied, profile of final users, expected demands, foreseen technological evolution, national or international regulations). In this sense, ICT investments in the public sector are becoming more challenging in relation to budget size and management, as well as with regard to the choice of procurement methods, technical options and stakeholders' involvement (OECD, 2016).

Governments of OECD countries are adopting business-case methodologies and assuming a cross-cutting commitment to the development of project management and digital skills, as critical elements of the public sector's capability to develop a digital government sustainable approach (Principles 9 and 10 of the OECD Recommendation on Digital Government Strategics). The strategic planning of ICT investments, i.e. the process by which the public sector ensures the alignment of ICT projects with broader objectives set by national/or and institutional strategies, helps governments to evaluate the benefits of their investments, avoid gaps and overlaps in public sector efforts and provides for more accurate risk management strategies.

The adoption and regular use of common business-case approaches and project management tools can have a positive impact on the prioritisation of investments and the mobilisation of adequate financial resources, since they favour a more holistic mapping of public sector needs. Strategic planning mechanisms also enable the public sector to better spot synergies, integrate financial efforts and share returns, which are central features of the digital transformation of public sector organisations.

In Norway, ICT expenditures represent a substantial proportion of central government procurement (see Figure 3.1). The Ministry of Health reports that ICT procurement represents 30% of total procurement expenditures. ICT procurement represents 28% of total procurement expenditures for the Ministry of Economic Affairs and 27% for the Ministry of Education (OECD, 2017a). Regarding the distribution across levels of government, the central government spends as much as 57% of total public sector ICT expenditures, against 35% for municipalities and 8% for counties (OECD, 2017a).

Figure 3.1. **ICT expenditures in Norwegian ministries**

By individual ministry, in %

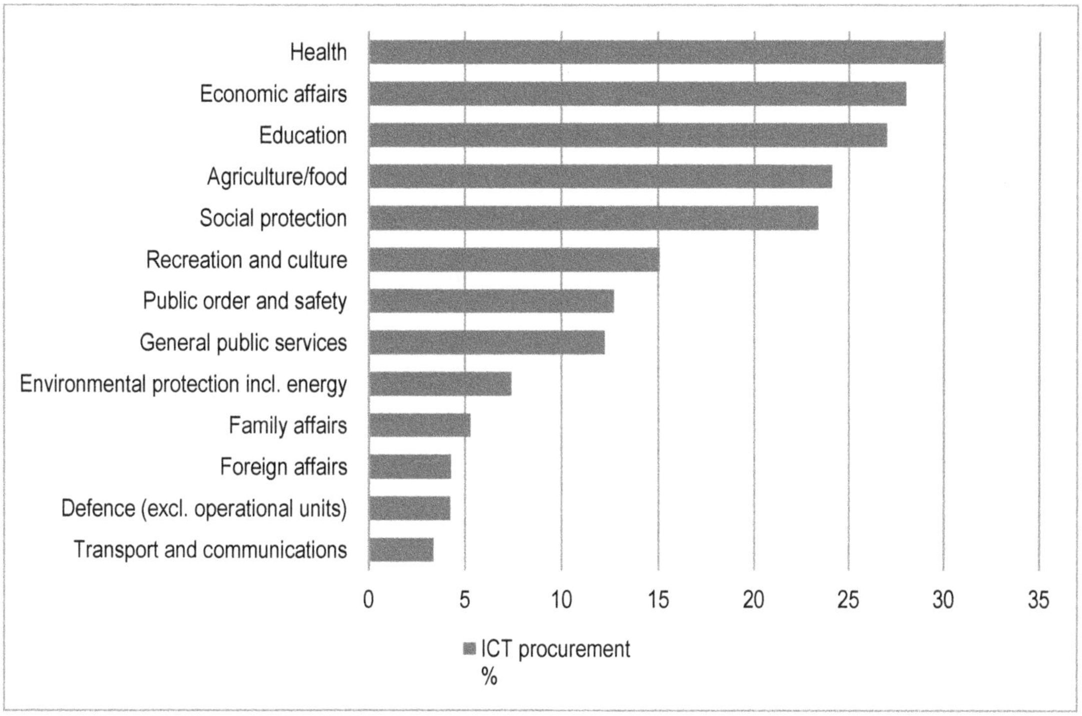

Source: OECD (2017a), "Digital Government Survey of Norway", central version, OECD, Paris. Based on the question, "Percentage of ICT procurement of the total procurement by individual ministry".

The significant weight of ICT expenditures on the Norwegian public sector highlights the relevance of ensuring robust and strategic ICT planning and management. This chapter provides a general assessment of the status of ICT planning and management within Norway's public administration. The next section advances an overview of the use of cost-benefit analysis, namely the use of business-case methodologies to guide ICT investments. The following section focuses on the importance of using standardised models for ICT project management across the public sector. The chapter continues by exploring how the needs in terms of digital skills are being tackled by the public sector, assessing in particular the need to ensure a proper balance between outsourcing and insourcing of the management of core tasks related to digital government development. The chapter concludes with an overview of the Norwegian public sector's strategic management of ICT procurement.

Reinforcing strategic planning and management of ICT projects

In order to fully realise the benefits of digital government, the public sector should be able to strategically prioritise, adequately structure and co-ordinate ICT expenditures across different sectors of government. This has led a majority of OECD countries to adopt tools for enhanced ICT project management and governance. Given the cross-cutting role of digital technologies, various policy mechanisms are used to optimise and rationalise ICT expenditures in the public sector, to make it more streamlined and coherent.

For instance, 80% of OECD countries use budget thresholds to structure the governance of ICT projects (OECD, 2014a). In these countries, ICT projects above a pre-determined budgetary value should meet certain administrative, financial, management or technical requirements in order to be approved. The level and scope of the thresholds is an important dimension to consider, as very different levels are used to make the evaluation mandatory or not with very different implications. In some countries, like Portugal and Spain, the value is substantially low, while in others, like Denmark, only large and structural ICT projects require the full development of a business-case proposition and all the phases of the ICT project management model (OECD, 2016).

Ex ante *evaluation mechanisms for sound ICT investments*

During the peer review mission in Oslo, the Norwegian stakeholders fully recognised the importance of value proposition practices to support ICT investments. The country's institutional framework to strengthen coherence and secure the sustainability of ICT expenditures comprises several elements.

The Ministry of Local Government and Modernisation (KMD) is the main co-ordination body for digital government development in Norway. KMD's subordinate agency, the Agency for Public Management and eGovernment (Difi), encourages the co-ordinated and cost-efficient use of ICT within the public sector. The Strategic Cooperation Council for Management and Coordination of eGovernment Services (SKATE) is a strategic collaborative council and advisory body meant to ensure co-ordination of the digitalisation of the public sector (see Chapter 2).

It is worth highlighting the role of the KMD in advising the Ministry of Finance on prioritisation of ICT investments within the yearly Budget Investment Proposal programme (Statsingsforslag). This policy mechanism is useful to align ministerial ICT projects with the national digital government strategic goals, e.g. as set in the national Digital Agenda. To apply projects to the Budget Investment Proposal programme, ministries must submit a form that includes information about the project's value creation. This information is used by the KMD to rank the submitted projects and for the final decision about the availability of funding.

The Digitalisation Council (Digitaliseringsrådet) is another collective body of the Norwegian digital government institutional framework. It was established in 2016 to assist public sector institutions succeed in their digitalisation efforts through the provision of quality assurance for ICT projects (KMD, 2016). Chaired by Difi, the Council has representatives from the public sector (central and local government), the private sector and the academia (see Box 3.1).

Box 3.1. **Norway's Digitalisation Council (Digitaliseringsrådet)**

Mission

"The government has established a digitisation council that will help public agencies to succeed in digitisation projects. The council will also help state agencies to learn from each other's successes and mistakes." (Difi, 2017)

Members

- Svein R. Kristensen, Difi (Chair)
- Toril Nag, Executive Vice President of Lyse
- Nina Aulie, Director of the Directorate of Health
- Kjetil Århus, Director of ICT Group in Bergen Municipality
- Magne Jørgensen, Researcher at Simula Research Laboratory
- Jan-Olav Styrvold, Director of Economics and IT at Vinmonopolet
- Eli Stokke Rondeel, Project Manager in Hospital Partner
- Øivind Christoffersen, Special Advisor

Review process for ICT projects

The process is divided into three stages:

1. **Preparations**: The public body contacts the Digitalisation Council and reports the interest for a project's review. The timeframe and the group of documents to be submitted are agreed.
2. **Project review**: The Digitalisation Council takes around three weeks to treat the process. The documents are reviewed by the secretariat as a preparation for the council. The leader of the public body meets the council and the project is broadly discussed. After the treatment in the council, the public body receives a written recommendation.
3. **Follow up**: After consultation in the Digitalisation Council, the public body can get guidance from the secretariat.

Source: Difi (Agency for Public Management and eGovernment) (2017), www.difi.no, official agency website (accessed 1 April 2017).

The Digitalisation Council has a determinant role in ensuring coherence of decisions and respect of established standards for major ICT projects, since public institutions are advised to submit to this collective body project proposals with a budget between NOK 10 million and NOK 750 million. However, the guidance and coaching role of the Digitalisation Council is not mandatory, thus relying on the institutions' willingness to follow its recommendations or not.

A second *ex ante* evaluation mechanism for public projects (including ICT projects) is applied to initiatives over NOK 750 million. Over this threshold, a cost-benefit assessment - known as KS-ordningen or Quality Assurance scheme (QAs) - is required.

The assessment is carried out by the Ministry of Finance, typically with the support of external consultancy firms.

The Quality Assurance scheme mechanism was established in 2000 after several examples of national projects that had failed due to costs overruns, delays and lack of quality standards (NTNU, 2017). The Ministry of Finance signed a framework agreement with diverse consultancy companies to perform the QAs. Since then, the framework agreement evolved. The current QAs was established in September 2015 and will last two years, with the possibility of being extended for another two years by the Ministry of Finance. The QA scheme in place nowadays comprises two external reviews in an investment project's planning process (NTNU, 2017) (see Figure 3.2):

1. **QA1 – Quality assurance of choice of concept**

   The purpose of this stage is to ensure that alternative concepts are considered and subject to the political control of the Government's Cabinet in the decision to start a project. The stage is also important to guarantee that the documents informing the decision are of high quality.

2. **QA2 – Quality assurance of the management base and cost estimates**

   Developed before the project being submitted for Parliament's approval and consequent funding consent, its main purpose is to control the documentation behind the proposition. The cost estimates and the foresight scenarios for the management challenges in the following phases of the project are at the centre of this stage.

Figure 3.2. **Norwegian scheme for quality assurance of major public investments (the QA scheme)**

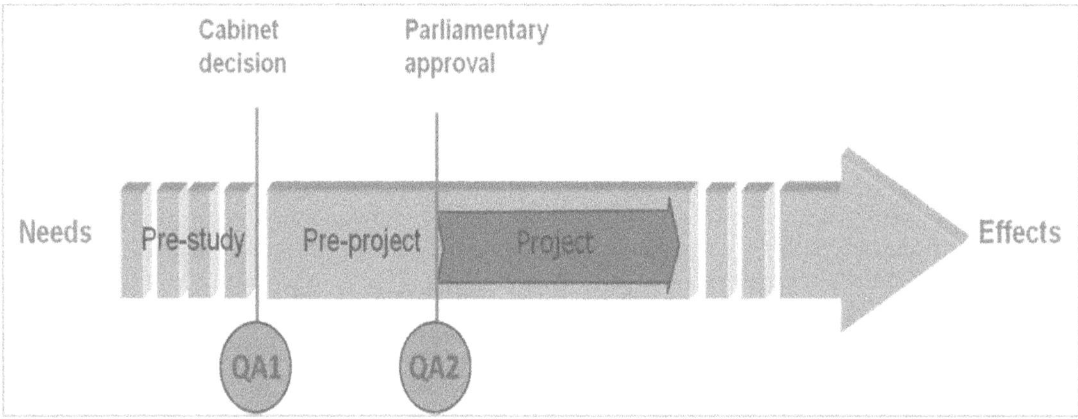

Source: NTNU (Norwegian University of Science and Technology) (2017), "The Norwegian scheme for quality assurance of major public investments (the QA scheme)", webpage, www.ntnu.edu/web/concept/qa-scheme1 (accessed 12 August 2017).

Although the two *ex ante* evaluation mechanisms – Digitisation Council and Quality Assurance Scheme – represent an important contribution to improving the efficiency and coherence of ICT initiatives, there was a general consensus among the public stakeholders during the peer review mission about the need to better use existing mechanisms for cost-benefit analysis of ICT projects. The recent establishment of the Digitisation Council, in 2016, might explain why even though an increasing number of actors is aware of its existence, insufficient awareness was found among the stakeholders about its advisory role. The Norwegian government would benefit from better promoting and clarifying the mission of the Council, inasmuch as it would help demonstrate the benefits for individual ICT projects' assessment and for the efficiency of the public administration as a whole.

The experience of OECD countries is diverse in terms of mechanisms in place to enhance projects' scrutiny and quality assurance. However, given the technical specificities and complexities of public sector ICT projects, governments have made efforts to streamline policy tools to guarantee the optimisation and increasing coherence of ICT expenditures, such as the acquisition and maintenance of hardware, deployment and development of software or contracting of ICT consultancy services (see Box 3.2).

Box 3.2. **ICT project assessment in Portugal**

The Portuguese Agency for Administrative Modernisation (AMA), an executive agency located at the Presidency of the Council of Ministers, has substantive powers in terms of allocation of financial resources and approval of ICT projects.

The AMA manages the administrative modernisation funding programme, which is composed of EU structural funds and national resources (SAMA2020). These funds are an attractive source of funding for agencies planning to develop ICT projects. This gives AMA important leverage as the approval of funding for digital government projects through this programme is conditioned on compliance with existing guidelines.

Similarly, every ICT project of EUR 10 000 or more must be pre-approved by AMA, which verifies compliance with guidelines, the non-duplication of efforts, and compares the prices and budgets with previous projects in order to ensure the best value for money.

Source: OECD (2016), *Digital Government in Chile: Strengthening the Institutional and Governance Framework*, OECD Digital Government Studies, OECD Publishing, Paris, http://dx.doi.org/10.1787/9789264258013-en.

In line with the progressive importance conceded by the Norwegian government to cost-benefit assessments, two relevant initiatives were implemented in 2016 to improve the quality of ICT projects:

1. **Difi's co-financing mechanism (Medfinansieringsordningen)**

This funding scheme led by Difi is intended to improve the digitalisation of the Norwegian public sector, investing in small- and medium-sized ICT projects that must be economically viable. To be considered for funding, ICT projects should have a total cost that ranges between NOK 5 million to NOK 50 million, and able to receive co-financing support from Difi of up to 50% of total costs, with a limit of NOK 15 million.

All submitted projects must present a simplified cost-benefit analysis that shows that the investment is financially viable. Proposals are ranked based on "which projects provide the highest socio-economic return per invested krone over the public budget" (Difi, 2017).

In 2017, Difi received a budget of NOK 111.8 million from central government to co-finance new projects.

Although counties and municipalities cannot apply for co-financing, many of the projects that receive financing have significant benefits for the municipal sector. For example, projects funded in 2016 will provide benefits in the municipal sector in the range of NOK 133.7 million annually from 2018. Fourteen projects have received provisional funding commitments, from NOK 2.6 million to NOK 15 million. The total socio-economic profitability (net present value over ten years) is estimated at NOK 6.5 billion and the possible savings over public budgets are around NOK 3 billion for the same period (Difi, 2017).

The Norwegian government is also reinforcing the funding mechanisms for ICT projects in the municipalities. NOK 25 million were allocated in 2017 and the government plans to allocate NOK 100 million in 2018, to be administrated by Norwegian Association of Local and Regional Authorities (KS). This new funding mechanism envisages supporting ICT projects in municipalities that develop solutions that can be used by all municipalities.

2. Digitalisation Memorandum (Digitaliseringsrundskrivet)

This yearly KMD's policy document is addressed to all the ministries and underlying/subordinate agencies and directorates. It compiles orientations about requirements and provides recommendations to promote the digitisation of the public sector (see Chapter 2). The areas covered in 2016 are very diverse, ranging from the use of national components to the "digital first" initiative (Digitalt førstevalg) (see Chapter 4).

One of the orientations of the memorandum is the requirement that ICT projects over NOK 10 million should use a best practice project management model. The model should have "clear phases and decision points, and requirements for which management documentation will be available at each decision point" (Difi, 2017) (see the next section, Improving ICT project management).

Difi's co-financing mechanism and the Digitalisation Memorandum are good examples of the Norwegian government's commitment to spreading cost-benefit analysis across the public sector, improving the quality of ICT projects.

Business cases for improved cost-benefit analysis

The use of common business-case methodologies is one of the central policy tools used by OECD countries to structure and secure strategic and efficient planning of ICT investments through cost-benefit analysis (see Figure 3.3). Some countries use it as a mandatory mechanism for all ICT projects in central government – e.g. in Denmark, Korea and Luxembourg. Others have more flexible approaches, considering it mandatory when specific criteria are met (e.g. Canada, New Zealand). The mandatory use of business-case methodologies above a certain threshold is the most common scenario.

Figure 3.3. **Business-case methodologies mandatory for ICT projects in central government in selected countries**

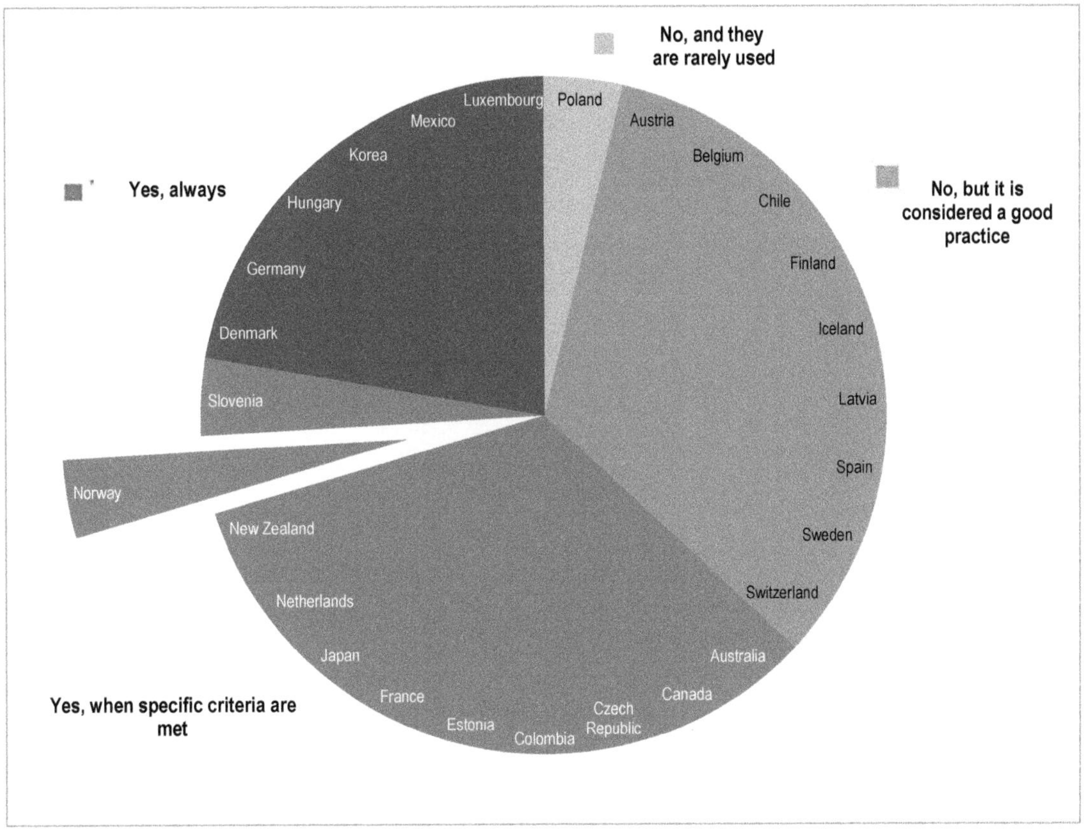

Source: OECD (2014a), "OECD Survey on Digital Government Performance" (dataset), OECD, Paris, http://qdd.oecd.org/subject.aspx?Subject=6C3F11AF-875E-4469-9C9E-AF93EE384796.

In Norway, the use of a business-case model is mandatory when a project is above NOK 750 million. As previously mentioned, a detailed cost-benefit assessment of such large-scale projects is required by the Ministry of Finance. Projects of small and medium scale are not required to follow this requisite and a standard model at national level for ICT project cost-benefit evaluation is not currently in place in the Norwegian public sector.

Nevertheless, when asked about the effective use of mechanisms for cost-benefit analysis for ICT projects, the majority of Norwegian institutions states using business-case models. Some 24% use it for all ICT projects and 29% use it for projects that meet specific criteria (Figure 3.4). The Brønnøysund Register, a public entity responsible for managing several Norwegian basic registries, was one of the stakeholders that stressed the utility of using business-case methodologies in all ICT projects.

Figure 3.4. **Business-case usage in Norway's central government**

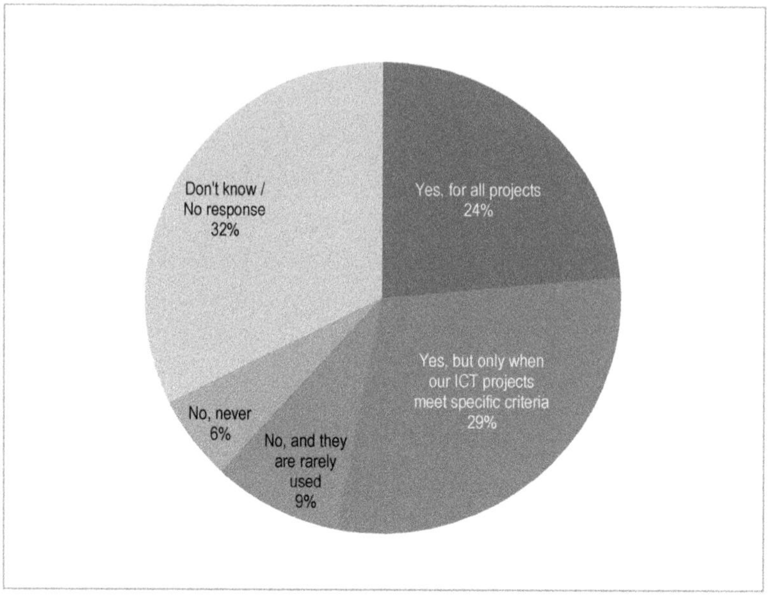

Source: OECD (2017b), "Digital Government Survey of Norway", public sector institutions version, OECD, Paris.

Beyond the use of business-case models, 89% of the Norwegian public institutions estimate the financial benefits for ICT projects (*ex ante*) (Figure 3.5 further below). This practice demonstrates that, although a standard business-case model has not been established and is not being used in Norway, and tight mechanisms for ICT project evaluation and financial approval are also missing, a culture of efficiency – with a strong focus on financial benefits - is grounded in the overall culture of the public sector, which is a key requirement for the success of the Norwegian model. The model is based on recommendations, guidelines and incentives, as opposed to strong requirements and obligatory practices found in other jurisdictions. The model provides the example of a high degree of compliance achieved without having to resort to obligatory measures.

Several institutional tools are also in place, applicable to all policy domains, supporting the Norwegian culture focused on efficiency and financial benefits. For instance, in the Budget Investment proposal (Satsingsforslag), there is a requirement to develop a business case. The Instructions for Official Studies (Utredningsinstruksen) aimed to provide a good basis for decisions about government measures, such as reforms, regulatory changes and investments, and include requirements such as: 1) What is the problem and what will we achieve?; 2) What measures are relevant?; 3) What fundamental questions do the measures take?; 4) What are the positive and negative effects of the measures, how long are they and who will be affected?; 5) Which measures are recommended and why?; 6) What are the prerequisites for successful completion? The Rules for Financial Management in the Staten (Regelverk for økonomistyring i staten) also require a cost-benefit analysis (Government of Norway, 2017).

Nevertheless, improving the performance of ICT investments requires going beyond the institutional culture and cost-benefit mechanisms applicable to all policy areas. The adoption and use of standardised tools for ICT projects could lead to even higher coherence of practices and financial decisions. When asked about monitoring (*ex post*) the financial benefits of ICT projects, less than half of the Norwegian institutions (47%) that responded to the OECD questionnaire report that they do so (Figure 3.5). This substantial gap between the use of *ex ante* and *ex post* mechanisms for financial benefits calculation demonstrates that there is still room for improvement in the Norwegian digital government landscape.

Figure 3.5. ***Ex ante* and *ex post* financial benefits: Practices employed by Norway's central government**

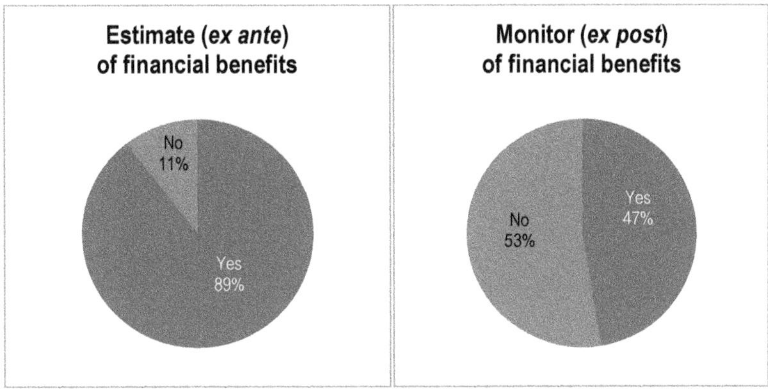

Source: OECD (2017b), "Digital Government Survey of Norway", public sector institutions version, OECD, Paris.

The Norwegian public sector would also benefit from a broader assessment of financial benefits of ICT projects, looking at the broader ecosystem of digital government stakeholders (e.g. private sector, third sector, citizens) beyond the public sector. According to Norwegian central government institutions that answered the OECD survey, the calculation of financial benefits of ICT projects for businesses, citizens or specific groups of the population is still an exception (Figure 3.6).

Figure 3.6. **Measurement of financial benefits outside the public sector by Norway's central government**

In %

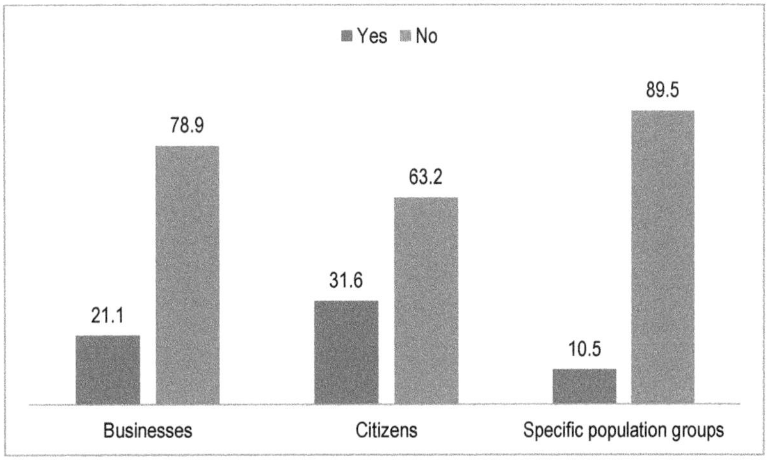

Source: OECD (2017b), "Digital Government Survey of Norway", public sector institutions version, OECD, Paris.

Sound financial approval mechanisms, connected with agile and streamlined cost-benefit analysis, can improve the strategic organisation and systemic governance of ICT projects. In this sense, given the considerable dimension and significant financial risks of the projects assessed by the Digitalisation Council (between NOK 10 million and NOK 750 million), the Norwegian government would benefit in shifting from a non-mandatory to a mandatory approach. Building on the consensus found among the stakeholders for the need for more consistency, it may be worth considering establishing a new non-mandatory mechanism for pre-evaluation of projects below NOK 10 million to increase the overall performance of ICT investments across the entire public sector.

The development of a clear, specific and standard business-case models that can be used as a mandatory requirement in the pre-evaluation of ICT projects is also a policy lever to be considered to promote greater coherence in cost-benefit analysis across sectors and levels of government. The model could be articulated with the best practice ICT project management model used in the framework of the Digitalisation Memorandum for projects above NOK 10 million.

Improving ICT project management

Due to the constant development of digital technologies, their rising scope and the urgency for their rapid uptake – also within the public sector - the management of ICT projects is becoming increasingly complex. The technical, financial, legal and institutional variables to be considered demand project management models able to structure public sector's efforts to maintain the alignment of the stakeholders' technological choices with overall strategic objectives and secure the quality and sustainability of results (Principle 10 of the OECD Recommendation on Digital Government Strategies).

A growing number of OECD member countries has established standardised models of ICT project management to face this challenge (e.g. Denmark; see Box 3.3), and to secure better alignment, comparability and performance of public efforts in this policy area. Some 60% of the countries that responded to the OECD (2014a) Survey on Digital Government Performance confirm the existence of a model for the central government level (see Figure 3.7). These models complement business-case methodologies and provide a framework for the effective implementation of projects as planned.

Box 3.3. The Danish ICT Project Model

The Danish ICT Project Model provides a standardised way of managing ICT projects across the government administration. With clear reference to the UK ICT project model, Prince2, it provides guidelines for how to organise and manage ICT projects and delivers concrete templates for all generic products in the process. The overall phases covering all projects are illustrated below:

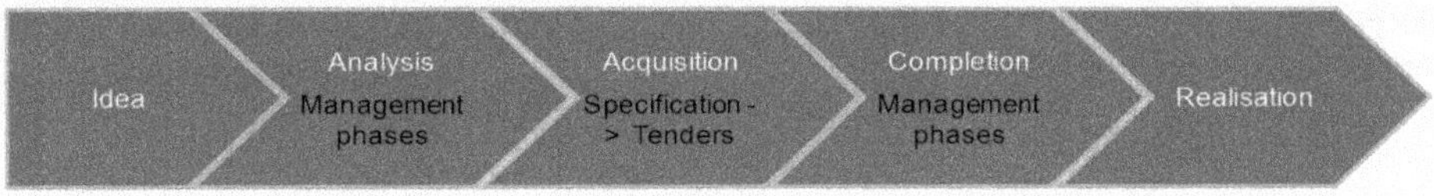

The model has enabled the establishment of a specific governance structure, for example requiring approvals of well-developed business cases, as well as ongoing approvals – so called "stop-go" decisions - each time a project passes from one phase to the next.

Source: OECD (2016), *Digital Government in Chile: Strengthening the Institutional and Governance Framework*, OECD Digital Government Studies, OECD Publishing, Paris, http://dx.doi.org/10.1787/9789264258013-en.

Figure 3.7. **Existence of standardised models of ICT project management at the central government level in selected countries**

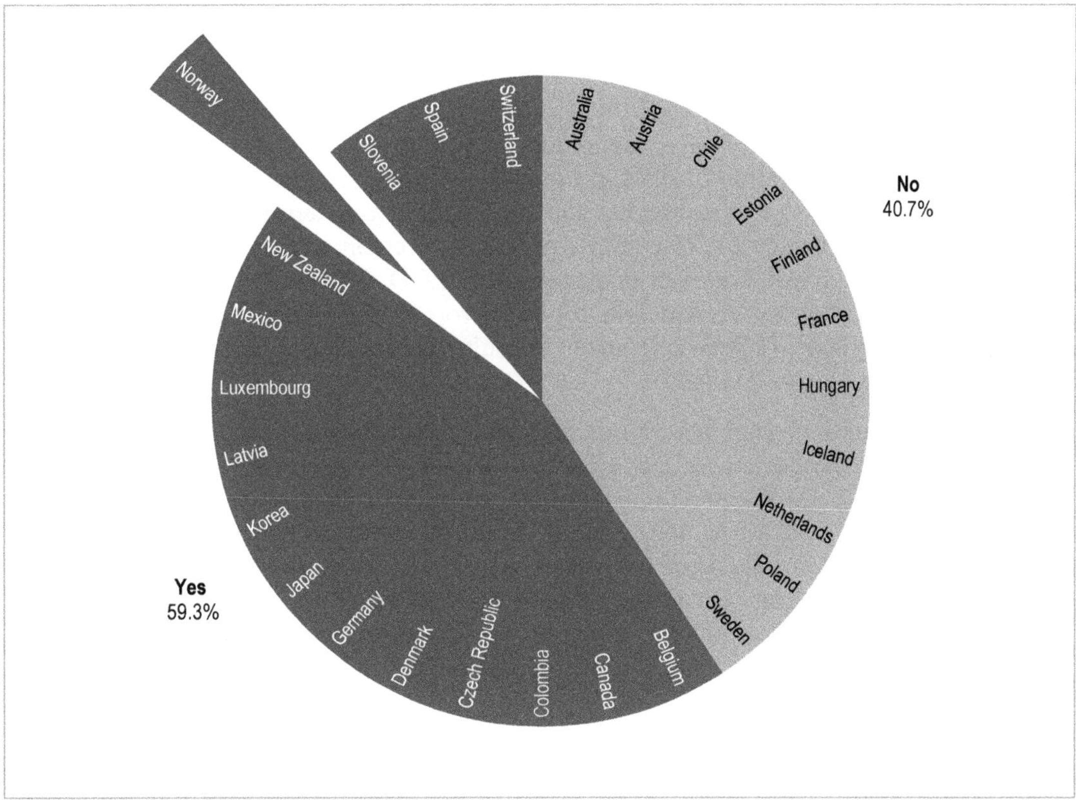

Source: OECD (2014a), "OECD Survey on Digital Government Performance" (dataset), OECD, Paris, http://qdd.oecd.org/subject.aspx?Subject=6C3F11AF-875E-4469-9C9E-AF93EE384796.

Norway has realised the relevance of such tools to ensure effective project delivery and has put in place its own model: Difi's Project Wizard (Projectveiviseren). Some 90% of the Norwegian institutions state being aware of the existence of this tool, and almost 80% of the institutions that are aware of it confirmed using it (Figure 3.8).

Figure 3.8. **Awareness of Difi's Project Wizard within Norway's central government**

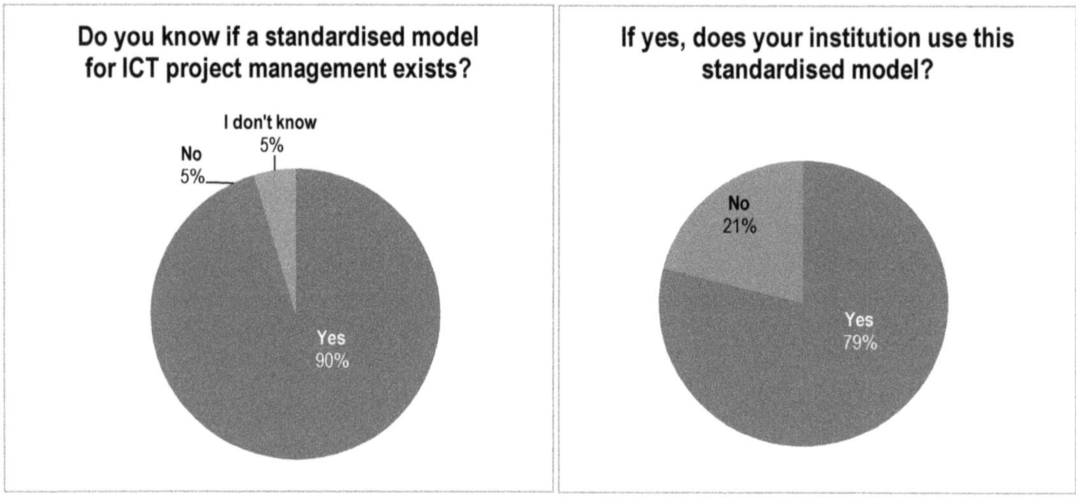

Source: OECD (2017b), "Digital Government Survey of Norway", public sector institutions version, OECD, Paris.

The involvement of external stakeholders in ICT project management is a practice that allows for the integration of different angles and perspectives in the development of the project, promoting shared ownership and encouraging a system-thinking culture in the public sector (see Chapter 2). Two-thirds of the Norwegian institutions state involving external stakeholders in ICT project management (OECD, 2017b). When asked to further specify, the line ministry responsible for the project, the executive agency, private information technology (IT) management consultancies and end users are most often stated as being frequently involved.

Norwegian public sector institutions also stated that they follow diverse guidelines and procedures in the design and development of their ICT projects (Figure 3.9). These are followed mostly for the procurement of IT goods or services, for the use of shared services (e.g. ICT infrastructure, shared business processes), the use of digital authentication or the management of cyber risks. The connection of these guidelines or procedures with existing or future digital government policy levers – funding mechanisms, pre-evaluation of ICT expenses, business-case models – is a key step for integrated policies able to drive the digital transformation of the public sector.

Figure 3.9. **Guidelines or procedures followed when managing IT projects in Norway's central government**

In %

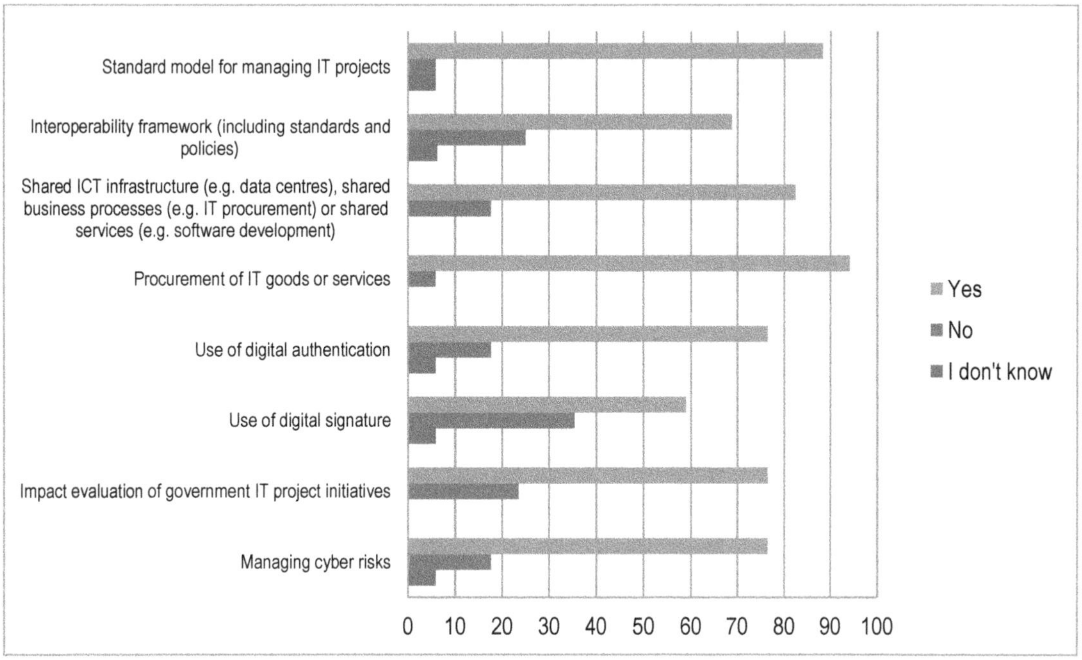

Source: OECD (2017b), "Digital Government Survey of Norway", public sector institutions version, OECD, Paris.

The Norwegian public sector landscape seems to be significantly mature in the cross-cutting use of ICT project management approaches. The requirement established by the 2016 Digitalisation Memorandum regarding the mandatory use of a best practice project-management model for ICT projects over NOK 10 million should contribute to increasing the country's capacities to maintain high levels of performance in the development of digital government, providing new opportunities for coherence and promoting the capturing of synergies. The requirement is also an opportunity to better map and share knowledge about the government's practices, contributing to strengthening the foundations of the digital transformation of the public sector.

Difi's Project Wizard is the recommended (although not mandatory) project management model indicated by the Digitalisation Memorandum. Understood as a common project-management model for the public sector, this online tool directed to project managers aims to reduce complexity and risks in public ICT projects. Based on the internationally renowned PRINCE2® (PRojects IN Controlled Environments) projection method, Project Wizard describes a set of phases that projects must go through, with specific decision points. It covers the full scale project management, including benefits' realisation.

The fact that a common model is available on line - Difi's "Project Wizard" platform www.prosjektveiviseren.no – is a very positive sign of progress and commitment from the Norwegian government to streamline ICT project management at the central and local levels of government. At the time of the drafting of this review, the launch of Project Wizard 3.0, including several new and relevant features, was still recent and its adoption was at the very early stages; thus, a full evaluation of its impact across the Norwegian Public sector was not possible. Nevertheless, the way the platform is structured and the fact that its usage benefits from substantial institutional support – Digitalisation Memorandum – set the stage and expectations for this promising initiative.

Project Wizard can indeed be assumed as a strategic tool for better development as well as monitoring of digital government projects across the Norwegian government. In fact, this standardised ICT project management model offers new possibilities to monitor projects' implementation in articulated ways, thus enabling smarter project management and data-informed improvements. The alignment of Project Wizard with the previously mentioned need for an ICT business-case model to be commonly used is one of the key developments that the Norwegian government could consider to improve the performance of its ICT investments.

On the other hand, this common project management tool can also improve institutional learning and knowledge sharing on successes and failures in ICT projects. The Norwegian government, through KMD and Difi, has an interesting opportunity to leverage and spread public sector experience, building on that knowledge for more robust and sustainable policy approaches to strengthen public sector capabilities to support the implementation of digital government.

Balancing public and private sector roles: Developing internal capacities vs. outsourcing

Public sectors are experiencing a shortfall in ICT professional skills (see Box 3.4). Public sectors across OECD countries are finding it challenging to satisfy internal demand for ICT professionals capable of responding to the rising complexity of users' needs associated with the rapid uptake of digital technologies. This is partly driven by a supply of emerging digital skills that does not currently respond to, or match, the demand of the labour market (see Box 3.4). One of the possible solutions adopted by governments is to increasingly contract external service providers. The complexity of the tasks involved and the lack of the necessary internal capabilities to carry them out are some of the most cited reasons used to justify the outsourcing of ICT services from the public sector. Another typical argument used to explain or justify outsourcing is that some routine ICT tasks are performed in a more cost-efficient way by specialised companies. For instance, general user assistance, development of software security tests or management of the IT infrastructure are some of the activities commonly outsourced in many countries.

Box 3.4. **The European skills gap in ICT professionals**

Following a trend that has been identified among its 28 member countries over more than a decade, the European Commission forecasts a 500 000 ICT professionals gap in Europe in 2020.

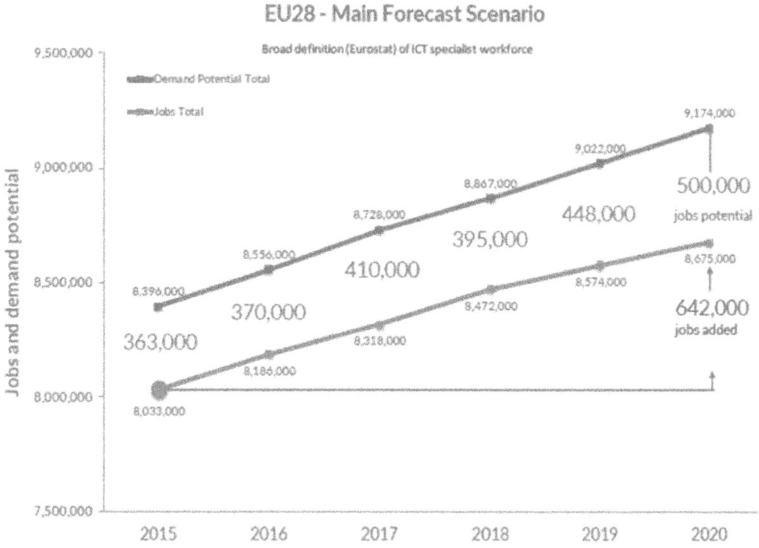

Source: European Commission (2017), "Digital Skills and Jobs Coalition", webpage, https://ec.europa.eu/digital-single-market/en/digital-skills-jobs-coalition (accessed 8 April 2017); Hüsing, Tobias and Eriona Dashja (2017), "Innovation Leadership Skills for the High-Tech Economy - Demand, Supply and Forecasting", presentation at the High-Tech and Leadership Skills for Europe Conference, Brussels, 26 January 2017, empirica, https://www.slideshare.net/TobiasHsing/innovation-leadership-skills-demand-supply-and-forecasting.

Outsourcing approaches generate some risks for the global management of digital technologies in the public sector. The creation of dependencies from big consultancy firms and situations of vendor-locked hardware and mostly software are frequent scenarios identified by senior digital government officials.

Alongside the use of outsourcing solutions to respond to the increasing demand for ICT related skills – including emerging needs for new digital skills, e.g. for data analysis - some OECD countries have dedicated strategies to attract, develop or retain digitally skilled civil servants in government. Given the competitive working conditions for this profile is high in the market, some OECD countries developed special career conditions to attract and maintain these professionals in the public sector. The Presidential Innovation Fellows programme of the United States is a good example of a fluid approach to attract highly qualified ICT professionals to the public sector (Box 3.5). Australia, Canada and Ireland have also taken important steps with relation to the formulation of initiatives and strategies aimed at increasing the availability of the necessary digital skills across the public sector.

Box 3.5. **Presidential Innovation Fellows programme of the United States**

Established by the White House in 2012, the Presidential Innovation Fellows programme is an initiative that brings together top innovators from the private sector, civil society, and academia with innovators in government to collaborate on the development of concrete solutions in a short period of time. Presidential Innovation Fellows serve for 12 months at federal agencies to which they are assigned, during which they work on one or several initiatives.

The Fellows' goal is to transform ideas into tangible results at startup speed, tackling issues at the convergence of technology, policy, and process. Fellows operate with wide latitude for individual initiative in planning and executing solutions to problems, and spend a significant portion of their time co-working and collaborating with other Fellows.

Throughout the programme, Fellows receive support from partners and change agents in the White House across various federal agencies.

Source: US General Services Administration (n.d.), "Presidential Innovation Fellows", webpage, www.presidentialinnovationfellows.gov (accessed 12 August 2017).

When questioned about the existence of a specific strategy at national level to attract, develop or retain ICT-skilled civil servants, more than half of the respondent countries answered affirmatively (Figure 3.10).

Figure 3.10. **Existence of national strategies to attract, develop or retain ICT-skilled civil servants in selected countries**

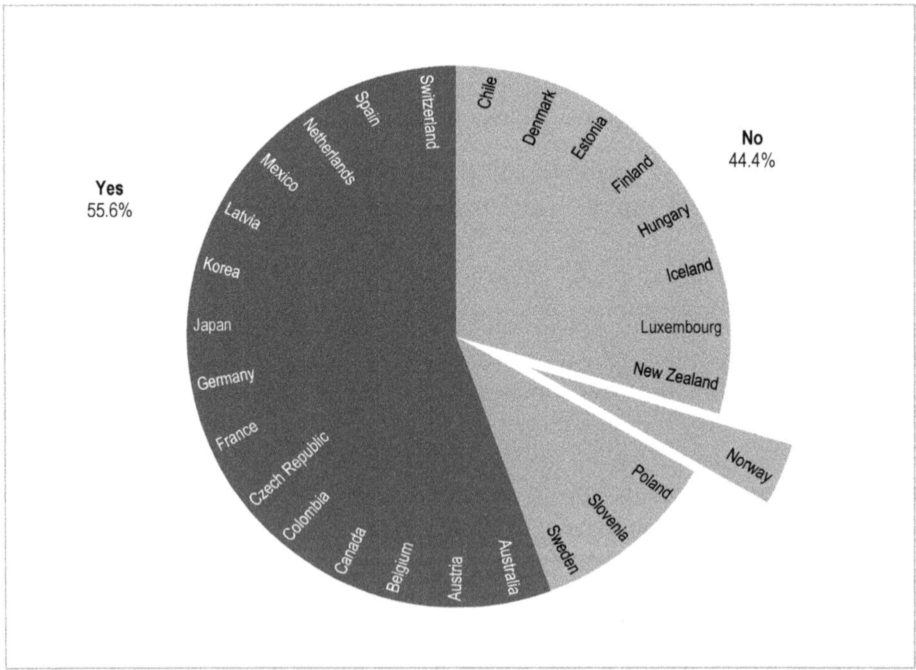

Source: OECD (2014a), "OECD Survey on Digital Government Performance" (dataset), OECD, Paris, http://qdd.oecd.org/subject.aspx?Subject=6C3F11AF-875E-4469-9C9E-AF93EE384796.

In Norway, KMD's Programme for Better Governance and Leadership in the Public Sector gives substantial relevance to the reinforcement of skills of public officers from central and local government. The programme focuses on – and highlights the urgency of - defining actions at the policy implementation and public management level, centring on five transversal areas of work (see Figure 3.11). The relevance of public managers is underlined based on their role as strategists. As such, managers should be capable of translating high-level policy objectives into co-ordinated actions at the institutional level and being accountable for delivering results.

Figure 3.11. **KMD's Programme for Better Governance and Leadership in the Public Sector**

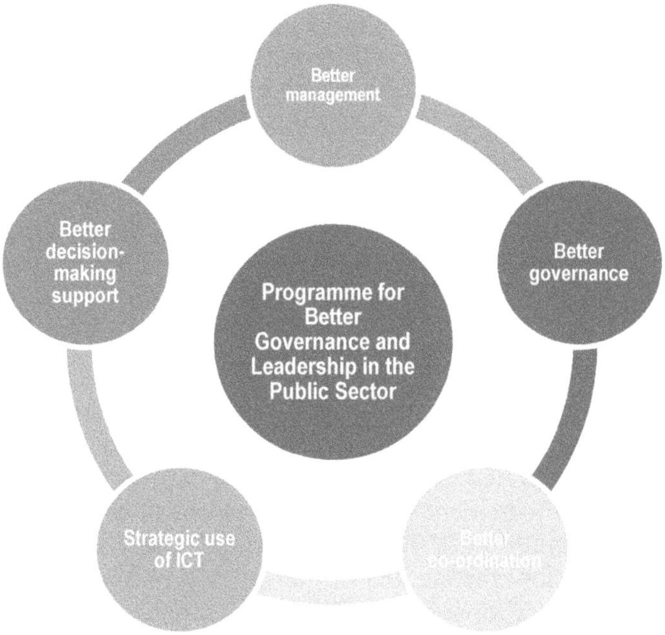

Source: Author, based on information provided by the Norwegian government.

While building ICT competencies among public managers is a key element of the programme, evidence from the OECD survey shows that building ICT-related and digital skills might not be seen as the most urgent digital government challenge to be tackled. The level of priority attributed to the development of ICT skills for public officers in the Digital Agenda for Norway is not substantial (OECD, 2017a). As shown in Figure 3.10, Norway belongs to the group of countries that does not have a specific strategy dedicated to attracting ICT professionals, nor to attract foreign highly skilled ICT workers. In addition, no ICT-specific policy is in place to spread ICT skills among public servants or develop digital skills (OECD, 2017a).

The need for specific policies to develop ICT skills and capabilities in the public sector is in line with growing worries about the risk of overdependence of the Norwegian public administration on ICT external suppliers. Overdependence on consultancy firms was identified as critical from an economic perspective, since the cost of outsourcing some ICT tasks may be higher than the adoption of in-house development, or management of, solutions. The excessive reliance on external providers was also considered responsible for a progressive deflation of ICT knowledge and capabilities in the public sector. Since external ICT providers are responsible for a growing number of core tasks within the Norwegian public sector (e.g. reviewing ICT projects or ideas for new projects), many public agencies are overloaded with the co-ordination and management of these services and dedicate fewer efforts to the development of in-house knowledge or solutions.

In opposition to the overdependence highlighted by public sector officials regarding ICT external companies, the Norwegian private ICT industry stressed, on the other hand, the reluctance of the public sector to outsource ICT development efforts The public sector officials and the private stakeholders present, in this sense, contradictory visions about the range and scope of their roles.

As found in most OECD member countries, a need to better balance the public and private responsibilities towards the digital transformation was identified in Norway. Clarification with regard to the areas and aspects for which the government considers itself ultimately responsible to maintain its leading role in the digital transformation, and those that can be outsourced to the private sector, would help. This discussion should be aligned with a national vision of ICT strategic human resources management in the public sector, with an eye on the need to consider the development of new digital skills, as it also relates to the strategic procurement of ICTs.

ICT procurement as a strategic asset

The OECD Recommendation on Digital Government Strategies (2014b) highlights the importance of an adequate ICT procurement framework for the sound development of digital government (Principle 11). As previously mentioned, the constant evolution and increasing complexity of digital technologies create significant challenges for public sector institutions. ICT procurement is a strategic aspect of digital government policies made even more challenging today by the strict legal and regulatory environment the public sector needs to follow for the acquisition of ICT products and services – due to requirements for transparency, openness and inclusive procurement processes.

The challenges created by the uptake of digital technologies and related trends – such as cloud computing, cloud-based forms of service provision, open data) that have emerged in recent years (e.g. infrastructure as a service, platform as a service, software as a service) illustrate the importance of updated ICT procurement frameworks. The public sector needs to have properly updated procurement mechanisms and strategies, enabling news forms of acquisition of products and services. The changing needs in a context of digital transformation of public sectors – e.g. in terms of innovative services relying on testing and prototyping, of engaging new actors like start-ups, of enabled use of open source and open standards - generate considerable challenges for existing procurement frameworks.

More than half of responding countries (52%) report having an ICT procurement strategy for the central government (Figure 3.12). Besides addressing the acquisition of emerging digital technologies, several reasons justify why a specific procurement strategy can be an asset for digital government development, including:

1. **Demand aggregation**: Given the frequent common needs for ICT products and services, a common procurement approach supports the creation of mechanisms that aggregate the demand across sectors and even levels of government (e.g. software, hardware), benefiting the public sector capacity of negotiation with private suppliers and rationalising needs.

2. **Promotion of common standards**: An ICT procurement strategy is a perfect policy lever to promote the use of common standards and the application of guidelines since criteria need to be established for the acquisition of products and services. A procurement strategy contributes, in this sense, to reinforcing the interoperability of ICT public platforms and the uptake of strategic approaches (e.g. cloud computing, open data).
3. **Increased transparency and accountability**: A structured approach for ICT expenditures boosts transparency and accountability in the public sector, helps better track the options made by public entities and keeps a better record of the service providers and the prices charged for the products.

Figure 3.12. **Existence of ICT procurement strategies across central government in selected countries**

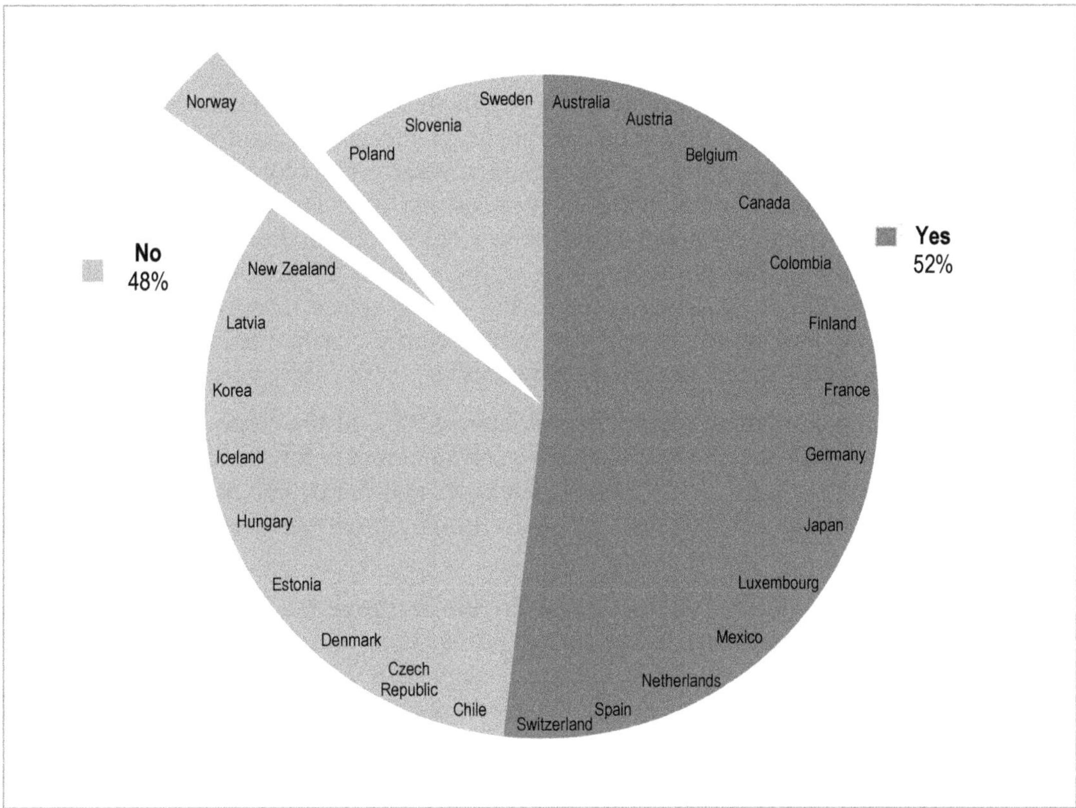

Source: OECD (2014a), "OECD Survey on Digital Government Performance" (dataset), OECD, Paris, http://qdd.oecd.org/subject.aspx?Subject=6C3F11AF-875E-4469-9C9E-AF93EE384796.

Norway does not have a specific procurement strategy dedicated to ICT. The OECD peer review mission in Oslo identified a consensus among stakeholders about the positive impact that such a policy lever could bring to the development of digital government in the country. The demand aggregation is expected to result in significant savings, and in the promotion of common standards.

Even though Norway does not have an integrated strategy for ICT procurement - which is an item covered generally in the Digital Agenda, but not coupled with an operationalisation of general guidelines with a specific strategic approach to be followed by public sector agencies consistently - a good practice identified is that Difi recommends the use of the State Standard Agreements (SSA) for ICT purchases. These non-mandatory agreements developed by Difi provide extended guidance and substantial support for public sector institutions. Through the website anskaffelser.no (*acquisitions.no* in English), Difi makes available extensive information about the State Standard Agreements, sharing several alternatives that can be used by public institutions, namely:

- assistance agreement standards (SSA-B) for the acquisition of consultancy IT services
- agreement on current services purchases (SSA-L) directed to software as a service approaches
- purchases agreement (SSA-K) for buying standard ICT hardware or software
- development and adaptation agreement (SSA-T) for the development of specific IT systems.

The newly established Government Procurement Centre (Statens innkjøpssenter), managed by Difi, is another important statement of the government's commitment to streamline public expenses. Joint agreements in several areas (e.g. personal computers [PCs] and mobile phones, consumables, professional and legal assistance) that are applicable to all central government institutions were being finalised at the time of the drafting of this review. The portal anskaffelser.no is also an important example of a knowledge gateway for ICT procurement in the public sector. Detailed information is provided in a clear and intuitive way for public entities, with recommendations and guidelines to support the public procurement processes.

Regarding the procurement methods used, almost 90% of the responding Norwegian public institutions confirmed the use of framework agreements for the acquisition of ICT products and services (Figure 3.13). Direct purchases and public-private partnerships are methods rarely or never used by the vast majority of the entities that responded to the OECD survey.

Since transparency is one of the central drivers for governments to adopt strategic ICT procurement approaches, the structured publication of information about public contracts is a key aspect to be considered. Although a culture of openness and transparency was generally found across the Norwegian central government's agencies, with active support for measures that can make the public administration more accountable to citizens and companies, no searchable repository exists with information on public contracts in the public sector. The Norwegian government didn't adopt the Open Contracting Data Standard (OCDS) (see Box 3.6) and no central database for ICT contractors' performance evaluations is available as a reference for future ICT procurement decisions (OECD, 2017b). In this respect, there is room for improvement for the development of this approach in Norway (see Chapter 5).

Figure 3.13. **ICT procurement methods used in Norway's central government**

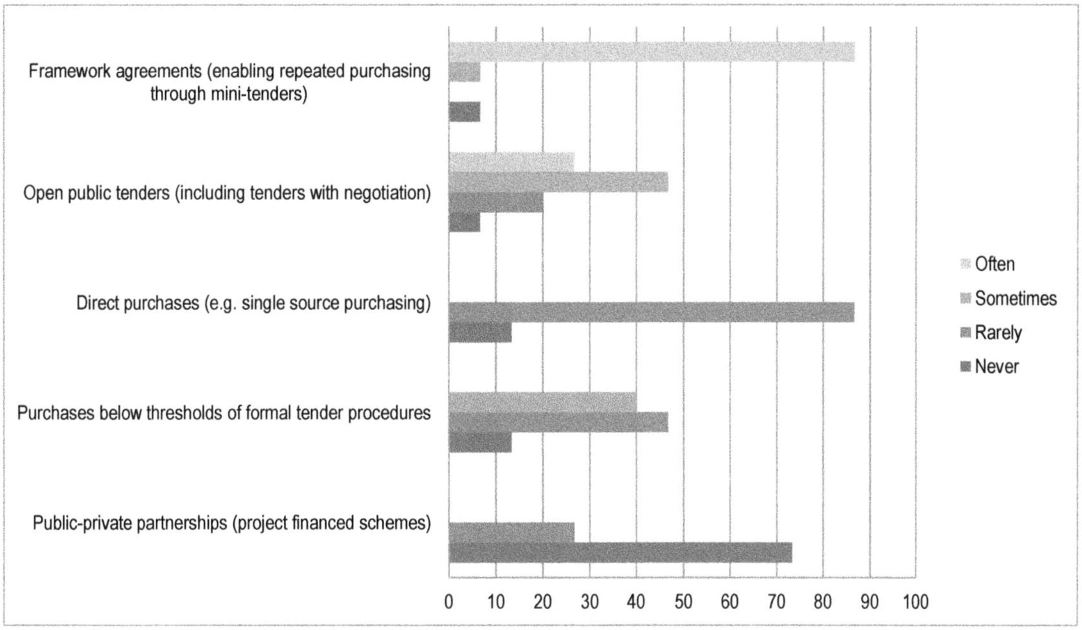

Source: OECD (2017b), "Digital Government Survey of Norway", public sector institutions version, OECD, Paris.

Box 3.6. **Open Contracting Data Standard**

The Open Contracting Data Standard (OCDS) enables the disclosure of data and documents at all stages of the contracting process by defining a common data model. It was created to support organisations to increase contracting transparency, and allow for deeper analysis of contracting data by a wide range of users. The OCDS was developed for the Open Contracting Partnership by the World Wide Web Foundation.

The OCDS approach is:

- publish early, and iterate: improving disclosure step-by-step
- simple and extensible JSON (JavaScript Object Notation) structure
- publish data for each step of the contracting process
- create summary records for an overall contracting process
- re-useable objects: organisations, tender information, line items, amounts, milestones, documents, etc.
- recommended data and documents at basic, intermediate and advanced levels
- common open data publication patterns
- guidance on improving data collection and data quality
- a growing community of users and range of open source tools.

Source: Open Contracting Partnership (2016), "Open Contracting Data Standard: Documentation", webpage, http://standard.open-contracting.org (accessed 12 August 2017).

When questioned about green IT procurement practices, the Norwegian government informed the OECD that the current regulations on public procurement of goods and services include considerations of environmental issues (e.g. Instructions for Official Studies – Utredningsinstruksen). This translates into some guidance and advice generally provided on green ICT procurement, but there is no formal requirement in Norway.

Norway has a propitious context for streamlining ICT strategic public procurement. The State Standard Agreements are a clear example of the importance attributed to structured procurement approaches. The Norwegian mostly consensus-based culture tends to be supported by soft policy levers (e.g. guidelines, recommendations). The adoption of some hard policy levers could help the Norwegian government to leverage ICT procurement as a strategic policy mechanism for coherent and optimised digital government development in the country. For instance, although the level of adoption of State Standard Agreements is very high according to the Norwegian government, its usage could be considered mandatory above the threshold of NOK 10 million. The mandatory use of State Standard Agreements could be connected with the mandatory application of project-management and business-case methodologies for ICT projects above the threshold.

In line with the efforts underway and the priorities set by the Digital Agenda for Norway, the development of a clearly identifiable and actionable ICT procurement strategy linked to the Digital Agenda, but recognised as a policy instrument to promote demand aggregation in the public sector, to foster the use of common standards, to strengthen collaboration across public sector entities and to increase the transparency and accountability of the procurement process, would provide the Norwegian government with the opportunity to further strengthen the soundness of its digital government policies. Building on the experiences of other countries, like the United Kingdom for instance (see Box 3.7), the development of a Norwegian public single digital marketplace would also be a strategic lever for an intelligent and sustainable ICT public procurement process.

Box 3.7. **Digital Marketplace in the United Kingdom**

Developed by the Government Digital Service, the United Kingdom's agency responsible for leading digital government policies, the Digital Marketplace is a portal where public sector organisations can find people and technology for digital projects. Three kind of agreements are available between the government and suppliers:

1. **Cloud services**: Around 20 000 cloud services on the Digital Marketplace through the G-Cloud framework (cloud hosting, cloud software and cloud support).
2. **Digital specialist services**: More than 1 000 suppliers provide digital specialist services, including digital outcomes (e.g. booking system or an accessibility audit), digital specialists (e.g. product managers or developers), user research studios, user research participants and data centre hosting services.
3. **Datacentre hosting services**: One supplier provides data centre hosting to government. It offers namely a flexible, pay-for-what-you-use model, secure facilities and leading environmental performance.

The Digital Marketplace is considered today a reference due to the amount of government frameworks agreements, making the buying of services faster and cheaper than entering into individual procurement contracts.

Source: UK Government (2017), "Digital Marketplace", webpage, www.digitalmarketplace.service.gov.uk/ (accessed 12 August 2017).

References

Difi (Agency for Public Management and eGovernment) (2017), www.difi.no, official agency website (accessed 1 April 2017).

European Commission (2017), "Digital Skills and Jobs Coalition", webpage, https://ec.europa.eu/digital-single-market/en/digital-skills-jobs-coalition (accessed 8 April 2017).

Government of Norway (2017), "Government.no", official government website, www.regjeringen.no/en/ (accessed 31 March 2017).

Hüsing, Tobias and Eriona Dashja (2017), "Innovation Leadership Skills for the High-Tech Economy - Demand, Supply and Forecasting", presentation at the High-Tech and Leadership Skills for Europe Conference, Brussels, 26 January 2017, empirica, https://www.slideshare.net/TobiasHsing/innovation-leadership-skills-demand-supply-and-forecasting.

KMD (Ministry of Local Government and Modernisation) (2016), "Digital Agenda for Norway in brief: ICT for a simpler everyday life and increased productivity", English version, KMD, www.regjeringen.no/en/dokumenter/digital-agenda-for-norway-in-brief/id2499897/sec1.

NTNU (Norwegian University of Science and Technology) (2017), "The Norwegian scheme for quality assurance of major public investments (the QA scheme)", webpage, www.ntnu.edu/web/concept/qa-scheme1 (accessed 12 August 2017).

OECD (2017a), "Digital Government Survey of Norway", central version, OECD, Paris.

OECD (2017b), "Digital Government Survey of Norway", public sector institutions version, OECD, Paris.

OECD (2016), *Digital Government in Chile: Strengthening the Institutional and Governance Framework*, OECD Digital Government Studies, OECD Publishing, Paris, http://dx.doi.org/10.1787/9789264258013-en.

OECD (2014a), "OECD Survey on Digital Government Performance" (dataset), OECD, Paris, http://qdd.oecd.org/subject.aspx?Subject=6C3F11AF-875E-4469-9C9E-AF93EE384796.

OECD (2014b), "Recommendation of the Council on Digital Government Strategies", OECD, Paris, www.oecd.org/gov/digital-government/recommendation-on-digital-government-strategies.htm

Open Contracting Partnership (2016), "Open Contracting Data Standard: Documentation", webpage, http://standard.open-contracting.org (accessed 12 August 2017).

UK Government (2017), "Digital Marketplace", webpage, www.digitalmarketplace.service.gov.uk/ (accessed 12 August 2017).

US General Services Administration (n.d.), "Presidential Innovation Fellows", webpage, www.presidentialinnovationfellows.gov (accessed 12 August 2017).

Chapter 4

From user-focused to user-driven service delivery in Norway

This chapter analyses the digital service delivery landscape in the Norwegian public sector. It discusses citizens' digital rights in regard to their interaction with the public administration, and assesses the culture and practices of openness and public engagement across the public sector in relation to the design and delivery of digital public services. It highlights those enablers that should be in place in order to properly support the digital transformation of the public sector, through the strategic integration of digital service delivery, underlying the potential of digital technologies for cross-border services in the Nordic and Baltic regions.

Introduction

An analogue government cannot serve a digital society and economy. Digital transformation calls for a digital government (OECD, forthcoming). The digital disruption brought about by new technologies, such as machine learning, open source algorithms, Internet of Things, big data analytics or quantum and cloud computing has the potential to leverage the interaction between citizens, businesses and the public sector. Communication processes are expected to be simple, efficient, intuitive, and tailored to the needs of service users. The use of new mechanisms for the exchange and analysis of data can support the development of data-driven service delivery models that can improve the experience of citizens and businesses in a revolutionary way when interacting with the public sector and accessing public services. However, emergent technological breakthroughs demand a paradigm shift for service delivery in the public sector.

Drawing upon leading innovative service delivery models provided by big, private digital trendsetters like Google, Amazon, Facebook, Uber or Airbnb, citizens expect similar experiences from the public sector in terms of usability, accessibility, friendliness, convenience and effectiveness. Government-centred online services, where the administration reproduces its analogic bureaucratic procedures in a digitised way, are far from fulfilling today's citizens' expectations. Siloed service delivery approaches, with multiple and sectoral public sector websites and fragmented service delivery that reflect the government's internal institutional structure are not compatible with today's need for simpler and more convenient services, which are expected to be seamless and integrated, and accessibile via multiple channels.

Nowadays citizens and businesses expect that their public services are designed with a user-driven perspective, adaptable to different user profiles. Through the intelligent re-use of data and information previously generated or provided by citizens, governments can today shift from reactive service delivery approaches to proactive service delivery practices. In reactive service delivery environments, the citizen is always responsible for starting the service demand, properly identifying him or herself and providing the required information. On the contrary, in proactive service delivery environments, the public sector knows its citizens, knows their life condition and current needs, as it provides them the space to voice and signal their requests and preferences (user-driven approach). This enables the public sector to inform citizens in a personalised fashion about their rights, their duties, the services available and to reach out to them to receive the authorisation to complete the services on their behalf (e.g. pre-filled tax forms).

By embracing a citizen and/or user-driven and proactive service delivery approach, governments commit to transfer a large share of service delivery transaction costs from users to the public sector. The capacity to collect, combine and process data in a useful and coherent way to better serve citizens and businesses is one of the features of the digital transformation of the public sector. This implies a whole-of-government co-ordination effort to exchange information across the public sector and to have key building blocks (e.g. common architecture, interoperability framework, digital identity system) in place that can enable integrated service delivery approaches.

Developing a user-driven approach also implies that public sector's capacities, workflows, business processes, operations, methodologies and frameworks need to be adapted to the rapidly evolving digital age. The challenge nowadays is not to introduce digital technologies into public sector activities, but to integrate and embed them right from the start into governments' efforts to modernise public administrations. Today's public policies need to be digital by design, mobilising new technologies to rethink and re-engineer business processes, simplify procedures and open new channels of communication and engagement with civil society, the private sector and the third sector, guaranteeing namely a more efficient, sustainable and citizen-driven public sector (OECD, forthcoming).

The digital transformation of the public sector, leveraging the power of data and assuming it as an asset, involves also earning citizen trust (see Chapter 5). Openness and transparency on the use of citizens' data by public entities should be considered a key prerequisite. Trust can also be gained through showing a coherent, transparent and responsible use of data (e.g. being transparent on algorithms' use by governments) while performing data analytics activities. Digital-by-design policies should ensure that the use of data always serves the public interest, without crossing legal and unethical lines in terms of security and privacy, which can erode public trust in government.

This chapter presents a general overview of digital service delivery in the Norwegian public sector. The analysis starts by addressing citizens' rights in terms of digital communication with the public sector and also the culture of openness and engagement in public services design. A second section will be dedicated to the key enablers that need to be in place to sustain the shift from an e-government approach to a digital government imperative (OECD, 2014a), allowing for a strategic integration of public service delivery. The chapter concludes with an analysis of the potential for cross-border services development in the Nordic-Baltic region.

Building on users' preferences

The development of user-centred services has characterised e-government strategies from OECD countries (OECD, 2009). Governments made considerable efforts to design service delivery models that, supported by information and communications technology (ICT), streamline the relationship between citizens/businesses and the public sector. The challenge, for instance, was to design public digital services that could reflect citizens' preferences and needs, if possible using life events and one-stop-shops models. Although this citizen-centred approach is an ongoing requisite to be fulfilled by governments, technological changes bring new opportunities and challenges for the public sector.

The following dimensions demonstrate how this new user-driven paradigm is changing public service design and delivery:

1. **Digital rights**: New rights are being established to allow users to benefit from the extra convenience and efficiency offered by digital technologies when communicating with the public sector. For example, the right to opt in to communicate digitally with the government or the right of not having to provide the same information more than once to public sector institutions are some of the legal trends being progressively adopted by OECD countries.

2. **Engagement by default**: Users' preferences should be the basis for the design and delivery of user-driven digital services. In order to obtain digitally transformed public services, citizens and businesses should be engaged and involved from the beginning, allowing the service designers to reflect their views, needs and aspirations right from the moment when the service and its content are being designed. This engagement-by-default model - in line with Principle 2 of

the OECD Recommendation on Digital Government Strategies (2014a) – capitalises on the availability of the digital government ecosystem to develop tailored services to citizens and businesses.

3. **Data-driven and proactive service delivery**: Beyond the direct involvement of users, citizen-driven approaches foresee the use of citizens and businesses' data to better deliver public services. Through the exchange of data across sectors and levels of government, public service providers can maintain an up-to-date view on citizens' life situations and related needs, allowing for a tailored digital service provision. The proper combination and use of data is the basis of the shift from reactive to proactive service delivery, enabling also the generation of feedback loops mechanisms that can help to improve the quality of public services.

These dimensions bring public service delivery to a new stage of development, allowing governments to strategically adopt digital technologies in order to provide the user experience that citizens and companies progressively demand.

Digital rights as a strategic policy lever

OECD countries are progressively adopting principles that try to safeguard citizen convenience, challenging the public administration to constantly improve its processes and mechanisms to align with the new digital age. The majority of countries that responded to the OECD Survey on Digital Government Performance (2014b) concedes the right to its citizens to communicate digitally with their public sectors (Figure 4.1). This allows citizens, for instance, to always expect a digital alternative to face-to-face analogic procedures. In Spain, a law from 2007 enshrined its people's right to communicate with public service administrations on line (see Box 4.1). In Mexico, the access to the Internet is a constitutional right since 2013.

Figure 4.1. **Digital communication by default with the public sector in selected countries**

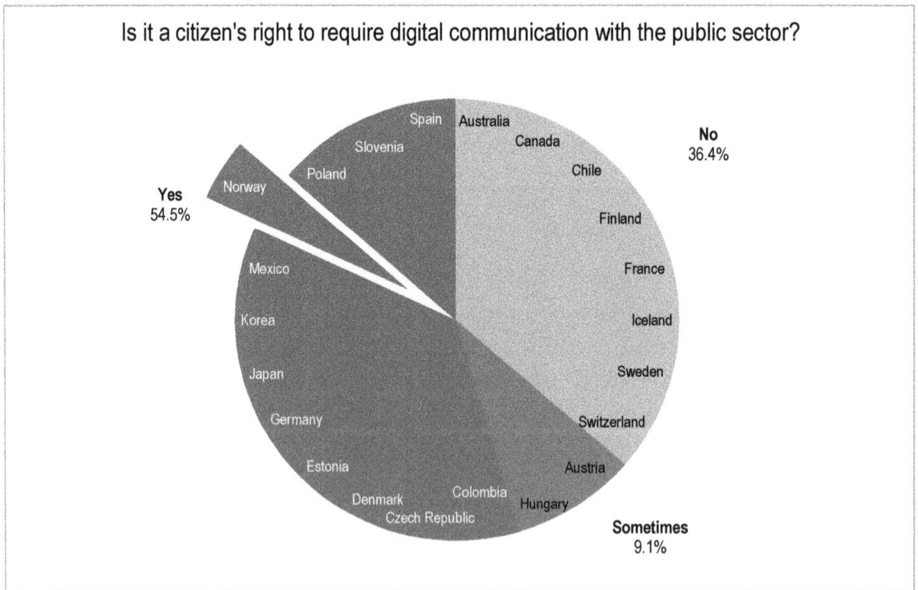

Source: OECD (2014b), "OECD Survey on Digital Government Performance" (dataset), OECD, Paris, http://qdd.oecd.org/subject.aspx?Subject=6C3F11AF-875E-4469-9C9E-AF93EE384796. Data from Norway based on OECD (2017a), "Digital Government Survey of Norway", central version, OECD, Paris.

Box 4.1. **The right to communicate digitally with the public sector in Spain**

In June 2007, the Spanish Parliament passed Law 11/2007, which enshrined its people's right to communicate with public service administrations on line. The law has played a pivotal role in determining the e-government approach in Spain and in clearing the path for progressive work in this area. The end of 2009 was the deadline it set the public service for complying with its provisions, of which the most important entitle citizens:

- The guarantee of digital service provision, whereby public administration bodies should ensure that all government transactions and services are fully available and updated on line.
- The right to choose among the service channels available when communicating with public authorities. The authorities are required to provide both analogue and digital communication and service processes as requested by citizens.
- The right not to supply data and documents already in the possession of other public administration bodies. Public authorities must organise data exchanges across all levels in formats that enable efficient interoperability.
- The right to secure and confidential storage of all personal data used in public authority files, applications and systems.
- The right to equality of access to public online services. Government services shall not discriminate against citizens using non-electronic forms of communication and services.
- The right to obtain an electronic ID and to use other approved electronic signatures.
- The right to access personal data and files about ongoing processes.

Law 11/2007 was followed by additional laws and royal decrees widening its scope to encompass the promotion of digital communication and procedures across all areas of government.

Source: OECD (2013), *Reaping the Benefits of ICTs in Spain: Strategic Study on Communication Infrastructure and Paperless Administration*, OECD Publishing, Paris, http://dx.doi.org/10.1787/9789264173224-en.

The application of this right in Norway is substantially advanced. The communication of the Norwegian public sector with citizens is digital by default; digital is assumed to be the preferential channel of communication by public entities, that is, they can communicate digitally with the population without receiving their consent. Nevertheless, according to the information provided by the Norwegian government (OECD, 2017b), citizens have the right to opt out, and can use public sector communication models that use non-digital means (e.g. traditional mail).

On the other hand, in order to boost digital service delivery across sectors and levels of government, the Norwegian Digitalisation Memorandum (Digitaliseringsrundskrivet) (see Chapter 2) sets ambitious objectives through its Digital First Choice initiative (see Box 4.2).

Box 4.2. **Norway's "Digital First Choice" initiative**

Norway's Digitalisation Memorandum (Digitaliseringsrundskrivet) established that public sector communication with citizens and businesses should be carried out via digital online services. These services should be comprehensive, user-friendly, safe and universally designed. To achieve this goal, the Memorandum foresees that:

- By the end of 2017, the ministries shall map the potential for digitising services and work processes, and prepare plans for how all appropriate services will be made available digitally.
- By the end of 2018, the ministries will assess the services that should be seen in conjunction with other services, and whether the services are suitable for the development of service chains. Plans/strategies for development of services will also be developed.

The mapping should include what services are already digitalised and which services are suitable to be digitalised. The mapping must also be used to assess whether existing digital services are user-oriented and user-friendly, or whether they should be redesigned, simplified or even eliminated. Relevant regulations must also be reviewed.

Source: Difi (Agency for Public Management and eGovernment) (2017), www.difi.no, official agency website (accessed 1 April 2017).

The right to only provide the same information once to the public administration – the "once-only principle" - is also being progressively adopted by OECD countries. In order to create an environment for the implementation of such a principle, governments have to advance integration efforts across sectors and levels of government so that public entities can exchange and re-use citizens and businesses' data and information, while ensuring the respect of national and international standards on data security and privacy protection. In Estonia, the once-only principle became a legal obligation in 1997. The political commitment to make the principle a reality led to the development of a national interoperability infrastructure (OECD, 2015).

Based on the OECD Digital Government Performance Survey (2014b) results, 44.5% of responding countries recognised the right of citizens to not have to provide the same data or information to the public sector more than once. Some 11% of countries stated that this right was recognised in specific situations and 44.5% stated that the right was not recognised at all.

In Norway, there is no formal requirement establishing the once-only principle for citizens, but public sector entities should work towards such a goal and establish procedures and regulations to enable it to a greater degree (OECD, 2017a). For instance, the Digitalisation Memorandum states that public institutions should re-use information available in other sectors of the administration, rather than requesting citizens to provide it again. During the peer review mission, the public and private stakeholders recognised that the progressive application of the once-only principle in Norway was one of the most challenging, but also more transformative, goals for improved service delivery to be targeted by the government.

Openness and engagement for better service delivery

As previously mentioned, citizens should be engaged in policy-design processes, to support the shift from a scenario where governments try to anticipate citizen and business needs (citizen-centric approaches) to an approach where citizens and businesses design and develop solutions to better respond to their needs in partnership with the government (citizen-driven approaches) (OECD, 2014a).

In Norway, 60% of central government institutions consider that the level of priority given to openness and engagement in the Digital Agenda for Norway (KMD, 2016a) is high (Figure 4.2), demonstrating a widespread culture that values transparency and citizen engagement in public policy processes.

Figure 4.2. **Priority given to openness and engagement in the Digital Agenda, according to Norway's central government**

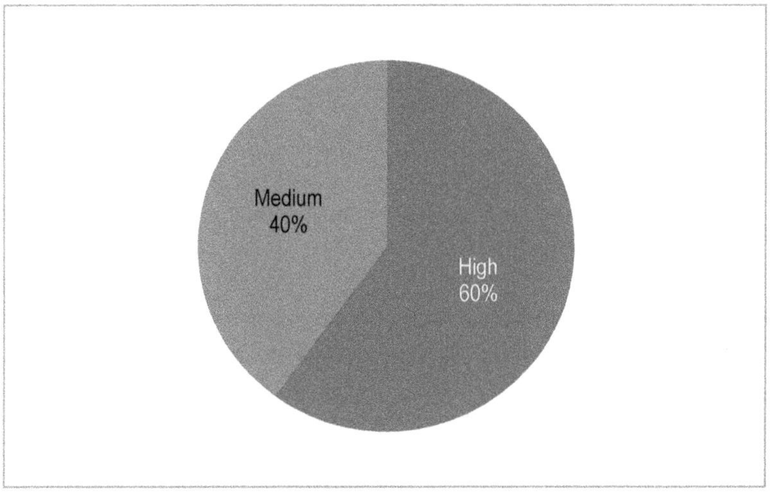

Source: OECD (2017b), "Digital Government Survey of Norway", public sector institutions version, OECD, Paris.

According to the Norwegian government, although there is no specific digital strategy in the country to foster a culture of openness and engagement among public officers, initiatives to spur openness and stakeholder engagement are widespread across other policy strategies, being a vital part of the Norwegian administrative culture and being supported through various laws, regulations and even the Constitution (OECD, 2017a). In fact, although only 30% of Norwegian public institutions report having an institutional strategy focused on openness, 57% state that they develop initiatives to spur institutional openness and stakeholder engagement (Figure 4.3).

Figure 4.3. **Strategies or Initiatives to foster openness and engagement in Norway's central government**

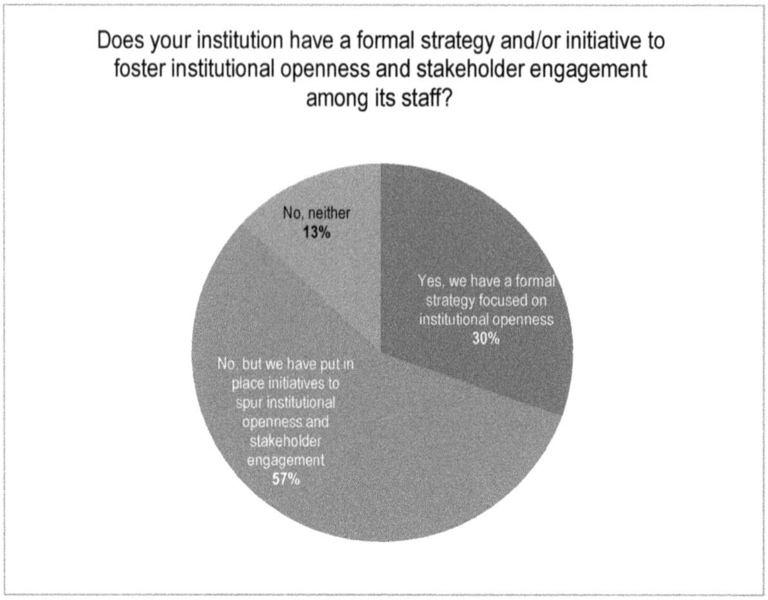

Source: OECD (2017b), "Digital Government Survey of Norway", public sector institutions version, OECD, Paris.

When questioned about the main reasons to promote openness and engagement at the institutional level, Norwegian public agencies reported that strengthening public trust in the institution and fostering transparency were their main drivers. The Norwegian institutions also highlighted the fact that openness and transparency are a priority for the central government (OECD, 2017b).

Throughout this review, we have observed various practices developed by Norway that demonstrate the commitment of its public sector to promote a culture of openness and engagement across sectors and levels of government. For instance, recognising social media as an increasingly important communication channel between the public administration and its constituencies, but also as a tool for engagement - namely for better service delivery (Mickoleit, 2014) - Difi (Agency for Public Management and eGovernment) is developing a new guide for social media use in the administration and is requesting input from public institutions and citizens to make it as rich as possible. The new guide will build on the work of the previous guide called "Social Media in Management – Reflections on Development 2010-2014" (Difi, 2009), and also on the addendum produced for social media administrators in the public sector (Difi, 2010).

The Norwegian Clear Language Project (Klarspråkprosjektet) is also a good practice that illustrates the importance accorded by the country's public sector to communicate with its citizens and businesses in a simple, friendly and understandable way (Box 4.3).

Box 4.3. Norway's Clear Language Project

Difi and the Norwegian Language Council collaborate on measures to stimulate the use of user-friendly language for the delivery of public services. These measures and joint initiatives include:

- **The Golden Pen**: A web course in plain language that helps public editors write in ways that citizens understand. The online course gives an introduction to the most important, and also simple, language skills.
- **klarspråk.no**: This website contains practical tools, advice and tips on how to make the language used in service delivery processes clear and user-friendly.
- **Funding schemes**: Agencies can apply for financial support for clear language work. In 2016, two support schemes were made available: one for textual vision and one for measuring the effects of language proficiency.
- **Clear Language Prize**: An annual award is given to public agencies that make an extraordinary effort to use clear, good and user-friendly language in its communication with citizens and businesses.

Source: Difi (2017), www.difi.no, official agency website (accessed 1 April 2017)..

In addition, according to the Regulations on the Universal Design of Information and Communication Technology Solutions, approved in 2013 (see Chapter 1), ICT solutions in Norway should be universally designed from 1 July 2014 and existing solutions should comply with universal design requirements by 1 January 2021. Both the public and private sectors should comply with the regulations (Difi, 2017). Difi supervises the compliance with the requirements, being responsible for providing information and guidance on this subject. The website www.uu.difi.com makes available information about the requirements and shares guidance materials to achieve, to create and to maintain webpages. Moreover, several initiatives underway, like the Digital First Choice initiative or the Clear Language Project, demonstrate Norway's willingness to use digital technologies to promote the openness of the public sector and the engagement of citizens in policy processes.

The practices reported through the OECD Digital Government Survey, administered as part of this review, as well as information collected during the peer review mission, demonstrate that a culture and mindset of transparency and collaboration with civil society is widespread across the country's public sector. Yet, some further improvements can be made if, in addition to the above-mentioned initiatives and the widespread mindset and culture, institutional mechanisms were developed to guarantee that the full potential of the country is exploited in terms of openness and engagement. For instance, an integrated and strategic approach for citizen engagement, supported by institutional levers, could help Norway achieve a more coherent approach to a citizen-driven public administration.

Better integrating digital service delivery

In the last two decades, most OECD member countries have focused on the development of digital services for citizens and businesses as one of the key drivers and most visible outputs of their digital government development. The level of access and uptake of digital services has improved as a clear sign of governments' commitment to digitalise their public services, making them more accessible and convenient to their constituencies. It also reflects the citizens' progressive adoption of digital channels as a preferred platform to interact with public administrations. In fact, the use of digital government services by individuals over the past decade has tripled, on average, among OECD member countries and non-member economies (Figure 4.4). In 2016, for example, about 36% of individuals submitted pre-filled forms via public authorities' websites.

Figure 4.4. **Individuals using the Internet to send pre-filled forms via public authorities' websites in the past 12 months, 2006-16**

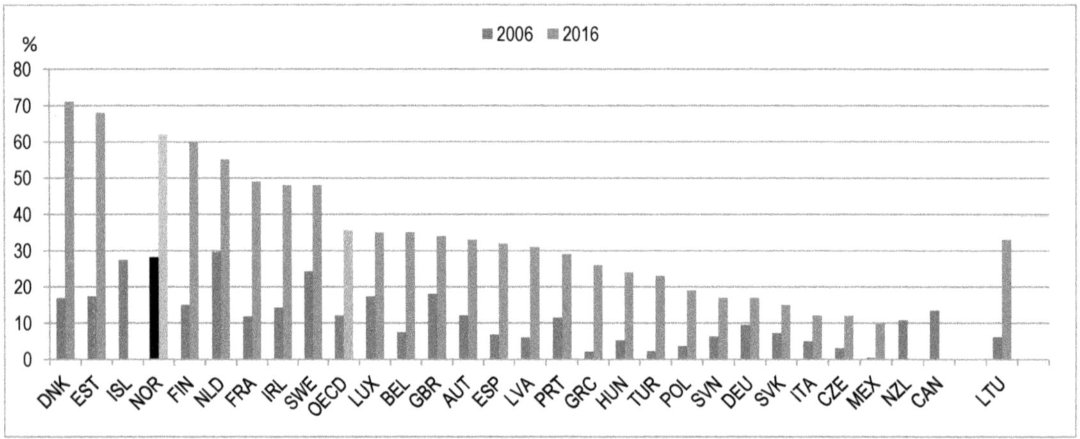

Note: Canada, Poland, Sweden, Turkey United Kingdom: 2007 rather than 2006. Mexico: 2015 rather than 2016. OECD average excludes Canada, Chile, Iceland and New Zealand due to missing time series.

Source: OECD (2017c), *Government at a Glance 2017*, OECD Publishing, Paris, http://dx.doi.org/10.1787/gov_glance-2017-en.

However, very different levels of usage of digital services persist among various segments of the population. Variables like education, income or age explain these different levels of uptake. For instance, on average across the OECD in 2016, about 54% of individuals with higher education submitted pre-filled forms via public authorities' websites, against 17% of individuals with low levels of education (Figure 4.5). Governments need to be aware of these substantial differences when designing and developing digital services, adjusting them to the specific contexts and users' needs, and complementing the development of the services with strategies aimed at building the capacities of users across society.

Figure 4.5. **Individuals using the Internet to send pre-filled forms via public authorities' websites in the past 12 months, by education level, 2016**

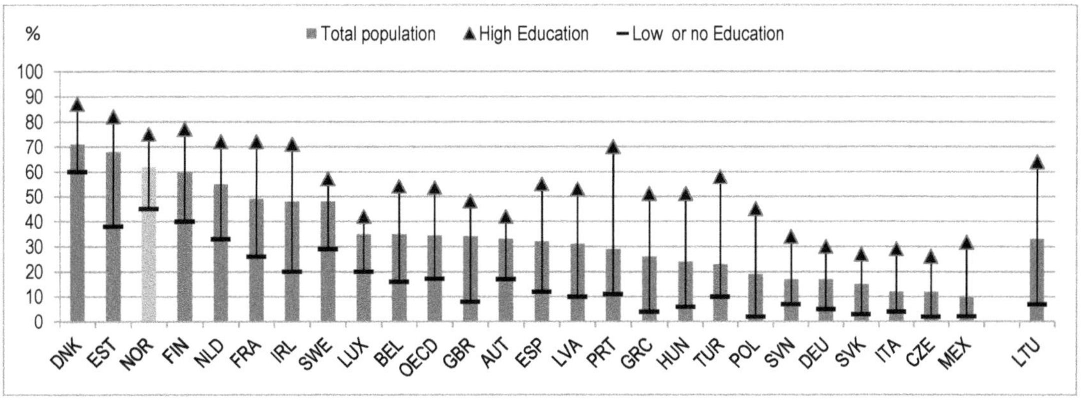

Note: Data for OECD non European member countries are not available. Mexico: 2015 rather than 2016.

Source: OECD (2017c), *Government at a Glance 2017*, OECD Publishing, Paris, http://dx.doi.org/10.1787/gov_glance-2017-en.

Governments' willingness to respond to citizens' expectations and needs was long reflected in the establishment of one-stop shops that became widespread across OECD public sectors, namely with the development of central portals of public services. For example, 92 % of OECD member countries state that they have a main national citizens' portal for government services (OECD, 2014b). Nevertheless, sector-specific approaches still seem to prevail in digital service delivery, with sector-specific public portals, diverse online navigating schemes, different usability standards and varied authentication mechanisms available to users. This situation results in fragmented accessibility and approaches in many instances, based on a prevailing agency-thinking approach rather than a system-thinking and user-driven approach.

In Norway, although considerable efforts have been made in terms of improving service delivery, with several public websites providing advanced interactive and transactional services to citizens and businesses, two critical dimensions of analysis provide a more refined perspective of the country's landscape of digital service delivery:

- the need for further adoption of cross-cutting digital key enablers that can sustain the development of a coherent digital service infrastructure
- the need for higher strategic integration of the national digital service delivery policy.

Building on digital key enablers

The development and use of common digital key enablers in the public sector is a fundamental requirement to enable the shift from e-government to digital government. Key enablers can boost the digital transformation of the public sector as they are important levers for change through integration and consolidation of common efforts across policy sectors and levels of government (Principle 6 of the OECD Recommendation on Digital Government Strategies).

Digital identification is one of the basic and overarching key enablers for digital government development. The existence of a common digital identification mechanism that can be re-used across sectors and levels of government to identify individuals and businesses constitutes a critical asset for the communication and interaction between citizens, businesses and the public sector. According to the OECD Survey on Digital Government Performance, 96% of responding countries confirm that they have a formally recognised digital identification mechanism in place (OECD, 2014b).

In Norway, the use of digital identity mechanisms for digital service delivery is widespread among public sector institutions. In fact, 77 % of the Norwegian public institutions that responded to the 2017 OECD survey confirmed using an electronic identification system to provide access to their services on line. Additionally, 68 % of the Norwegian institutions use digital signatures in transactions with individuals or businesses (Figure 4.6).

Figure 4.6. **Electronic Identification and digital signatures: Take up among Norwegian public sector institutions**

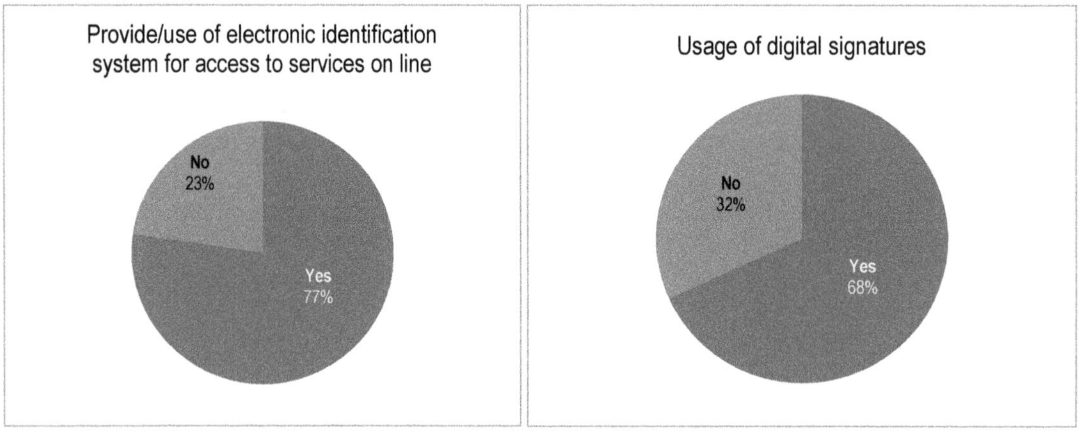

Source: OECD (2017b), "Digital Government Survey of Norway", public sector institutions version, OECD, Paris.

The ID-porten is a good example of a key enabler developed to provide an authentication solution to public services. Developed by Difi as an agile mechanism of online identification for citizens and businesses, the ID-porten is available on several Norwegian public websites, providing access to more than 1 100 services from over 600 government agencies and with more than 90 million logins in 2016.[1]

Besides digital identity, several other key enablers are available in the Norwegian public sector context. From access to base registries to shared data centres, the country has in place some critical enabling frameworks that can promote coherence and avoid overlapping mechanisms in the development of digital service delivery (Table 4.1). The level of adoption of some of these frameworks by the Norwegian institutions is substantial, e.g. the use of common base registries (Figure 4.7).

1. Information provided by the Norwegian government.

Table 4.1. **Availability of enabling frameworks in the Norwegian public sector**

Enabling frameworks	Not available	Available to central government institutions	Available to regional/county level institutions	Available to local/municipal government institutions	Available to private sector institutions
Common interoperability framework	X				
Base registries		X	X	X	X
Shared ICT infrastructure (e.g. shared data centres)		X	X	X	
Shared business processes (e.g. common logistics management)	X				
Shared services (e.g. joint software development)		X	X	X	
Support for the use of cloud computing		X	X	X	
Support for the use of open source software		X	X	X	

Source: OECD (2017a), "Digital Government Survey of Norway", central version, OECD, Paris

Figure 4.7. **Usage of enabling frameworks among Norwegian public sector institutions**

In %

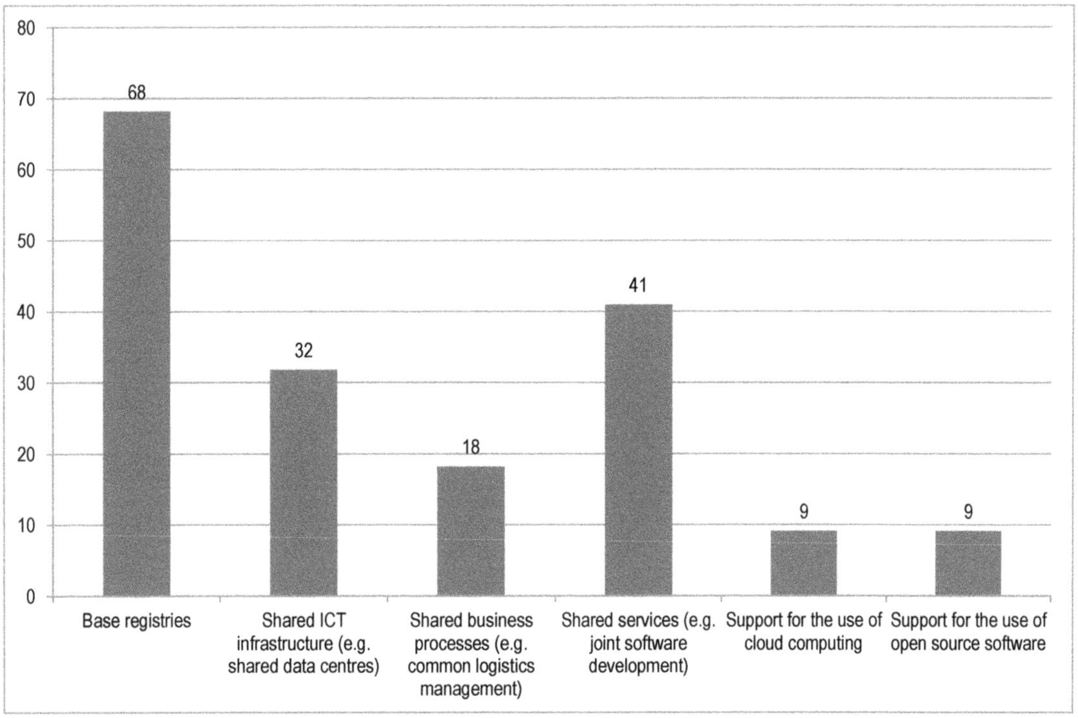

Source: OECD (2017b), "Digital Government Survey of Norway", public sector institutions version, OECD, Paris.

Cloud computing is also recognised by public entities as an important enabler for data storage, sharing and processing, as well as for service delivery. Given its disruptive role in todays' ICT management, a topic-specific strategy was developed by the Norwegian government with the purpose of spurring its use by public and private sector organisations (see Box 4.4). The Cloud Computing Strategy is a good example of the willingness of Norway's public sector to lead the adoption of new technological trends that are able to revolutionise service design, development and delivery and increase a culture of integration and sharing of common platforms and systems across the public sector.

Box 4.4. **Norway's Cloud Computing Strategy**

In 2016 the Ministry of Local Government and Modernisation (KMD) published the Cloud Computing Strategy (CCS) for Norway as an effort to assess the feasibility of developing cloud-based services in the country. The CCS underlines the relevance of cloud computing to public sector productivity drawing upon the development of cloud-based ICT solutions, public-private co-operation and cost-efficient ICT-based services.

The strategy assessed the current legal and regulatory challenges for cloud-based solutions in the country (e.g. cross-border storage and access of data) and centred cloud services procurement on five premises:

- **Sourcing**: Assessing the benefits and risks of outsourcing cloud-based solutions.
- **Architecture**: Forward-looking design of ICT architecture (based on Difi's ICT Architecture Guidelines) that would ensure migrating to the cloud in the future. The latter assuming that a scenario where the adoption of cloud-based solutions is not feasible or convenient for public sector organisations (e.g. an ad hoc solution is not available).
- **Information security** by default: The procurement of cloud-based services should be assessed with a risk-management approach. Ensuring the security of the information would require assessing the capacity of the provider to ensure the integrity, confidentiality and continuous availability of the information.
- **Data protection** by default: Measures should be taken to ensure protected data management processes. Co-responsibility is needed as contractors are obliged to comply with data protection regulations (e.g. the Personal Data Act) as public sector organisations have the obligation to assess and ensure such compliance.
- **Cost-efficiency**: Assessing procured cloud-based solutions in relation to in-house solutions centring on decision-making elements such as clear description of project objectives and exit costs.

The CCS for Norway highlights the role of Difi as the agency in charge of providing guidance to help central public sector institutions, and willing institutions at the local level, to outsource cloud-based solutions in line with public procurement, data protection, risk management and cost-benefit regulations, standards, and/or guidelines.

Source: Author, based on KMD (2016b), "Cloud Computing Strategy for Norway", English version, KMD, www.regjeringen.no/en/dokumenter/cloud-computing-strategy-for-norway/id2484403/.

To boost the use of some ICT building blocks, the Norwegian government has established a group of ICT common components to be adopted by public sector institutions across different sectors of the government (Difi, 2017). The following are highlighted in the 2016 Digitalisation Memorandum (KMD, 2016c) (see Chapter 2):

- **ID-porten**: Public institutions should use the digital ID port that requires login and authentication.
- **Altinn**: Public institutions will initially use Altinn's infrastructure and service platform for the production of relevant services. Digital services for business must be available on Altinn's portal.
- **Digital mailbox for residents**: Public institutions will use Digital Mailbox for residents, when this is chosen.
- **Contact and reservation register**: Public institutions will use the contact and reservation register for notification and transmission of individual decisions and other important digital inquiries.
- **Common public records**: To ensure up-to-date and accurate information about persons, businesses or properties, public institutions shall use the population register, unit registry and matrix, provided that Terms of Use are met.

Additionally, in order to develop the coherent and interoperable environment required for the development of digital government, Difi has published common IT Architecture Principles. The principles aggregate the orientations to be adopted by the Norwegian public sector for the management of IT solutions (see Box 4.4).

Box 4.4. **Norway's IT Architecture Principles**

Assumed as common guidelines for all IT systems in the public sector, Norway's IT Architecture Principles are an important contribution to a common public sector architecture.

- **Service orientation**: Functionality and performance level should be the main consideration in the development of IT solutions.
- **Interoperability**: The platform should be able to interact with other platforms at an appropriate level.
- **Availability**: Electronic services should be available when users need them, easy to find, user-friendly and universally designed.
- **Safety**: The IT solution itself and the information dealt must be protected in terms of confidentiality, integrity and availability, based on formal and risk-based requirements.
- **Openness**: The methods and processes of IT solutions should be explained.
- **Flexibility**: IT solutions should be designed in a way that minimises the changes in work processes, content, organisation, ownership and infrastructure.
- **Scalability**: IT solutions must be able to be scaled as a consequence of changes in usage.
- **References**: The references should refer to regulations, circular, documents, etc.

Source: Difi (2017), www.difi.no, official agency website (accessed 1 April 2017).

The Norwegian public sector seems to have in place the key requisites to support the further development of an integrated digital service delivery. From digital identity mechanisms to base registries and the enabling of frameworks like architecture principles, common instruments exist in Norway to be used by the public sector to guarantee the coherence of the government ICT infrastructure. However, these soft policy levers have a limited capacity of influence if not properly connected with other policy levers like the pre-evaluation of ICT projects or funding mechanisms for the development of digital government projects, e.g. that could require the compliance with certain principles, or the use of certain ICT enablers, as mandatory. By better leveraging the use of the key enablers in place, the Norwegian government could further advance a coherent service-delivery policy.

Integrating the service-delivery policy

Today, digital service designers face the challenge of conceiving multi-channel approaches that can fulfil users' increasingly demanding expectations in terms of simplicity, friendliness and efficiency while securing the public sector's efficiency and increasing its productivity. Nowadays, service-delivery portals need to be totally user-centred and even user-driven. Not only do they need to avoid reflecting the public sector's institutional settings and the complexity of internal public processes, e.g. by being based on one-stop-shop concepts and using life events approaches, but they need to support accessibility of services and same-user experiences regardless of the specific platform used (e.g. online portal, smartphone, tablet).

In Norway, digital service delivery reflects the level of digitalisation of the country's economy and society. The transactional nature of service delivery and the level of sophistication of the underlying platforms demonstrate the government's long-time policy to use digital technologies to improve the relationship between the public administration, citizens and businesses.

The central citizen service delivery portal – norge.no – guides citizens across the services provided by several sectors of government. The possibility of using life events, such as getting married, having a child, in Norway represents the citizen-centred approach, that today is assumed as a minimal requirement to assure convenience for the users of public services.

Other public portals like the Altinn Platform (Box 4.6) provide diverse public services to citizens and businesses. The My Health Portal demonstrates the Norwegian's institutions efforts on advanced digital service delivery approaches that aim to increase user satisfaction. The re-use of information and data within the public sector aims to limit the administrative burdens to citizens and businesses and common components like the ID-porten and the Digital Mailbox for residents are being used across sectors of government, providing users with more uniform and efficient communications with the public sector.

Box 4.6. **Norway's Altinn Platform**

Managed by the Brønnøysund Register, a public entity that is responsible for several public registers, Altinn is a digital infrastructure that links public agencies, municipalities and registers with 4 million inhabitants and 1 million enterprises. Interestingly, 100% of Norwegian adults have a user account in Altinn and 100% of Norwegian enterprises have a user account and a mailbox in Altinn.

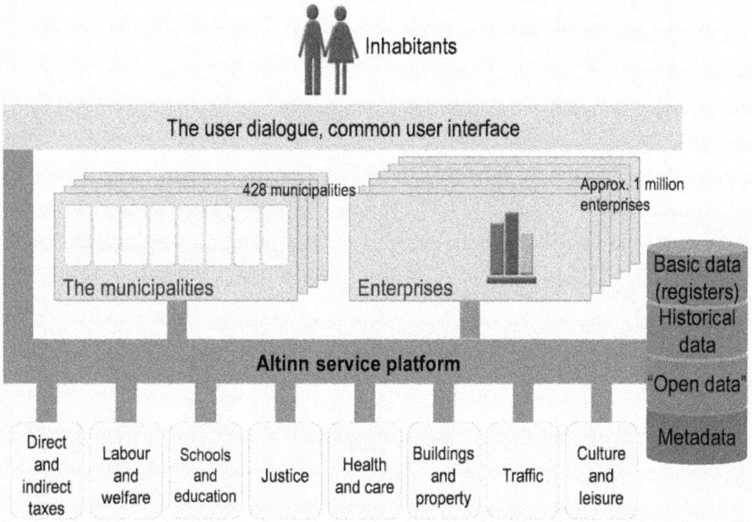

The three dimensions of Altinn:

1. The **platform**: Infrastructure for public communications with the government. Information about services and regulations for citizens and businesses.
2. The **organisation**: Specialised to support the service owners' objectives (simplification for the users and efficiency of the public sector). Responsible for operation, maintenance and further development of the platform management contracts with service owners and suppliers.
3. The **collaboration**: Venues for learning and information exchange and formalised co-operation with service owners. Manages the development of organisation formalised forums. Open innovation co-operation.

Source: Brønnøysund Register (2016), Presentation made during the OECD peer review fact-finding mission to Norway in September 2016.

Another good example of Norway's efforts to improve digital service delivery across sectors of government is the Quality Web Project (QWP). This project, led by Difi, conducts yearly assessments to map the quality of digital services and websites. The assessment is based on 33 criteria, such as: 1) how easy the content of the website is to identify; 2) whether or not the users have the opportunity to provide feedback; and 3) responsiveness to mobile devices. Based on the mentioned criteria, awards are attributed each year and the project works as a soft lever to promote the best Norwegian digital services being provided to citizens and businesses (Difi, 2017).

Projects like norge.no, the Altinn platform, the MyHealth Portal and the Quality Web Project demonstrate the significant level of maturity of the Norwegian public sector in digital service delivery. Nevertheless, there are still several areas where improvements are needed.

Although a central citizen service-delivery portal exists in Norway – norge.no – which make several services available to citizens using a comprehensive life-event approach, several other very relevant public services portals are still being used and developed, like the Altinn platform. This coexistence is difficult to justify from either a citizen-centred and/or even more a citizen-driven perspective. For instance, the Mexican digital one-stop shop – gob.mx – provides a good example of a strong national effort to concentrate in one single portal the public sector online presence (see Box 4.7).

Box 4.7. **Mexico's one-stop shop: gob.mx**

The Mexican national public portal - gob.mx - is a good example of a country-level, digital one-stop-shop approach. The portal has a simple and intuitive design, including a central search bar in the homepage that allows citizens to quickly search and navigate through the Mexican government digital presence. The portal integrates information and services in four areas:

- **public services**, with a scheme that allows the user to navigate through categories (e.g. education, health, taxes), through life events (e.g. start my business, I'm getting married, exit and enter the country) or through public institutions that provide the service
- **government information**, giving citizens access to specific areas or websites of Government Secretaries, public administration institutions, the Mexican states' administrations and the country's embassies and consulates around the world
- **public participation**, allowing access to public consultations underway, to submit public petitions or participate in citizen forums about diverse issues
- **open government data**, giving direct access to the Mexican open government data portal (www. datos.gob.mx).

The portal is responsive to mobile devices and accomplishes the level AA of W3C for motor, hearing and visual disabilities. From August 2015 until June 2017, the portal has received more than 385 million hits and provides high satisfaction to 85% of its users. Gob.mx receives more than 1.5 million visits per day.

Source: Author, based on www.gob.mx and on information provided by the Digital Government Unit, Ministry of Public Administration, Mexico.

The diversity of portals aimed at citizens can be a challenge for an integrated "look and feel" for users when interacting with the Norwegian public sector. The different visual identity patterns and diverse navigation standards applied create additional complexity for citizens with regard to navigating between the different platforms available, generating learning curves for the adoption of each platform by its target audience, and projecting a fragmented image of the government.

Stronger co-ordination seems necessary in Norway to achieve more integrated service delivery, and to render the government's online presence more coherent and intelligible to citizens and businesses. More than reflecting institutional legacies in the Norwegian public administration, the government service delivery practice should focus on serving citizens' needs to better take into account their contexts and life conditions as well as making service delivery more convenient.

To do this, additional clarification about the leadership and governance model for an integrated public service delivery policy might improve the relationship between the public sector and its constituencies. Although the responsibilities of the Ministry of Local Government and Modernisation (KMD) and Difi are substantial in these areas, a clear mandate along with the associated financial and human resources are needed to reap the full benefit of Norway's highly digitalised public sector.

The adoption of digital service standards, applicable to different policy sectors and levels of government, is a mechanism used by some OECD member countries to support more integrated service-delivery practices in the public sector. The United Kingdom and Australia developed standards for digital service delivery that are applied across the public sector (Box 4.8). A similar approach in Norway could be considered.

Box 4.8. Digital services standards: Examples from the United Kingdom and Australia

Digital service standards were developed in the United Kingdom and Australia to help public entities create and run good and coherent digital services. All the public services must meet the standard and are used to check whether a service is good enough for public use.

United Kingdom Digital service standard	Australia Digital service standard
1. Understand user needs.	1. Understand user needs.
2. Do ongoing user research.	2. Have a multidisciplinary team.
3. Have a multidisciplinary team.	3. Use an agile and user-centred process.
4. Use agile methods.	4. Understand tools and systems.
5. Iterate and improve frequently.	5. Make it secure.
6. Evaluate tools and systems.	6. Ensure consistent and responsive design.
7. Understand security and privacy issues.	7. Use open standards and common platforms.
8. Make all new source code open.	8. Make source code open.
9. Use open standards and common platforms.	9. Make it accessible.
10. Test the end-to-end service.	10. Test the service.
11. Make a plan for being off line.	11. Measure performance.
12. Make sure users succeed the first time.	12. Don't forget the non-digital experience.
13. Make the user experience consistent with GOV.UK.	13. Encourage everyone to use the digital service.
14. Encourage everyone to use the digital service.	
15. Collect performance data.	
16. Identify performance indicators.	
17. Report performance data on the Performance Platform.	
18. Test with the minister.	

Source: UK Government (2017), "Digital Service Standard", webpage, www.gov.uk/service-manual/service-standard (accessed 12 August 2017); Australian Government (2017), "Digital Service Standard", webpage, www.dta.gov.au/standard/ (accessed 12 August 2017).

Clear usability guidelines are also an important policy mechanism to support the development of more integrated user experiences for citizens and businesses when interacting with the public sector. For instance, Portugal has recently launched a public website – www.usabilidade.pt – dedicated entirely to the promotion of usability standards across the public sector.

Enabling cross-border public service delivery

Due to the levels of digital government development, economic integration and cultural ties, the Nordic and Baltic countries are probably the region world wide most able to advance expeditiously to the delivery of cross-border services, improving government's co-operation and boosting convenience for its citizens and businesses. Based on this assumption, in April 2017, the ministers in charge of digital development from Åland, Denmark, Estonia, Faroe Islands, Finland, Greenland, Iceland, Latvia, Lithuania, Norway and Sweden agreed on the need to create a common area for cross-border digital services in the public sector as part of the Declaration of the Nordic-Baltic Ministerial Conference on Digitalisation (see Chapter 1).

This high-level political recognition of digitalisation matters in the Nordic-Baltic region underlined the need to take strategic action at the regional level in order to fully reap the potential of cross-border services as tools to:

1. deliver better services for citizens
2. develop a more effective public sector
3. reduce the administrative burdens for businesses, improving their capabilities to innovate.

The OECD Recommendation on Digital Government Strategies (2014a) stresses the relevance of international co-operation (Principle 8) for knowledge sharing, for cross-border joint efforts and for the definition of common goals among countries' public sectors. The context for digitalisation across Nordic and Baltic countries favours positioning these countries as leaders and frontrunners in regard to the digital transformation of the public sector, namely through the development of cross-border services for citizens and businesses.

During the peer review mission in Oslo in September 2016, several public stakeholders considered that the development of cross-border services should be further explored in Norway. Following the mission, the OECD Digital Government Survey of Norway (2017b) confirmed that the majority of Norwegian institutions consider that its transactional services should benefit from cross-border delivery (Figure 4.8).

Figure 4.8. **Support for the development of cross-border services among Norwegian public sector institutions**

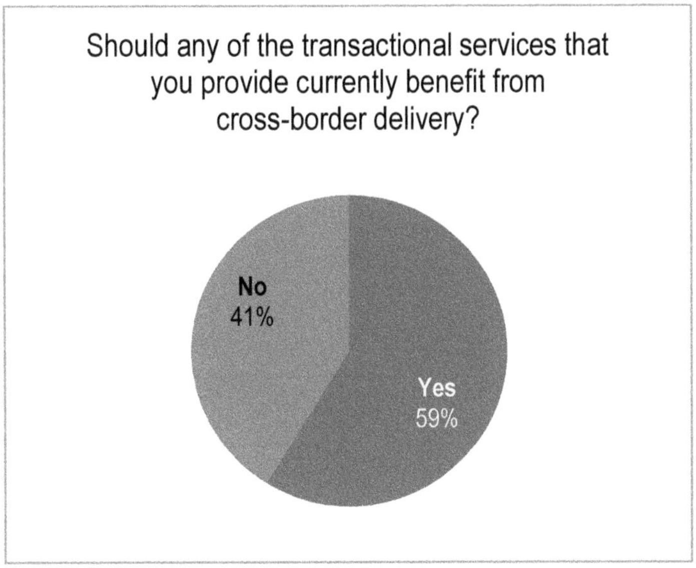

Source: OECD (2017b), "Digital Government Survey of Norway", public sector institutions version, OECD, Paris.

Norway has actively participated during recent years in the European Union's co-operation for the development of cross-border digital services. Projects include the following:

- The **TOOP project** is part of the EU eGovernment Action Plan 2016-20 and has the ultimate goal of applying the once-only principle through cross-border co-operation among European public administrations. TOOP will develop three pilot projects in different areas: 1) cross-border e-services for business mobility; 2) updating connected company data; and 3) online shipping and crew certificates to connect 60 information systems from at least 20 countries. The project was launched in January 2017, involving 21 countries (namely Norway) and has a budget of EUR 8 million (European Commission, 2017a).
- The **Connecting Europe Facilities** (CEF) is an EU programme focused on the development of cross-border infrastructures in the transport, energy and telecommunications sectors in Europe. CEF Digital is the part of this programme that includes the telecommunications sector. The programme lasts until 2020. Difi has the role of co-ordinator for CEF Digital in Norway (Difi, 2017) (see Table 4.2).
- The **ISA² programme** supports the development of digital solutions that enable public administrations, businesses and citizens in Europe to benefit from interoperable cross-border and cross-sector public services. ISA² commenced on 1 January 2016 and will run until 31 December 2020 (European Commission, 2017b). Difi is the secretariat of the programme in Norway and is responsible for co-ordinating the activities and establishing national networks.
- The aim of **eSENS** was to facilitate the deployment of cross-border digital public services through generic and re-usable ICT building blocks. Though the project ended in March 2017, it brought together 22 countries for the development of

pilots in the areas of e-procurement, e-health, e-justice, business life-cycle, citizen life-cycle and e-agriculture. As a core infrastructure for the pilots, the following building blocks for cross-border exchange of information were developed: e-delivery, semantics, e-documents, e-identity and e-signature. Difi was responsible for eSens in Norway (eSens, 2017).

Table 4.2. **Norwegian government involvement in the Connecting Europe Facilities programme**

Building blocks being developed with Norwegian involvement	
e-ID	eProcurement
eSignature	Europeana
eDelivery	Safer Internet
eInvoicing	BRIS (Business Registers Interconnection System)
eTranslation	EESSI (Electronic Exchange of Social Security Information)
Public open data	EJustice Portal
Cyber security	eHealth
Online dispute resolution	

Source: Difi (2017), www.difi.no, official agency website (accessed 1 April 2017).

Norway has also been involved, through KMD's and Difi's active participation, in the following Nordic cross-border co-operation initiatives:

- **Legal guide to cloud sourcing**: Study initiated by the Nordic Council of Ministers to promote and sustain the discussion on eID similarities and differences among Denmark, Finland, Iceland, Norway and Sweden. The project had the goal of investigating and mapping the eID systems of the these countries, uncovering key issues for cross-border access to digital services (Nordic Council of Ministers, 2013).
- **Nordic digital identification (eID) – Survey and recommendations for cross border cooperation**: Guidelines financially sponsored by the Nordic Council of Ministers to ensure the proper legal compliance, contractual efficiency and proper handling of risks to public sector institutions of the Nordic countries interested in procuring certain cloud ICT services (Nordic Council of Ministers, 2016).

Building on its involvement in the above-mentioned projects and programmes, on the support of the majority of public sectors institutions and on the Declaration of the Nordic-Baltic Ministerial Conference on Digitalisation, Norway can play an active role as promoter of cross-border services among Nordic and Baltic countries. An untapped opportunity seems to exist in the Nordic-Baltic region for this new stage of public service delivery, which has the potential to contribute to strengthening the economic co-operation between the countries and boost the convenience of citizens that live and circulate in the region.

As a result of previous collaboration with the Nordic and Baltic countries, the OECD has supported national efforts to identify untapped opportunities, and trigger the exponential benefits of the digital revolution for economies and societies. The joint Public Governance Review of Estonia and Finland (OECD, 2015) focused particularly on the development of cross-border services among the two countries. The report discussed how political intentions can be converted into tangible implementation, including the establishment of shared governance, co-ordination and management mechanisms. The report is a clear example of the OECD experience supporting the development of cross-border digital government co-operation.

References

Australian Government (2017), "Digital Service Standard", webpage, www.dta.gov.au/standard/ (accessed 12 August 2017).

Difi (Agency for Public Management and eGovernment) (2017), www.difi.no, official agency website (accessed 1 April 2017).

Difi (2010), "First in Social Media for Management", Difi.

Difi (2009), "Social Media in Management – Reflections on Development 2010-2014", Difi.

eSens (Electronic Simple European Networked Services) (2017), www.esens.eu, official website (accessed 12 August 2017).

European Commission (2017a), "The "Once-Only" Principle (TOOP) Project launched in January 2017", https://ec.europa.eu/digital-single-market/en/news/once-only-principle-toop-project-launched-january-2017.

European Commission (2017b), "ISA^2 – IT solutions for less bureaucracy", official website, https://ec.europa.eu/isa2/.

KMD (Ministry of Local Government and Modernisation) (2016), "Digital Agenda for Norway in brief: ICT for a simpler everyday life and increased productivity", English version, KMD, www.regjeringen.no/en/dokumenter/digital-agenda-for-norway-in-brief/id2499897/sec1.

KMD (2016b), "Cloud Computing Strategy for Norway", English version, KMD, www.regjeringen.no/en/dokumenter/cloud-computing-strategy-for-norway/id2484403/.

KMD (2016c), "2016 Digitalisation Memorandum", KMD, www.regjeringen.no/no/dokumenter/digitaliseringsrundskrivet/id2522147/.

Mickoleit, A. (2014) "Social media use by governments: A policy primer to discuss trends, identify policy opportunities and guide decision makers", *OECD Working Papers on Public Governance*, No. 26, OECD Publishing, Paris, http://dx.doi.org/10.1787/5jxrcmghmk0s-en.

Nordic Council of Ministers (2016), "Nordic digital identification (eID): Survey and recommendations for cross border cooperation", NCM, http://norden.diva-portal.org/smash/get/diva2:902133/FULLTEXT01.pdf.

Nordic Council of Ministers (2013), "Legal guide to public organisation cloud sourcing in the Nordic countries", Working Paper prepared for Nordic Council of Ministers' informal forum for IT directors, 17 December, http://norden.diva-portal.org/smash/get/diva2:701093/FULLTEXT01.pdf.

OECD (forthcoming), "The digital transformation of the public sector: Helping governments respond to the needs of networked societies", *OECD Working Papers on Public Governance*, OECD Publishing, Paris.

OECD (2017a), "Digital Government Survey of Norway", central version, OECD, Paris.

OECD (2017b), "Digital Government Survey of Norway", public sector institutions version, OECD, Paris.

OECD (2017c), *Government at a Glance 2017*, OECD Publishing, Paris, http://dx.doi.org/10.1787/gov_glance-2017-en.

OECD (2015), *OECD Public Governance Reviews: Estonia and Finland: Fostering Strategic Capacity across Governments and Digital Services across Borders*, OECD Public Governance Reviews, OECD Publishing, Paris, http://dx.doi.org/10.1787/9789264229334-en.

OECD (2014a), "Recommendation of the Council on Digital Government Strategies", OECD, Paris, www.oecd.org/gov/digital-government/recommendation-on-digital-government-strategies.htm.

OECD (2014b), "OECD Survey on Digital Government Performance" (dataset), OECD, Paris, http://qdd.oecd.org/subject.aspx?Subject=6C3F11AF-875E-4469-9C9E-AF93EE384796.

OECD (2013), *Reaping the Benefits of ICTs in Spain: Strategic Study on Communication Infrastructure and Paperless Administration*, OECD Publishing, Paris, http://dx.doi.org/10.1787/9789264173224-en.

OECD (2009), *Rethinking e-Government Services: User Centred Approaches*, OECD Publishing, Paris, http://dx.doi.org/10.1787/19901054.

UK Government (2017), "Digital Service Standard", webpage, www.gov.uk/service-manual/service-standard (accessed 12 August 2017).

Further reading

Government of Norway (2017), "Government.no", official government website, www.regjeringen.no/en/ (accessed 31 March 2017).

OECD (2016), *Digital Government in Chile: Strengthening the Institutional and Governance Framework*, OECD Digital Government Studies, OECD Publishing, Paris, http://dx.doi.org/10.1787/9789264258013-en.

OECD/International Telecommunication Union (2011), *M-Government: Mobile Technologies for Responsive Governments and Connected Societies*, OECD Publishing, Paris, http://dx.doi.org/10.1787/9789264118706-en.

Chapter 5

Building a data-driven public sector in Norway

This chapter seeks to understand the actions required to unleash the power and strategic use of data for the digital transformation of the Norwegian public sector. It discusses the governance of the public sector data value chain, including the role and legacy of the Norwegian basic data registries and open government data. Consequently, it addresses the development of skills and competencies and a propitious organisational environment inside Norwegian public sector institutions as a precondition to fully reap the benefits of data-driven technologies for public sector productivity and growth.

Introduction

The rapid expansion of digital technologies and the increasing access of citizens and businesses to the Internet have led to the increased availability of digitalised processes and information. The digitalisation of the economies and societies created new business models that centre on human-machine interaction and machine-to-machine communication. The transition from analogue to digital daily activities has placed data at the core of these activities.

Data has become a valuable commodity in the 21st century. The analogue-to-digital shift engendered the exponential production and storage of digitalised information. Academic research (see Hilbert and Lopez, 2011) points to the fact that by 1986 only 0.8% of information (e.g. documents, music, and video) was available in digital formats. This figure rose to 94% by 2007. The underlying digitalised data creating such information (which, as a whole, creates knowledge) has become a "gold mine". Such data represent indeed a valuable asset for economic actors and the civic tech communities that can re-use it to increase business intelligence, but it can also support evidence-based decision making, accountability and improved service delivery across public sectors (Ubaldi, 2013).

Norway, like many OECD countries, is not exempt from undergoing this transition. The digitalisation of business models within public sector institutions has created the need to establish models for the effective management of the data value chain in order to trigger the strategic value of data for digital government. In optimum conditions (e.g. interoperable, accessible, discoverable, open), data can be continuously produced, collected, shared and re-used by all actors involved in the data ecosystem (see Figure 5.1), including public sector institutions, thereby incentivising public sector efficiency and productivity, and spurring social and business innovation.

Norway has the opportunity to capitalise on its previous achievements related to e-government (e.g. eID [electronic identification system], one-stop-shop portals, information technology [IT] architecture principles) towards a data-driven public sector that transforms the design, delivery and monitoring of public policies and services through the strategic management and use of data (OECD, 2016a). This requires revising legacy data management models, highly influenced by traditional siloed public sector governance structures (see Chapter 2) in relation to digital government principles in order to re-engineer processes and enable a propitious environment that, as a result, contributes to fully reaping the benefits of data for all actors in the ecosystem.

Governing the data value chain (from data collection to opening up government data and re-using data) within the public sector is crucial to capitalise on data as a strategic asset. Building a data-driven public sector requires understanding how the data value chain is linked to the achievement of overarching policy goals. Conceiving all the stages of the value chain - and their outputs (e.g. data registries and open government data [OGD]) - as inter-connected elements of the data value chain process, and recognising how specific key factors (e.g. human, technology, organisational models) influence - in a positive or negative fashion – and interact throughout the whole process is vital to construct a data-driven public sector.

This chapter centres on data governance within the Norwegian public sector, drawing upon the analytical framework developed by the OECD. Norway's policies and initiatives are discussed from the perspective of their contribution to the use of data as a strategic asset for the public, private and social sector.

Figure 5.1. **Data provision and consumption: Main stakeholders and their roles**

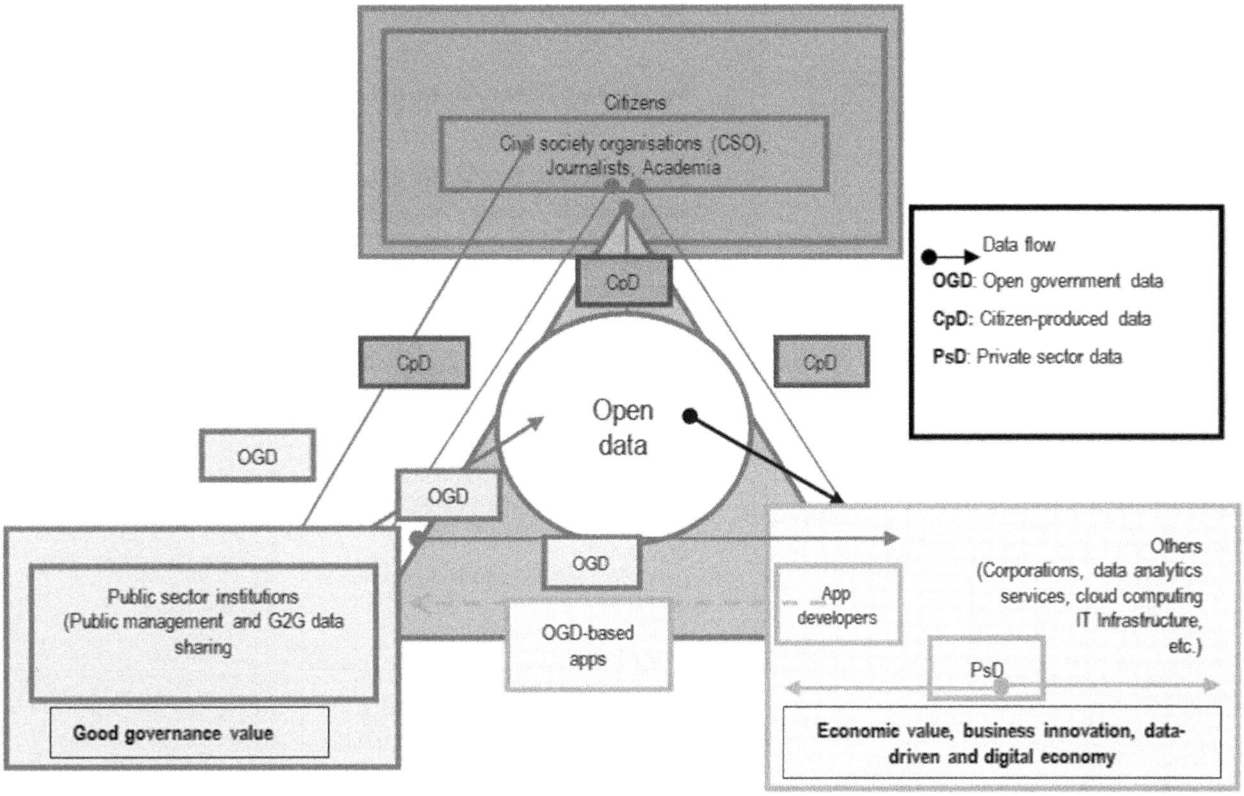

Source: Adapted from Rivera Perez, J.A. (2015), *Beyond Open Data Disclosure: Fostering The Impact Of Open Government Data Towards More Efficient Public Institutions*, London School of Economics and Political Science, Department of Management, London.

As shown in Table 5.1, the analytical framework places the data value chain (from data production/collection to data re-use), as a core component of digital government. The framework can be used to scale up the understanding of data from the technical to the policy level, therefore grouping and connecting the components of the data value chain, along the three key dimensions of data policies: availability, accessibility and re-use. These dimensions are equally used as the three umbrella composites of the OECD OURdata Index (OECD, 2017a).

Table 5.1. **Data governance in the public sector: Leading, governing, enabling and guiding data-driven institutions**

Overarching conditions	Data policy dimensions (incl. OURdata Index composites)	Data value chain		Key components of the data value chain		Ruling OECD digital government principles
Governing the data value chain (e.g. governance , regulations, CDOs, data stewards, horizontal co-ordination) *Enabling* data as a strategic asset (eID, IT architecture, one-stop portals) *Guiding* the data value chain (Guidelines, standards) Supporting an effective data governance: Skill and capacity development (external and internal actors) (taskforces, trainings)	Data availability	Collection and production	Data integrity / Data corruption	Data collection tools (e.g. human-machine interaction, offline collection, automated collection) Data sources (internal, external) Data ownership Data crowdsourcing	E-government approach (crganisational efficiency, citizen-centred) Digital government approach (open, inclusive, digitalised, user- and data-driven institutions)	Once-only principle Digital by design
	Data accessibility	Processing and computing		Raw data Metadata (e.g. data documentation, contextual and processing information, data owners) Data qualities: Completeness/comprehensiveness, validity, timeliness, accuracy, consistency, formats) Data quality certification vs. laissez-faire approach Data interoperability (semantics, common identifiers) Structured/non-structured data Data granularity		Digital by design Open by default (e.g. use of non-proprietary software and data formats)
		Storage		Data silos (data fragmentation) Data lakes (from raw to structured data) Data consolidation vs. connected and linked data silos Data catalogues (open or not) Data graveyards Cross-border data sharing and server locations (e.g. cloud computing)		Privacy by default/design
		Security		Restricted and/or enabled data access Data privacy, anonymisation, encryption		Privacy by default/design
	Data re-use (incl. Using data for the policy cycle)	Sharing		Linked data and data relationships Data interoperability (Semantics, common identifiers) Government-to-government data sharing (e.g. basic data registries)		Once-only principle
		Publishing and opening up data		Consultations and prioritisation Data catalogues and one-stop OGD portals Data infrastructures Data visualisation and data story-telling		Open by default Engagement by default
		Re-using data and engaging the ecosystem		Reach, promotion and communication Consultations Data discoverability Value co-creation (e.g. datalabs, datatons) Digital inclusion		Engagement by default/design
		Monitoring and measurement		Feedback loops		Engagement by default/design

Source: Author (original content created for this review).

The above-mentioned dimensions serve as a guiding policy backbone useful to highlight the need to implement effective data governance models as the basis of a data-driven public sector across OECD member countries, including Norway. This requires ensuring the availability of a propitious institutional, technological, cultural, and regulatory environment that favours the use of digital government strategies as the basis for the construction of a data-driven public sector that uses data as a strategic input. This is in line with ruling OECD principles for digital government (OECD, 2014a).

Together, all the above-mentioned components are strategic levers for digital government policies. This is highlighted by the OECD (2014a) Recommendation on Digital Government Strategies - in particular Principle 3, which recommends that OECD countries, including Norway, create a data-driven culture within the public sector (see Box 5.1).

Box 5.1. **OECD Recommendation of the Council on Digital Government Strategies (extract)**

Principle 3

Creation of a data-driven culture in the public sector

The Council, on the proposal of the Public Governance Committee, recommends that government develop and implement digital government strategies which:

Create a data-driven culture in the public sector, by:

1. developing frameworks to enable, guide, and foster access to, use and re-use of, the increasing amount of evidence, statistics and data concerning operations, processes and results to (a) increase openness and transparency, and (b) incentivise public engagement in policy making, public value creation, service design and delivery
2. balancing the need to provide timely official data with the need to deliver trustworthy data, managing risks of data misuse related to the increased availability of data in open formats (i.e. allowing use and re-use, and the possibility for non-governmental actors to re-use and supplement data with a view to maximise public economic and social value).

Source: OECD (2014a), "Recommendation of the Council on Digital Government Strategies", OECD, Paris, www.oecd.org/gov/digital-government/recommendation-on-digital-government-strategies.htm.

The importance of sound institutional governance for government data in Norway

Difi as a driver of a data-driven public sector in Norway

The Agency for Public Management and eGovernment (Difi) has played an instrumental role in governing the public sector data value chain in Norway. It does so as part of its mandate and instructions received via an annual letter of allocation and any additional instructions that might result from the Digitalisation Memorandum – both issued by the Ministry of Local Government and Modernisation (KMD) on a yearly basis (see Chapters 1 and 2). As a result of Difi's mandate, the agency developed the Framework for the National IT Architecture. The framework places information management and the basic registries as core components of one out of the five areas of work that guide the work of the agency on information and data governance (see Table 5.2).

Table 5.2. **Difi's Framework for the National IT Architecture**

Main areas of work: Information management

Administration (internal)	Users: Communication	Task (or assignment) solving	Information management	Security, privacy and infrastructure
Salaries, personnel and human resources	Communication with users	Payment and collection	Information management	Information security
Governance	Making information available	Processing, case management	Basic data	Infrastructure for interoperability
Procurement	Democratic dialogue	Specialised case management		Authentification and user management
Service design and development		Document management		

Source: Provided by the Agency for Public Management and eGovernment (Difi).

Difi also developed an information governance (IG) model (see Figure 5.2), which places public sector information and data at the core of its work to develop a national IT architecture for the public sector. While open government data appears to be somehow disconnected from the actual conceptualisation of Difi's IG model and IT architecture (mainy focused on e-government and inter-institutional data sharing), the model sets an advanced starting point to leverage the strategic use of government data by all actors of the ecosystem.

Figure 5.2. **Difi's information governance model**

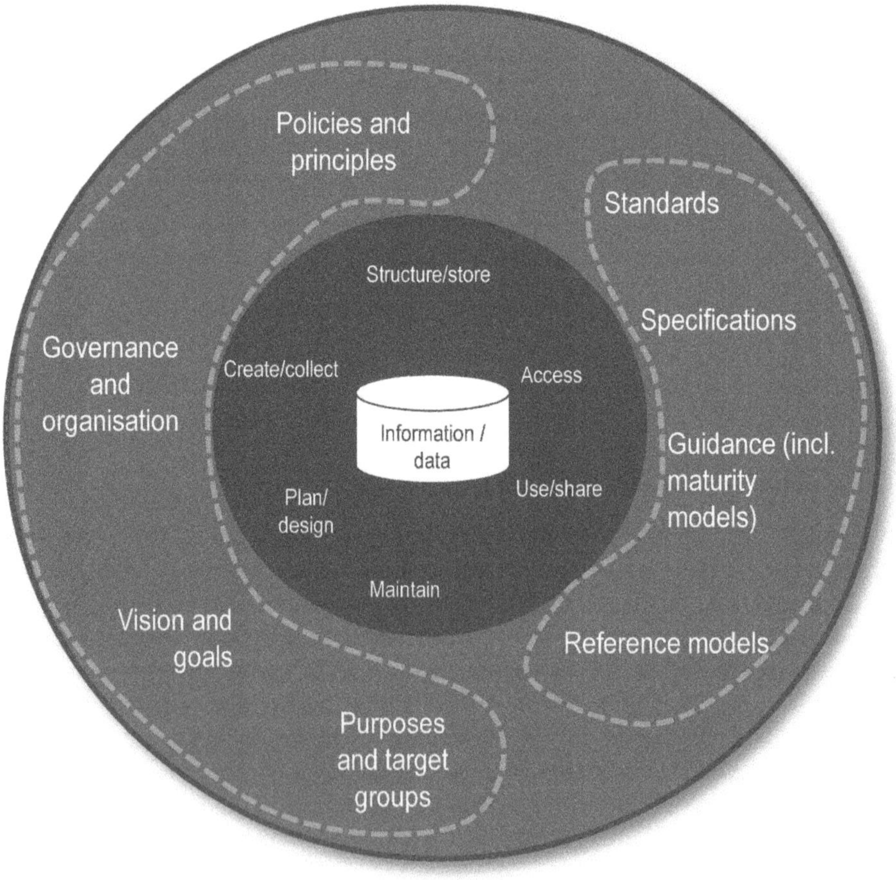

Source: Provided by the Agency for Public Management and eGovernment (Difi).

Highlighting Difi's efforts to place data at the core of the IG model, and as a key component of the national IT architecture as a whole, is crucial to understand the role that Difi has played to govern and rule (e.g. through guidelines and standards) the data value chain within the Norwegian public sector.

As a result of the IG model, Difi has developed, and published for public access on www.difi.no, a rich set of guiding instruments (e.g. open up guides, guidelines and data standards) that set clear rules to better govern the data value chain. Among others, these instruments include:

- **Standards for Description of Data Sets and Data Directories** (DCAT-AP-NO).
- The **"Order your Own House" Guide**, aiming to help public sector institutions understand, organise, catalogue, and structure their own data.[1]
- **Metadata standards**.[2]
- **Guidelines for the publication of open government data**[3] (e.g. under an open licence, for free, in machine, open and non-proprietary formats and with the appropriate metadata). These guidelines, published on 7 January 2017, support the directives on open government data included on the 2016 Digitalisation Memorandum.

Horizontal co-ordination

The role of the Strategic Cooperation Council for Management and Coordination of eGovernment Services (SKATE) (see Chapter 2) is also relevant to understand data governance in the Norwegian public sector. In this regard, the work of the SKATE (integrated by 12 directorates and agencies, a representative from the local government association [KS], and chaired by Difi) has been crucial to reach an agreement on what measures are relevant for ministries and agencies, and which are not, in order to govern the data value chain, and better support and guide the overall implementation of digitalisation efforts across the broad public sector.

For instance, as highlighted by some public officials during the OECD mission to Oslo, the co-ordinating work of the SKATE is useful in guiding ministries and agencies towards the development of their institutional data catalogues. Data catalogues are a crucial component of the data value chain as they can contribute to increasing institutional awareness on those data collected, managed and stored by the organisation; facilitate inter-institutional data sharing; and, eventually, spur the publication of open government data. Most ministries and agencies providing an answer to the OECD survey (a total of 35) reported that an institutional data catalogue was neither available nor under development, or reported no scheduled plans – as of December 2016 - to develop one.

In addition, there is important, broad, cross-sectoral, public, long-lasting co-operation on digital spatial information access, governed by KMD, with both the National Geodata Board (representatives from the private and public sectors) and the National Coordination Committee on Spatial Information (representatives from 12 ministries, local and regional authorities). Some 600 public agencies and municipalities are offering data and are actively using information in the spatial data infrastructure, showing one of the broadest practical data-sharing initiatives in Norway.

The work of the Standards Council (Standardiseringsrådet) also contributes to setting clear rules governing the data value chain. While the activities of the council are not strictly focused on data standards but on broader standardisation efforts (e.g. management standards for procuring external services), the council exerts an advisory role for Difi in regard to matters related to data standardisation across the public sector (e.g. the DCAT standard). The work of the Standards Council (integrated by 15 central and local level public sector institutions) focuses on discussing standardisation measures that are then presented to Difi and the KMD – which decide on the need to issue these standards as recommendations (decision made by Difi) or as mandatory standards (decision made by the KMD) (as found in the Regulations on ICT Standards in Public Administration).[4]

Leading data governance: From consensus-based decision making to strategic implementation

The SKATE and the Standards Council reflect the organisational culture within the Norwegian public sector. As widely discussed in previous chapters, this culture is characterised by consensual decision making, but also by the fragmented implementation of joint decisions and initiatives within sectors where agencies play a key role. This organisational culture is typical of the Norwegian public sector and has not changed since the publication of the OECD e-Government study of Norway (see Chapter 1). However, while this culture could favour innovation in specific sectors, it can also hinder the possibilities of achieving systemic change in a structured and co-ordinated fashion.

The work of the SKATE and the Standards Council has contributed to promoting a more co-ordinated policy implementation through consensus and the development of standards. Nonetheless, driving change within the above-mentioned organisational context requires strengthening the current institutional governance model in order to leverage data as a strategic asset for, and within, the public sector and build a digital government under strong and clear leadership.

Currently it is not clear who leads the overall *de facto* data governance policy in Norway. On the one hand, as the policy co-ordinating agency, the KMD defines the priorities of the digital agenda, but implementation takes place at the agency level. On the other hand, Difi plays a key role with regard to the governance of the data value chain, and the overall digital government agenda; nevertheless, as discussed in Chapter 2, the agency lacks the right set of policy levers at hand to rightfully execute a stronger mandate.

From a data governance perspective, the Norwegian government, through the KMD and Difi, has succeeded in developing different governance instruments to co-ordinate, regulate, guide and support effective data value chain management models inside public sector institutions and across the broad public sector.

In this line, it is important to differentiate policy definition and co-ordination responsibilities (under the KMD), and instrumental/technical support roles (Difi) from leadership and championship. Despite the availability of a forward-looking policy, advanced enablers (e.g. eID, IT architecture), and a good set of instruments governing the data value chain, clear and strong leadership leading the data governance and management strategy in the country is still lacking in Norway.

Some OECD countries have addressed these leadership issues by creating formal chief data officer (CDO) positions within the central government. In Norway some of the responsibilities of CDOs across OECD countries (see Box 5.2 later in this chapter) are shared between the KMD and Difi. In other words, the role of the KMD is to set the vision and goals for digitalisation in the country (including digital government) and Difi is in charge of supporting public sector institutions towards the achievement of the former.

This being said, the responsibilities of these institutions lag in regard to the active role that CDOs have across different OECD countries as the implementation of key data-related initiatives, if done, are the full responsibility of agencies. For instance, in some cases, the creation of dynamic CDO offices (e.g. Mexico) have been used as *de facto* innovation or data labs to test data-driven initiatives to address specific policy challenges, providing a set of good practices that could be scaled up and transferred to other line ministries to ensure their resilience and sustainability, once these initiatives have been tested and proved. Such a dynamic approach is absent in Norway.

In addition, the location of the office of the CDO as a body within the centre of government (e.g. Cabinet Office in the United Kingdom, Office of the President in Mexico, Office of the Prime Minister in France) grants them high-level political support to advance the data governance strategy in the country. This model is also absent in Norway as of November 2016, and the clear support of the Office of the Prime Minister was not at the level of these OECD countries.

Data collected through the OECD Open Government Survey 3.0 shows that, as of December 2016, 14 out of 31 OECD countries and partners had CDO positions (see Figure 5.3). Such a position, together with the Chief Information Officer (CIO) role (see Chapter 2), is not yet available within the Norwegian government (June, 2017).

Figure 5.3. **Availability of chief data officer positions across selected countries**

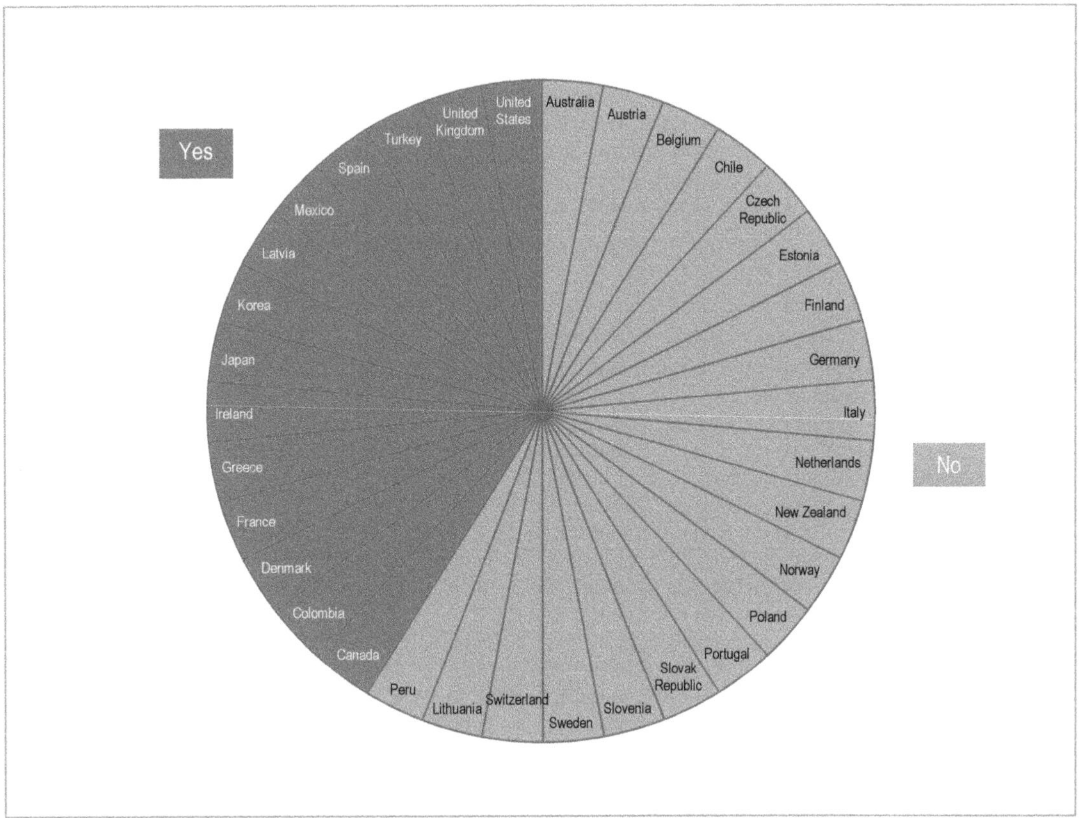

Source: OECD (2016b), "OECD Open Government Data Survey 3.0", OECD, Paris.

In Norway, there is a need to invigorate and leverage the sense of urgency of doing better in regard to data governance. This requires moving beyond the definition of policy goals or the development of standards and guidelines for data sharing or open government data. OECD reviews on open government data (see OECD, 2015a and 2016c) highlight the emerging yet key contribution of the CDO role as a core component of data governance in front-running countries like France, the United Kingdom and the United States (see Box 5.2). As data champions, CDOs can lead data governance strategies thereby connecting the strategic vision of the central government with the overall data value chain of the public sector. The CDO should be able to deliver policy quick wins in a structured fashion, based on how processes work inside the public sector, and the skills and technology needed across the public sector to do so. This is crucial to ensure that those structured quick wins are translated into long-term and sustainable impacts. Building a data-driven public sector requires not only formal policy or guidelines in place, but also a strategy designing how the policy goals will be achieved. Leadership is crucial for this purpose.

Box 5.2. **The role of the Chief Data Officer in France, the United Kingdom and the United States**

France

In France, the work of the CDO contributes to ensuring the quality of the data produced by the French public sector, and facilitates data sharing among administrations, researchers, companies and citizens. The CDO role sits within the Etalab, the French Task Force for Open Data at the Prime Minister's Secretariat-General for Modernisation of Public Action. The CDO is in charge of stimulating the dissemination of new data-based decision methods within the administration: big data approaches, optimised allocation of public resources.

The CDO co-ordinates administrative actions related to the data value chain (e.g. data catalogues, governance, production, circulation and exploitation of data by administrations). He/she is also in charge of organising its circulation, while respecting the protection of privacy and secrets as defined by law. The CDO is empowered to request from administrations (if needed) information on the data they produce, receive, or collect, and provides a yearly report to the Office of the Prime Minister on the inventory, the governance, the production, the dissemination and the use of data by administrations. Finally, he/she is authorised to conduct experimentations on the use of data, to reinforce the efficiency of public policies, to contribute to a better management of public spending and resources, and to improve the quality of public services provided to citizens.

United Kingdom

In March 2015, the UK government appointed its first chief data officer following the launch of a set of principles designed to improve transparency in government contracts. These principles laid out requirements for the release of information pertaining to dealings between government and its suppliers.

The CDO was held alongside the position as head of the Government Digital Service (GDS) at the UK Cabinet Office. The objective of the CDO is to spearhead the government's digital revolution by taking the UK world-leading approach to open data even further, while strengthening data analysis skills in the UK civil service. The CDO champions the government's approach to open data access and use, and the use of data to better inform decisions across the public sector. In his/her role, the CDO will need to strike a balance between open data and inspiring confidence in the general public in how government uses their data.

The original responsibilities of the CDO involved:

- transforming the management and use of data within government, by setting standards and principles and opening up data flows across government (i.e. overseeing the definition and enforcement of a new government data standard
- championing open data, and opening up existing government data wherever possible
- driving the use of data as a tool for making decisions in government.

In February 2017, the United Kingdom published its Digital Transformation Strategy for 2017-20, which includes the new appointment of the next chief data officer in the country.

United States

In February 2015, the White House named the first Deputy Chief Technology Officer (CTO) for Data Policy and Chief Data Scientist (CDS) in the Office of Science and Technology Policy. The CDS:

- helps shape policies and practices to help the United States remain a leader in technology and innovation
- fosters partnerships to help responsibly maximise the nation's return on its investment in data
- helps to recruit and retain the best minds in data science to serve the public
- provides data science leadership on the administration's momentum on open data and data science.

The CDS is also expected to work on the administration's Precision Medicine Initiative, which focuses on utilising advances in data and healthcare to provide clinicians with new tools, knowledge, and therapies to select which treatments will work best for which patients, while protecting patient privacy. As part of the CTO team, the CDS works with colleagues across government, including the Chief Information Officer (CIO) and the US Digital Service.

Source: Adapted from OECD (2015a), *Open Government Data Review of Poland: Unlocking the Value of Government Data*, OECD Digital Government Studies, OECD Publishing, Paris, http://dx.doi.org/10.1787/9789264241787-en.

The role of institutional data stewards

When published in 2013, the Korean Open Data Law succeeded in foreseeing the relevance and need to ensure the availability of institutional chief data officers (or data stewards) in order to ensure the strategic implementation of data governance strategies across the public sector that could contribute to the overall achievement of central, sectoral and institutional policy goals (see Box 5.3). Data stewards have a similar role to that of the national CDO, championing data-related initiatives and/or formal strategies (e.g. open government data) at the institutional level.

Box 5.3. **Data stewards: Leveraging the strategic and systemic role of data at the institutional level**

While national chief data officers (CDOs) are in charge of translating international and national open data policy goals into strategic actions, and co-ordinating central bodies towards a synchronised and well-structured policy implementation, the role of institutional data stewards centres on translating those policy goals, guidelines and standards into well-structured public data management strategies. Data stewards are therefore able to connect strategic vision with the overall governance and management of data at the institutional level.

Data stewards act as change drivers and data evangelists inside public institutions. Their role is key to moving from a centralised government-user co-operation (led by central co-ordinating agencies) to a more proactive and direct approach that enables closer and more direct collaboration with stakeholders (inside and outside the public sector), aligned to sectoral and policy/value specific goals.

In general, the data stewards should:

- be involved in, and in many cases responsible for, any activities along the data management value chain
- connect his/her work to organisational governance, from delivering services and institutional results to protecting the public or public interest
- identify and exploit the potential and value of data disclosure for sectoral, policy and institutional objectives, and closely co-operate with the national CDO towards the achievement of central policy goals
- focus on helping the organisation get more value and insight from the data it collects and on helping people accomplish their goals by aligning them with the process and technology components that are critical to organisational strategic goals
- be an evangelist for the increased use and publication of data in many contexts (e.g. elevating the awareness and discussion internally regarding the importance of well-run data operations, supporting organisational culture change, and championing and evangelising a data-driven culture)
- provide data governance and data management services to the organisation (e.g. spanning divisional silos, setting and implementing central data standards and guidelines in the process)
- collaborate with other institutions to set common sectoral goals, and standards for data internally, and externally, to ensure interoperability and so that users, suppliers and the whole ecosystem can understand them
- engage on a regular basis with developers and data users to know their data needs and obtain feedback on the institutional data strategy.

Source: Adapted from OECD (2015a), *Open Government Data Review of Poland: Unlocking the Value of Government Data*, OECD Digital Government Studies, OECD Publishing, Paris, http://dx.doi.org/10.1787/9789264241787-en.

As of December 2016, only 2 out of the 35 Norwegian ministries and agencies that responded to the OECD survey reported the availability of a data steward. In some cases, while not formal, other institutions reported a disperse distribution of responsibilities among different public officials and/or bodies (e.g. IT architects/managers, institutional CIOs, department managers).

Despite the relevance of data stewards, the existence of such a strategic position is not yet widespread across OECD countries either. By December 2016, only 16 out of 34 OECD countries and partners (e.g. Colombia) (see Box 5.4) report the formal recognition (e.g. through legal instruments) and/or the availability of data stewards or institutional officers across public sector institutions (OECD, 2016b). The role is often strongly linked to open government data and not with the government data value chain as a whole. Yet, the latter should not be understood as the complete absence of this role inside public sector institutions *de facto*, but as a lack of formal recognition of the strategic contribution of data stewards to the construction of data-driven public sectors (e.g. data governance is often still understood as a merely technical role).

Box 5.4. **The role of data stewards in Colombia**

In Colombia, Decree 415/2016 mandates all public sector institutions to designate a Chief Data Officer (iCDOs) (data stewards) at the directive level. Among others, the main responsibilities of iCDOs include:

- focusing on generating public value, thereby enabling the necessary technological capacities and services inside public sector institutions in order to foster digital transformation, organisational efficiency and government transparency
- ensuring the implementation and maintenance of the IT enterprise architecture of the entity in accordance with central guidelines, the e-government strategy and according to the strategic vision, digital transformation needs and the available legal framework specific to the entity or policy sector
- identifying opportunities to adopt new technological trends that might contribute to creating further impact at the sectoral and national level
- leading the processes of acquisition of technology goods and services
- articulating with other actors from the public sector, private sector, civil society and academia that could contribute to a more evidenced-based IT and data policy design and implementation
- developing information management strategies to ensure the relevance, quality, timeliness, security and exchange and efficient flow of public sector information within and between public sector institutions
- proposing and implementing strategic actions to promote the open government strategy through the publication and interoperability of government data towards greater civic participation, multi-stakeholder collaboration, and public sector transparency
- appointing those public officials responsible for leading the development, implementation and maintenance of information and digital services systems in line with the central Strategic Plan for Information and Communication Technologies, taking into consideration the needs of information inputs for the design of citizen services
- promoting and facilitating the use and adoption of information technologies, digital information systems and services by public servants, citizens and other stakeholders
- promoting the effective use of the right of access of all persons to information and communication technologies, within the limits established by the Colombian Constitution and the law.

Source: Information provided by the Colombian Government through the OECD Open Government Data Survey (OECD, 2016b).

The data governance policy in Norway

While the governance of the public sector data value chain, as such, is not explicitly included in the Digital Agenda for Norway (see Chapter 2), its core components are strategically embedded throughout the overall goals of the agenda. This is in line with the current work of other leading OECD countries, such as the United Kingdom, who are explicitly scaling up the strategic use of data as part of their digital transformation strategies (see Box 5.5).

Box 5.5. **Better use of data as part of the UK 2017-20 Digital Transformation Strategy**

In February 2017, the UK government launched its Digital Transformation (DT) Strategy for 2017–20. The strategy identifies five key priority areas guiding the work of the Government Digital Service (GDS) of the UK Cabinet Office, including the delivery of world-class services for citizens drawing upon the digital transformation of operational processes and the development of the right set of skills and culture inside public sector institutions in order to support the digital transformation of the UK public sector. The UK DT Strategy has placed data at the core of its strategy therefore aiming to support the better use of data in the public sector. In this line, the GDS will focus its efforts on the following (GDS, 2017):

- making better use of data as an enabler for public services, particularly where those services cross organisational boundaries
- removing barriers to effective data use by all parts of government through the data-sharing provisions of the Digital Economy Bill, once it is passed by Parliament
- making better use of data to improve decision making, by building and expanding data science and analytical capability across government, for analysts and non-analysts alike
- managing and using data securely and appropriately, ensuring that public sector workers understand the ethics of data sharing - including what is and what is not permissible
- building a national data infrastructure of registers (authoritative lists that are held once across government) and ensuring that they are secured appropriately
- opening up government data where appropriate
- continuing to open up government services internally and externally through the use of application programming interfaces (APIs) where appropriate
- improving data discovery tools for users both within and beyond government
- transforming the way that government's major repositories of data are stored and managed.

The achievement of the UK DT Strategy is that it conceives the data value chain as an inter-connected process affecting the overall digital transformation of the public sector. This means that instead of conceiving fragmented and disconnected areas of work (e.g. opening up government data and the development of basic registries infrastructure), data-related objectives are all covered under a single stream of work of the DT strategy (the better use of data). This holistic approach reduces the risks of scattered and siloed efforts and increases the possibilities of better governing the overall value chain within the public sector.

Source: Author, with information from UK Government (2017), "Government Transformation Strategy: Better use of data", Policy paper, Cabinet Office, Government Digital Service, www.gov.uk/government/publications/government-transformation-strategy-2017-to-2020/government-transformation-strategy-better-use-of-data.

Components such as the development of data catalogues/inventories by agencies (data storage), the support for the publication of public sector information in open and machine-readable formats (data publication), data privacy/safety, and the use of big data analytics by public sector institutions (data re-use) are included as key measures of the Digital Agenda for Norway. Results from the OECD survey administered for the purpose of this review corroborate the identification of the aforementioned topics as key parts of the Norwegian digital agenda from the perspective of public sector institutions. These measures aim to enable and spur organisational efficiency and value creation (KMD, 2016) and mirror the efforts of Difi to instrument an efficient strategy for information and data governance in Norway (see the previous section).

Yet, according to data collected through the OECD survey, the view of the central policy co-ordinating body (namely KMD's Department of ICT Policy and Public Sector Reform, AIF), Difi, and other ministries and agencies with regard to the operational prioritisation of specific components related to the data value chain varies between these bodies (see Figure 5.4). This evidence highlights inter-institutional agreement and alignment in relation to core policy areas, but also underscores disagreements, namely:

- There is joint agreement between the central co-ordinating agency, Difi and other public sector institutions on the level priority given to increase the use of basic registries.
- However, the publication of open government data is a priority for the KMD and Difi, but not for other ministries and agencies.
- The opposite case is observed in regard to topics related to the use of data analytics by public sector institutions (e.g. foresight activities and data crowdsourcing) – a priority for ministries and agencies, but not for the KMD.
- In some cases, Difi did not provide a response in relation to specific topics (e.g. use of cloud computing for more effective data management across public sector institutions) relevant for the overall work on digital government and data governance and management in Norway (such as the Cloud Computing Strategy) (see Chapter 4).

Capturing and addressing the above-mentioned untapped synergies and existent discrepancies concerning views on policy priorities is needed to build a common vision within Norwegian ministries and agencies with regard to the construction of a data-driven public sector. This is also necessary to increase the engagement of ministries and agencies towards the accomplishment of the goals of the digital agenda (e.g. open government data).

Driving change across the Norwegian public sector based on a system-based approach requires understanding the underlying factors supporting the-above mentioned evidence. This would help to identify what the drivers of change are across public sector institutions.

In broad terms, Figure 5.4 points to organisational efficiency (e.g. in regard to public service delivery) as the underlying factor supporting those policy elements ranked the highest by public sector institutions. Therefore, it would be necessary to further connect the contribution of specific policy goals (e.g. open government data) to the achievement of greater organisational efficiency in order to strengthen the business case for these initiatives among ministries, directorates and agencies in Norway.

Figure 5.4. **Main goals of the data governance strategy in Norway by priority level: Perception of public sector institutions**

1: Not relevant, 7: Highly relevant

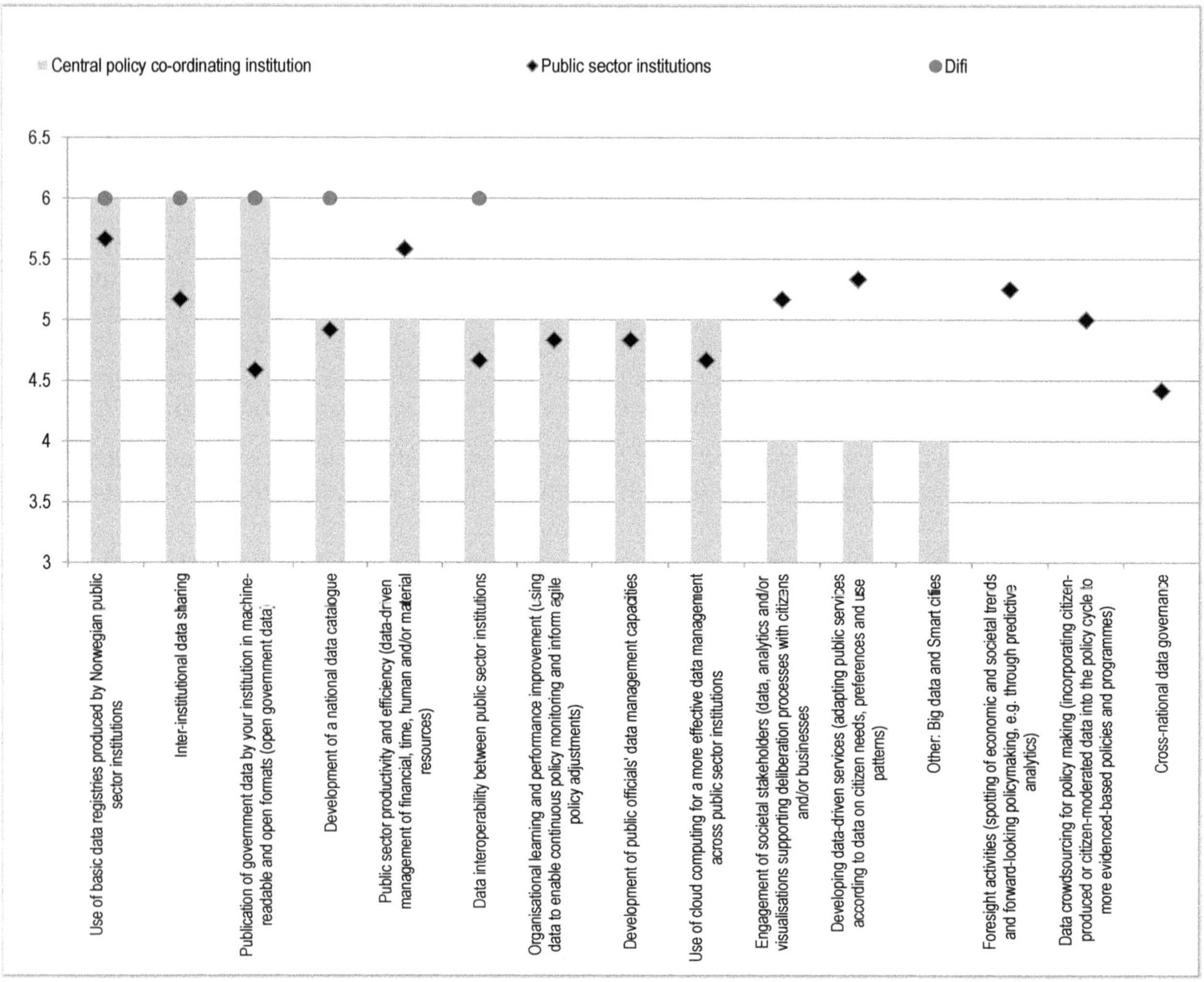

Notes: Public sector institutions responding to the question: "Which is the level of priority in practice given to each by the national data governance strategy? (1: Highly relevant; 7: Not relevant)"

Original ranking scale: 1: Highly relevant, 7: Not relevant. Scale modified for data visualisation purposes.

Source: OECD (2017c), "Digital Government Survey of Norway", central version, OECD, Paris (Question 115a); OECD (2017d), "Digital Government Survey of Norway", public sector institutions version, OECD, Paris (Question 127a).

Main regulations governing the data value chain

Like many other countries, Norway faces the challenge of keeping pace with the digital era, thereby enabling a regulatory framework that mirrors the digitalisation of the society and the market, and favours achieving digital policy goals (Chapter 1). A sound legal and regulatory framework can contribute not only to enabling streamlined data-sharing processes, but it also ensures the legitimacy of data policies, in line with social expectations and ethical principles, all of which are key to gaining and maintaining public trust.

In Norway, the urgency to create a more adequate regulatory framework for effective management of data governance inside the public sector is driven by: 1) external factors (e.g. the digitalisation of the economy and society requires fully digital governments capable of using data as a strategic asset to respond to the changing needs of citizens and businesses); and 2) the willingness of the central government to fully reap the opportunities of technology in order to digitalise the public sector (e.g. by enabling data value chain governance frameworks that allow for the effective implementation of digital government principles, such as open by default, digital by default or once-only principle), thereby contributing to achieving the goals of the Digital Agenda for Norway (see Chapter 2).

Regulations concerning basic data registries

The basic data registries are regulated by specific laws and regulations that set the rules on who collects and produces these data (data ownership), what public sector institutions can access it and under which conditions (e.g. data anonymisation and data protection). For instance:

- The **1970 Census Act** (Folkeregisterloven) regulates the confidentiality of, and public sector institutions' access (e.g. health authorities) to, the data registered in the **National Population Registry** (managed by the Norwegian Tax Authority). The Census Act also regulates the provision of these data for research activity (within the limits of confidentiality and private protection).
- The **1994 Act on Legal Entities** (Enhetsregisterloven) established the creation and management of the **Central Coordinating Register for Legal Entities (CCR).** The CCR - created in 1995 - gives all private sector enterprises a unique identity number and it is managed, together with other public registries and the Altinn Portal, by the Brønnøysund Register Centre.
- The **2004 Regulations on e-Administration and Management** (eForvaltningsforskriften), which authorises the creation of the **Digital Contact Information Register** used to record citizens contact information that is later used to provide online or mobile-based services to citizens (e.g. Digital Mailbox).
- The **2005 Act on a National Register for Land Information (Cadastre Act)** (Matrikkelloven) with direct implications on the **Land and Cadastre Registry** managed by the Norwegian Mapping Authority (with most data being provided by municipalities).
- The **2012 A-information Act** (a-opplysningsloven), which regulates the collection of employment and salary information and data from employers. These data, which are collected through the A-ordningen platform,[5] is used by the Brønnøysund Register Centre to create one of the basic registries database managed by the centre and accessed by different public sector institutions, such as the Tax Authority, the Labour and Welfare Directorate and Statistics Norway.
- The **2014 Act on the Management of Health Records and Data** (Helseregisterloven), which regulates the management of health data, including

the collection by specific public sector institutions of data from the National Population Registry.

- The **2014 Regulations on the Norwegian State Educational Loan Fund** (Utdanningsstøtteloven), Educational Loan Fund (Lånekassen) access to public sector information. The regulations set the basis for the ELF to access data held by other public sector institutions in order to assess applicants' eligibility to obtain governments' financial support for education. These public sector institutions include the Labour and Welfare Administration (NAV), Children Welfare services, the Norwegian Directorate of Immigration (UDI), and the National Population Registry.

Regulations concerning open government data

As a member of the European Economic Area (EEA), and not a European Union member state, Norway is obliged to transpose European Single Market legislation into national law. As a result, the 2003 EU Directive on the re-use of public sector information and the amending EU directive of 2013 has been implemented in Norwegian law through provisions in the Freedom of Information Act (Offentleglova) (Government of Norway, 2006) – which, as a transparency and open government instrument – defines the reach and limitations of open government data. This is in line with the approaches taken by many other OECD countries where the re-use of open government data is also mainly regulated by the freedom of information (FOI) acts.

Yet, one could argue if the more traditionally passive approach of FOI acts (e.g. focusing on citizens' right to request public sector information) is the most suitable legal environment to develop a proactive and open-by-default approach driving open government data development with a strong focus on re-use for value creation. While the adoption of EU directives strengthens the governance framework for OGD, the creation of OGD-driven economic, social and good governance impacts still requires the definition and implementation of coherent OGD policies and initiatives that ensure: 1) user- and demand-driven approaches; and 2) the strategic proactive publication of open government data) - all required conditions to enable value creation that entails re-use.

FOI acts – when amended – provide a strong legal lever for the development of open government data strategies and initiatives across OECD countries and partners. For instance, in 2015 the Mexican government included for the first time the concepts of "open data" and "open formats" in the General Law on Transparency and Access to Public Information (which superseded the 2002 Freedom of Information Act) (OECD, 2016a). In addition, the Mexican General Law on Transparency also promotes the publication by public sector institutions of public sector data in open formats whenever possible. Latecomers in the adoption to laws on access to information, such as Spain, have also ensured that their FOIs contains requirements relevant to OGD (OECD, 2014b). While the Spanish FOI act does not make a direct reference to open data, it foresees that newly available public sector information accessible on line will have to be made available as clear, structured, understandable data and preferably in re-usable formats (OECD, 2017b). A few OECD countries, namely Germany and Korea (see Box 5.6), have put in place specific laws on open government data.

Box 5.6. Korea's Act on the Promotion, Provision and Use of Public Data

Korea enacted the Act on the Promotion, Provision and Use of Public Data in June, 2013, which entered into force at the end of October, 2013. The law mandates the opening of public data and provides the legal basis for commercial usage of open data.

The Korean Open Data Law:

- Creates the Open Data Strategy Council (ODSC); providing specific guidelines for the OSDC's work. The Council is co-chaired by the Korean Prime Minister and one individual (designated by the Prime Minister) with sufficient literacy on open data's disclosure and consumption. The ODSC is integrated by members (35 maximum) from heads of public institutions, administrative agencies and local governments plus open data experts from non-governmental organisations.
- Defines the responsibility of the Korean government to create a periodic three-year Master Open Data Plan that, among other components, should include action lines to promote the re-use of OGD by the private sector. The Master Plan is a multi-agency effort lead by the Minister of Security and Public Administration in consultation with the Minister of Science, ICT and Future Planning and it should integrate specific areas of work for the national government and for local governments.
- Establishes that, in line with the Master Plan, central administrative agencies and the heads of local governments should publish an Open Data Implementation Plan on a yearly basis. Implementation plans should include performance assessments related to open data disclosure and use, and one-year budget allocation planning.
- While consultation is not mandatory, the law highlights the importance of running consultation exercises to identify data demand, and to obtain and receive policy feedback and complaints from citizens and private sector organisations towards more efficient policy implementation and data provision.
- Makes a distinction between the Institutional Chief Data Officer (data steward) ("Officer Responsible for the Provision of Public Data") and data managers ("working-level employees"); therefore contributing to the definition of and distinction between managerial/strategic roles and administrative/technical roles. Strategic activities includes the overall co-ordination of, and support for, OGD policies, and the co-ordination and alignment of central OGD policies with institutional policies, plans, etc. Administrative/technical responsibilities are related to open data management, disclosure, use, quality, etc.
- Creates the National Open Data Centre (ODC), which provides policy and technical advice for the implementation of open data initiatives. The ODC is in charge of the management of the national open data portal www.data.go.kr, assists the public sector in opening their data, and facilitates private sector's use of open data.
- Highlights institutional independence related to: 1) the promotion of open data's re-use among individuals, businesses, non-profit organisations, etc.; and 2) international co-operation to support the exchange of technologies related to and human resources working on open government data; the adoption of international standards; research; and the use of OGD by the private sector.
- Establishes that the list of institutional datasets should be registered with the Ministry of Interior (MOI, formerly MOGAHA) - the lead Ministry on open data initiative – in order to make open data available for public access within the limits of privacy and other regulations.
- Provides immunity to public sector staff from civil and criminal liability for damages incurred to users or third parties due to quality of data (except in cases of intent or serious negligence), etc. The Korean government took this approach to facilitate the disclosure of open government data.
- Creates the Open Data Mediation Committee (ODMC) as a dispute resolution mechanism between citizens and public sector organisations.
- Provides general clauses on foundations for open data, including data quality management, standardisation, training, etc.

Source: Text from OECD (2016c), *Open Government Data Review of Mexico: Data Reuse for Public Sector Impact and Innovation*, OECD Publishing, Paris, http://dx.doi.org/10.1787/9789264259270-en; based on information provided by the Korean government to the OECD; Fact-finding mission to Mexico, November 2015.

In other cases, the publication of executive decrees on open government data has also supported the definition and implementation of the open government data policy in some OECD countries and partners (e.g. Argentina, Brazil, France, Mexico, United States) (see Box 5.7). Other countries (e.g. Lithuania) have drawn upon the use of soft-law instruments (for instance, recommendations on OGD issued by specific ministries) as an effort to support the OGD policy.

Box 5.7. **Using Executive Decrees as drivers of value-driven OGD publication: Examples from Argentina and Brazil**

Argentina

In January 2016, Argentina's President Mauricio Macri passed an Executive Decree mandating central ministries to develop institutional open data plans by September/October 2016, in accordance with the policy framework for open data developed by the Chief of Cabinet Office and the Ministry of Modernization. The decree is framed within a broader open data initiative at the central level, which has involved the Ministry of Modernization, the Chief of Cabinet, and key partners such as the Anti-corruption Office and the Ministry of Finance.

The decree acts as a mechanism to encourage the development of institutional open data plans and the Argentinian central open data portal, and defines categories of public sector information to be prioritised by the central government for their publication as open data to fight corruption in the country, including:

- structure of the Executive Branch
- salaries and asset disclosure of senior-level authorities at the Executive Branch
- salaries of all civil servants and public sector employees
- salary scales applicable to different public employment regimes
- budgetary credits
- all procurement procedures, include in the Electronic Public Procurement System
- access to information requests
- all lobbying meetings held by members of the Executive Branch.

Brazil

In Brazil, former President Dilma Rousseff published an Executive Decree in May 2016 establishing the Brazilian national open data policy. Among other objectives, the policy aims to improve government-to-government data-sharing practices towards greater public sector efficient, increase citizen engagement through digital technologies, improve digital public service delivery and encourage private and public sector innovation. The decree provides a definition of open data while establishing an institutional governance for policy co-ordination led by the Ministry of Planning Development and Management (Ministério de Planejamento, Desenvolvimento e Gestão, MP) through the National Open Data Infrastructure (INDA).

The INDA acts as a multi-participatory, transparent, collaborative and democratic governance mechanism, composed by public agencies and private sector representatives. The Ministry of Transparency, Oversight and Office of the Comptroller General is given the responsibility to monitor the open data policy in the country.

Box 5.7. Using Executive Decrees as drivers of value-driven OGD publication: Examples from Argentina and Brazil *(continued)*

The decree establishes that each federal government body must develop an Open Data Plan, conducting an internal survey and inventory of the available databases and prioritising, in a defined timeframe, the availability of databases in an open format. As observed in the Argentinan case, the Brazilian decree has equally identified public sector information categories to be necessarily prioritised for their publication in open and machine-readable formats, including:

- civil servants in managerial and directive positions in state-owned enterprises and subsidiaries
- data from the Integrated Financial Management System (Siafi)
- information on the corporate structure and ownership of companies collected by the National Register of Legal Entities
- public procurement information collected through the Integrated General Services Administration (Sistema Integrado de Administração de Serviços Gerais, Siasg)
- cadaster and registration information related to the control of the execution of parliamentary amendments.

The Brazilian Ministry of Transparency, Oversight and Office of the Comptroller General (CGU) has also released, by virtue of the decree, data on state-owned companies' directors and managers. At the same time, the Brazilian Ministry of Finance should release the registry of businesses' beneficial ownership. By releasing those data, the Brazilian government aims to reduce the risk of conflict of interest resulting from the potential relationship and partnerships between private sector organisations and civil servants.

Source: Text from OECD (2017b), *Compendium on the Use of Open Data for Anti-corruption: Towards Data-driven Public Sector Integrity and Civic Auditing*, OECD, Paris, www.oecd.org/gov/digital-government/g20-oecd-compendium-open-data-anti-corruption.htm.

The 2016 version of the Digitalisation Memorandum (Digitaliseringsrundskrivet) (see Chapter 2) has also been used as a regulatory lever to spur the publication of OGD by public sector institutions. The memorandum, published by KMD on a yearly basis, instructed public sector institutions to dedicate further efforts to open up government data, in line with Difi's guidelines on open government data.

At the sectoral level, the Norwegian 2010 Spatial Information Act (Geodataloven), which implements the INSPIRE, Directive for Infrastructure for Spatial Information in Europe (European Directive 2007/2/EC), focuses on the publication and re-use of geographic data thereby setting rules on data interoperability (e.g. through metadata) and data sharing for private or public purposes, including cross-border data sharing with other countries (e.g. EEA). Norway's Mapping Authority (Kartverket) is in charge of co-ordinating the work of public sector institutions in this domain through the national co-operation on spatial data infrastructure. For such a purpose, the Authority created the portal Geonorge.no where public sector institutions can publish documentation about all available spatial data. Data is available for download or as online data services/APIs. The main underlying principle is to have a decentralised infrastructure where each organisation is publishing its own spatial data according to agreed standards. In order to avoid the fragmentation of efforts and avoid the propagation of different access points for geodata, a new national Geoportal is being developed with the objective of centralising publication of geographic data by Norwegian public sector institutions and ease users' access to it. However, the new Geoportal will not necessarily publish these data in machine-readable and open formats or for free, which may have a negative impact on users' access and data re-use.

The Geodata Act, its regulations and the Geonorge.no portal are in line with Norway's obligations through the EEA and the efforts of the central government to implement the EU INSPIRE Directive 2007/2/EC.[6]

Assessing regulatory challenges with an overarching approach

Norway's main challenge with regard to the current regulatory framework governing the data value chain within the public sector is related to regulatory adaptability. As discussed in Chapter 1, results from the OECD survey and from the OECD mission to Oslo indicate the lack of major legal and regulatory challenges for digital government in the country. Yet, further work is needed to fully align specific policy goals with some regulations affecting the full-scale management of the data value chain. The challenges include:

- **The current legal and regulatory framework governing data and privacy protection in Norway restrict the access of public sector institutions to citizens' (anonymised) data.** While specific laws and regulations are in place to allow, for instance, the use of anonymised data for research purposes, these restrictions have an impact on the possibilities to design automated data-driven services or perform big data analytics. Further exploring the increasing availability of advanced technologies for data analytics and their interaction with data protection regulations will play a key role in ensuring the development of a legal and regulatory framework that strikes the right balance between data protection and data re-use.
- **While inter-institutional and inter-sectoral data sharing is limited** as a result of the current regulatory framework restricting or preventing data access by public sector institutions, some regulations have been developed to address this issue. Yet, these regulations are often very specific on which data can be used or shared and by which institutions (e.g. the Educational Loan Fund, the Tax Authority or the NAV). this scenario is aggravated by: 1) a highly sectoral public sector that promotes co-operation within policy sectors, thereby hindering more horizontal and inter-sectoral co-operation; 2) the ruling Principle of Ministerial Responsibility, which makes Norwegian ministers responsible and accountable for the actions of public sector official in their ministries, contributes to risk-averse public institutions that avoid exploring new organisational models due to the negative impact these decisions may produce (if any); and 3) the strong approach on data-sharing models based on inter-institutional agreements and access by request. This scenario inhibits inter-agency and inter-sectoral co-ordination, affects the development of streamlined data-sharing processes, and has negative implications for the further development of initiatives that can contribute to better implementing key digital government principles. For instance, the implementation of the once-only principle is affected as institutions' data-sharing capabilities are restrained by legacy matters due to existing regulations and inefficient inter-institutional data-sharing models.

- **Cross-border data management and sharing** are limited by some legislation still in place restricting cross-border data storage (such as the Archives Act and the Accounting Act). This obstructs the possibility to further develop **cloud-based services** that may require storing data in servers outside Norwegian borders; limits Nordic co-operation on this subject; and prevents putting the recommendations on cloud computing of the 2016 Digitalisation Memorandum into action. These legal and regulatory barriers were widely explored by the KMD as part of the 2016 Cloud Computing Strategy for Norway (see Chapter 2), which included an assessment of the current legal and regulatory environment for cloud-based solutions in Norway (e.g. cross-border storage and access of data).
- **Open government data:** While the FOI act, as the main legal instrument supporting the publication of government data, was updated to include requirements for the publication of public sector information in digital formats, the law is still lagging behind when compared to other OECD countries. Despite the application of amendments to the law in April 2017 in line with EU directives and the objectives of the Digital Agenda, the law still lacks a clear definition on open government data that could contribute to building a common vision and agreement among public sector institutions on what open data is, its limitations and its purpose.
- At the time of this review, the Norwegian government has showed its commitment to identifying and removing unjustified data localisation barriers in Norwegian legislation. Norway supports EU initiatives to further the free flow of data, while respecting concerns for national security. For example, the Norwegian government is of the opinion that harmonised legislative measures to ensure that no country in the EEA practices unjustified data localisation requirements is the most appropriate action to ensure this.

While the Norwegian government has taken action to evaluate the legal and regulatory framework affecting the implementation of specific digital government initiatives (such as the above-mentioned cloud strategy) directly linked to specific stages of the data value chain (e.g. data storage), the overall context for the development of a data-driven public sector would benefit if these efforts were to be scaled up. This would require implementing a whole-of-government and system-based approach, supported by timely and coherent assessments in line with the goals of the Digital Agenda as a whole. As a result, matters concerning the management of the data value chain would be dealt with as part of an integrated process affecting all stages. This would imply assessing the barriers for the efficient governance of the entire data value chain within the public sector, instead of tackling single issues as if they were relevant only to specific aspects or moments of such chain (e.g. cross-border data storage and opening up government data).

The closest initiative to an overarching regulatory exercise to assess the overall digitalisation of the public sector, including elements related to the data value chain, took place within the framework of the Tidstyv project (Norwegian for "Removing time thieves") (Difi, 2015). This project (led by Difi) focused on simplifying daily citizens' lives though more improved and simplified organisational processes within the public sector. The project took place mainly at the agency level, thus agencies were required to perform self-assessments in order to identify and remove unrequired and bureaucratic processes, simplify regulations and, whenever possible, digitalise procedures. As a result, challenges were addressed with a sectoral/agency mindset, and not with the conception of how the project would have contributed to the construction of a data-driven public sector.

Systemic common challenges (such as data governance) were not widely discussed, nor were Difi's knowledge-sharing tools widely used by public sector institutions (e.g. pools of best practices developed for the purpose of the project).

In addition, this project highlighted the potential of legal and regulatory instruments (e.g. such as KMD's Digitalisation Memorandum, see Chapter 2) as (hard) levers that could be used by ministries to enforce the observance of central guidelines for the design of public services, and recommended the mandatory implementation of regulatory simplification exercises by agencies as tools to maintain streamlined organisational processes - at the agency level. It is not clear if the goals of the project conceived data-sharing exercises. The KMD has also commissioned additional external reports that included assessments to identify regulatory barriers for the digitalisation of the private sector and economic activity (see KPMG, 2014).

From a data governance perspective, evidence shows that, in practice, overarching regulatory assessments related to digitalisation are limited to the private sector (e.g. reduction of red tape and administrative simplification exercises for businesses), but these exercises leave behind the assessment of these barriers for the digitalisation of the public sector as a whole, including those affecting data governance and the construction of a data-driven public sector. If any, efforts to assess the governance of the data value chain within the Norwegian public sector are topic-specific, siloed and disconnected from each other.

Ensuring the right balance between data governance regulatory control and regulatory flexibility

New regulation affecting data governance in the Norwegian public sector is expected to come into force soon as there is an effort of the government to address the above-mentioned issues. By July 2017, work was underway to develop a new Census Act, and a new General Data Protection Regulation which will come into force by 2018 will address issues relating to the once-only principle and the possibilities to perform big data analytics. These are important for the construction of a digital government propelled by data infrastructure. In addition, by July 2017, an official committee was established by the Norwegian government in order to assess potential revisions to the Public Administration Act. The committee is expected to present its findings in 2019 which will inform the overall revision and amendments process of this legal instrument. In addition, the European General Data Protection Regulation (entering into force in 2018) will also be implemented in Norwegian legislation.

However, by implementing measures to ensure the sustainability of a supportive and adequate regulatory environment the Norwegian government would sustain the establishment of a context propitious and flexible enough to cope with and adapt to the digital evolution. Such an approach is in line with:

- Principle 5 of the 2012 OECD Recommendation on Regulatory Policy and Governance, which advises OECD countries (including Norway) to "conduct systematic programme reviews of the stock of significant regulation against clearly defined policy goals, including consideration of costs and benefits, to ensure that regulations remain up to date, cost-justified, cost-effective and consistent, and deliver the intended policy objectives." (OECD, 2012)
- Principle 12 of the 2014 OECD Recommendation on Digital Government Strategies, which advises OECD countries to review and assess current and new

legislation and regulation in order to "ensure that general and sector-specific legal and regulatory frameworks allow digital opportunities to be seized." (OECD, 2014a)

Norway's tradition of government openness and public engagement during the initial stages of the regulatory process (e.g. *ex ante* stakeholder online consultation, central-local co-ordination, and regulatory impact assessments) (OECD, 2015b) contributes to the quality of new primary legislation (laws issued by the parliament). For instance, the activities of the Norwegian Better Regulation Council (Regelrådet, BRC), a body within the Norwegian Ministry of Trade, Industry and Fisheries, focuses on assessing the potential impact of new regulations on business activity. However, despite Norway's use of regulatory review and control instruments such as sunsetting[7] provisions, a 2014 OECD assessment on regulatory policy found evidence that *ex post* evaluation for primary laws are not common practice in Norway when compared with other OECD countries (see Figure 5.5), and the activities of the BRC are restricted to business activity.

Figure 5.5. ***Ex post* evaluation for primary laws in OECD countries**

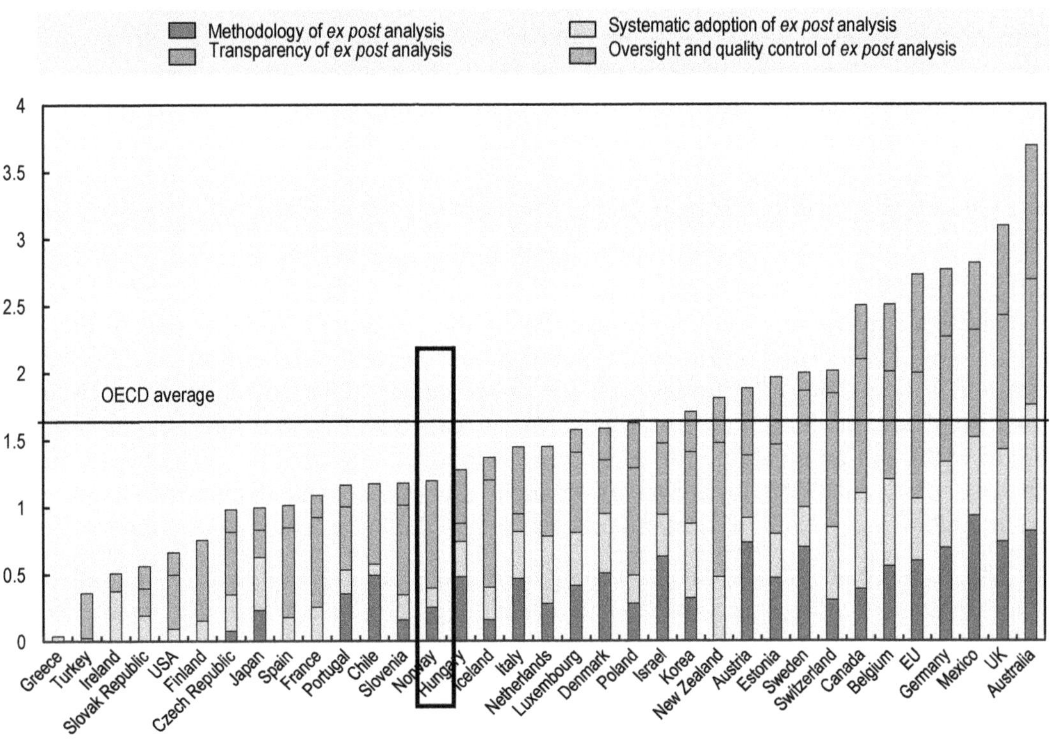

Source: OECD (2014c), *Regulatory Indicators Data* (dataset), OECD, Paris, www.oecd.org/gov/regulatory-policy/measuring-regulatory-performance.htm.

The scenario above could have an impact on the possibility to maintain an optimal legal and regulatory stock capable, on the one hand, of ensuring the availability of key data-related regulations (e.g. privacy and data protection, data sharing), and, on the other, contributing to the quality of the regulatory environment for a data-driven digital government in Norway.

For this purpose, it would be also necessary to go beyond one-time *ex post* and/or one-time regulatory assessments (e.g. as done in regard to cloud computing and Difi's

Time Thieves project) and develop a governance framework enabling the regular evaluation of the impact of existing legislations on the development of the data-driven public sector, and assess the effects of new legislations on data governance arrangements within the public sector.

Sharing data inside the public sector: The basic registries in Norway

Norway's long-time and well-established efforts to develop basic data registries and facilitate inter-institutional data sharing provide the foundations to further construct a data-driven public sector, e.g. by exploiting the potential of data to develop a smart government capable of foreseeing citizens' needs, anticipating societal trends and designing intelligent public services.

In Norway, the focus on organisational efficiency and citizen-centred services (e-government) contributed to the development of digital components and tools that have underpinned more effective data management activities across public sector institutions. For instance, the relevance of the Altinn platform (see Chapter 4) goes beyond its value for citizens and businesses, but comes from its nature as IT architecture supporting the automated exchange of data between public sector institutions. As a result of such an approach, the Norwegian government, as other Nordic countries, has put in place different basic data registries to facilitate data sharing within the public sector. The overall goal is to better serve Norwegian citizens and businesses using this context to apply strategic digital government principles ruling government-citizen interaction (e.g. once-only principle) (Chapter 2).

For some registries, analogue information processing models were developed dating back to the 1980s. For instance, large-scale computer systems for mass processing of student loan applications were developed during the 1980s and 1990s as part of the State Educational Loan Fund information management system. According to information collected by the OECD during the peer review mission to Oslo, by September 2016, the Loan Fund was in charge of processing information from 1.05 million users, processing roughly 900 000 applications for educational support per year. The current activities of the fund produce NOK 30 billion of financial remittance and disbursement per year, totaling NOK 155 billion of outstanding educational debt (the lending portfolio) by 2016.

The Loan Fund information processing model is an example of how the digitalisation of information-sharing processes, and its underlying data, has contributed to the need to better design data-management processes. As part of its digital transition, the Fund launched the LØFT renewal programme in 2003 with the objective of using digital tools to reduce operational costs, comply with regulations and, moreover, better serve citizens. The programme, which finished in 2014, included the creation of the Fund online portal in 2003, the implementation of a digital-only rule since 2008 (paperless and digital by default) applying to applications for funding, and the redesign of the data management and data-sharing model between the Fund and other public sector institutions (e.g. the Tax Administration, the Directorate of Immigration, the Norwegian Health Economics Administration and Statistics Norway [SSB]) (see Figure 5.6). As a result, the programme led to an estimated reduction of the average operational cost per client from roughly NOK 500 in 2002 to NOK 300 in 2013.[8]

Figure 5.6. **Norway's Educational Loan Fund: Information and data management model**

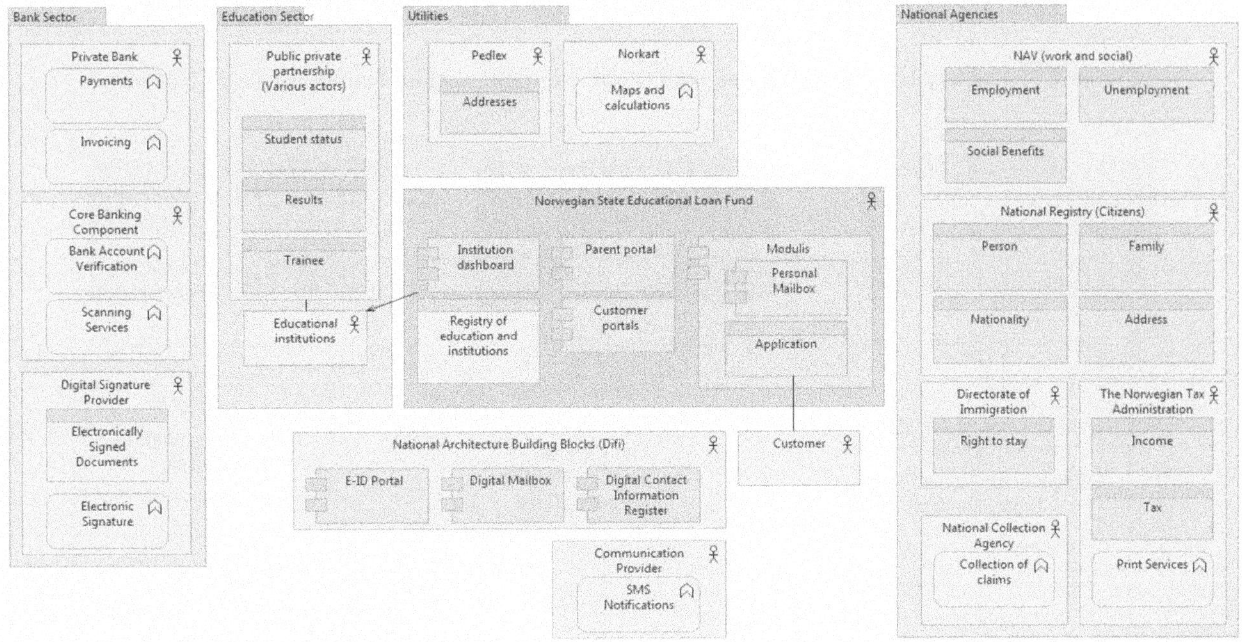

Source: Information provided by the Norwegian Educational Loan Fund to the OECD.

Yet, data collection processes varies in relation to the different registries. For instance, the Land and Cadastre Registry (Matrikkelenregister), managed by the Norwegian Mapping Authority (the Kartverket), centralises data provided by local authorities, which is then shared with other public sector institutions. The Mapping Authority plays mostly an oversight role during the data management process ensuring that data complies with the minimum quality requirements necessary to make it useful for users (data certification). The Mapping Authority during the OECD mission to Oslo indicated that the provision of metadata (i.e. data that makes other data understandable) is sometimes the real challenge for some registries. Still, according to the Authority, only 10% of the data provided by local authorities requires some additional quality assurance action from the Kartverket, proving that, in general terms, the right controls have been put in place by local agencies and the Kartverket to ensure the integrity of 90% of the data managed by the register.

The Land and Cadastre Registry currently provides data on 4 million buildings, 3 million properties and 2.3 million addresses in Norway and, together with the Business Registry and the National Population Registry (see Figure 5.7), it is part of the four key basic registries considered as strategic for the digital agenda of the Norwegian government. Still, challenges remain with regard to spurring the re-use of these and other basic registries across the Norwegian public sector, across different policy sectors, and by Norwegian businesses and society.

Despite the availability of a relatively mature data infrastructure in the country, results from the OECD mission to Oslo and the OECD survey administered for the purpose of this review show that most data-sharing sharing activities take place within the framework of inter-institutional agreements or as a response to data access requests (see

Figure 5.8). Personal and business data are identified as the most used registries by public sector institutions in Norway.

Figure 5.7. **The key basic registries as part of the common national components in Norway**

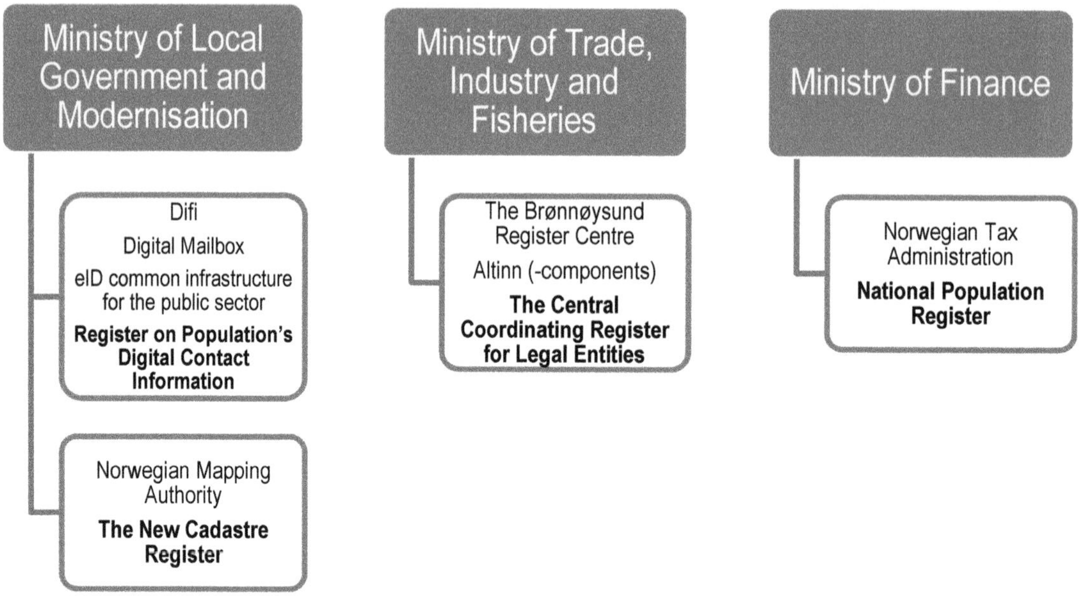

Source: Author, with information provided by the Norwegian government.

Figure 5.8. **Inter-institutional data sharing: Main access mechanisms**

Aggregated data for 18 different data categories

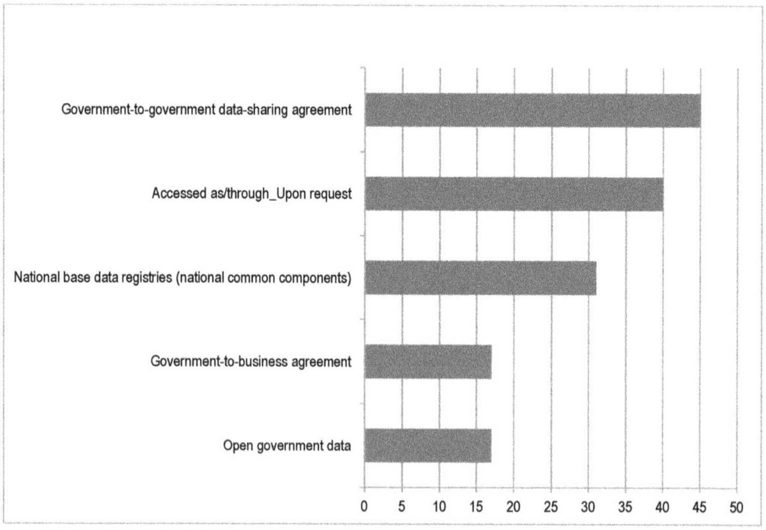

Source: OECD (2017c), "Digital Government Survey of Norway", central version, OECD, Paris. Institutions responding to Question 138, "Please indicate what type(s) of data your institution regularly collects from other public institutions and how these data are accessed."

In relation to the increasing use of basic data registries within the public sector, the view from public sector institutions is heterogeneous. Yet, evidence from the OECD survey and the OECD mission to Oslo can be used to draw some conclusions:

- Breaking down **data silos** (e.g. institutional data storage systems are not consolidated or inter-connected) - especially within same sectors e.g. health, transport - would help to better design **efficient data management systems**, foster data re-use and streamline organisational processes in order to move away from outdated data-sharing models centring on inter-institutional agreements and access by request.
- Increasing the use of the registries would depend on ensuring that the accompanying **metadata** is also provided in order to ensure that the registries (or any other data being shared) can be **identified and understood** by all users.
- Ensuring the availability and facilitating the use of **machine-to-machine communication tools** (e.g. APIs) and other **automated data collection** tools would contribute to a more efficient access to data in the registries.
- Overcoming registries' fragmentation (e.g. a **single-access window** to access information on the registries, and the data itself, is not available).

The big untapped opportunity: Underpinning open government data

Norway, like other Nordic countries, enjoys a well-established culture of openness and transparency within the public sector, but there is an opportunity to do better. The level of digitalisation of the Norwegian society and the increased availability of citizens literate in information and communications technology (ICT) and data (see Chapter 1) provide an ideal knowledge base to promote civic tech, incentivise economic development and contribute to public sector good governance.

The digital era has made opening up government data a key element of the data value chain. Business innovation and entrepreneurship, citizens' empowerment, e-participation, online activism, public sector accountability and data-driven journalism are only a few of the vast array of positive outcomes that can result from the publication of open government data (OGD) by public sector institutions. The Norwegian government and its public sector need to respond to the demands of businesses, citizens and the third sector regarding the proactive publication of OGD, engage with actors of the ecosystem towards greater data re-use for, and design OGD initiatives that can contribute to finding joint solutions to policy challenges, co-create public value, and lever organisational efficiency.

The state of OGD in Norway

Results from the 2017 OECD OURdata Index – which benchmarks OGD policies across OECD countries and partners – show that Norway scores slightly above the OECD average (see Figure 5.9). The underlying data supporting the OURdata Index provide evidence on the level of advancement achieved in Norway in terms of ruling open government data in the country and guiding public sector institutions during the opening up process (e.g. Difi's handbooks, guidelines and standards on open government data, and the Norwegian Data Protection Authority guidelines on data anonymisation), but also reflect that the Norwegian government could do better in terms of supporting the re-use of OGD by external actors.

Figure 5.9. **Open-Useful-Reusable Government Data Index (OURdata), 2017**

OECD countries and partners

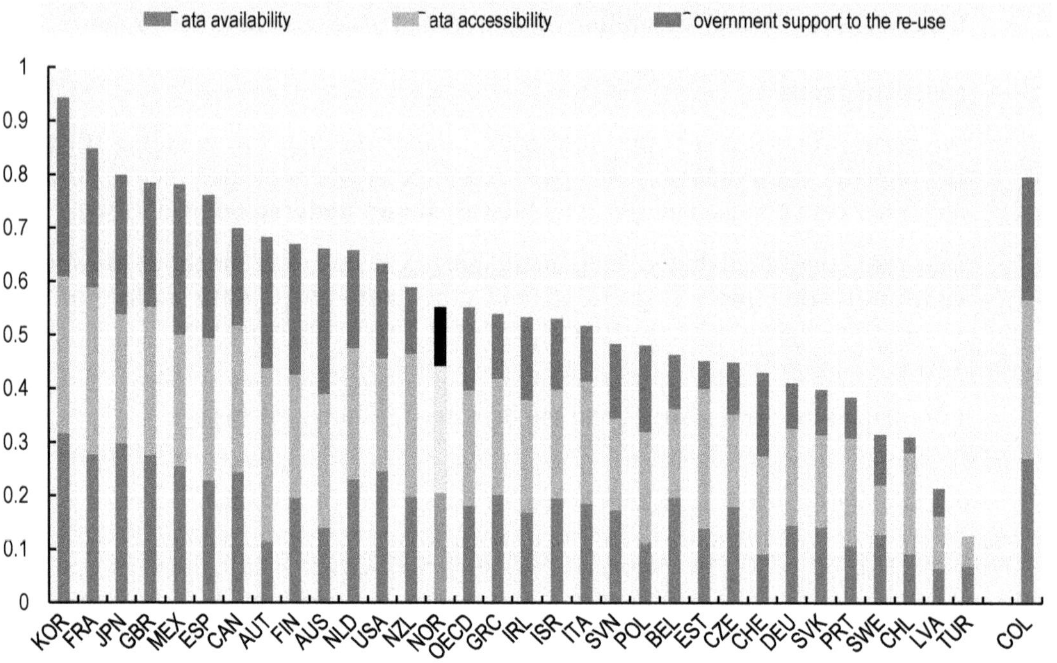

Source: OECD (2017a), *Government at a Glance 2017*, OECD Publishing, Paris, http://dx.doi.org/10.1787/gov_glance-2017-en.

At the same time, the FOI act and the Personal Data Act provide clear formal requirements on the limitations for the publication of public sector information (which comprise open government data) in line with data protection and personal privacy restrictions. Yet, when these instruments are in conflict, the provisions of the FOI act supersede those of the Personal Data Act, therefore supporting the principle of maximum information disclosure within the limits of privacy and data protection regulations.

Despite the absence of a formal open government data strategy and a government CDO in charge of leading the OGD policy, the legal support provided by the FOI act, the guidelines of the 2016 Digitalisation Memorandum, and the policy priorities on OGD included in the Digital Agenda (see Box 5.8) strengthen the current governance framework for OGD in Norway.

Box 5.8. Main OGD policy objectives included in the Digital Agenda for Norway (extract)

Chapter 14.4. ICT policy for value creation and inclusion

The [Norwegian] government will:

- Initiate studies to map the sharing economy from a Norwegian perspective, including current initiatives and the economic and value-adding potential.
- Support the work, and consider following up the recommendations, of the committee appointed to assess the challenges and opportunities presented by the sharing economy.
- Make certain amendments to the Freedom of Information Act's provisions concerning re-use of public-sector information. These amendments will make it easier to make public sector data accessible, with a view to making more datasets accessible and increasing re-use.
- Prepare strategies and action plans for increasing the accessibility of data pertaining to culture, geodata, and public expenditure.
- A strategy for making transport-sector data accessible shall be included in the new National Transport Plan due to be presented to the Storting in 2017.
- Prepare a strategy or action plan for making research data more accessible by the end of 2017.
- Follow up requirements for machine-readable formats by revising Guidelines for making public data accessible.
- Monitor technology developments in big data and consider the need for a strategy for using big data in the public sector.
- Strengthen participation by Norwegian public agencies in relevant EU research projects.
- Return to the use of ITS in connection with the white paper on the National Transport Plan 2018–2029 due to be presented to the Storting in spring 2017.
- Assess the need for facilitating smart city development in Norway.

Source: Text from KMD (Ministry of Local Government and Modernisation) (2016), "Digital Agenda for Norway in brief: ICT for a simpler everyday life and increased productivity", English version, KMD, www.regjeringen.no/en/dokumenter/digital-agenda-for-norway-in-brief/id2499897/sec1.

Like many other OECD countries, the Norwegian government has put in place central portals - data.norge.no - as an effort to provide direct and indirect public access to open government data that is published by different public sector institutions. Difi is the main agency in charge of managing the central OGD portal, and developing OGD-related instruments to ensure the quality and potential re-use of the data published on the portal. Besides controlling the publication of open government data on the portal, the agency ensures that the data is provided strictly in non-proprietary formats so it can be freely re-used, and with the accompanying metadata. Difi also developed the Norwegian License of Open Data[9] which, together with the use of other open data (OD) licences (e.g. Creative Commons), is mostly used for the publication of OGD by public sector institutions.

The Norwegian government has identified five data categories as a priority for publication: government spending, geodata (in line with EU directives), transport, research, and culture data. Among these, according to the information provided by the Norwegian government through the OECD Open Government Data Survey, the most common commercially used government data in the country is Geodata (managed and published by the Norway's Mapping Authority).

In regard to the current availability of OGD on the central portal, results from the OECD Open Government Data Survey indicate that Norway has made available for public access 34 data categories of a total of 48 categories (see Table 5.3) identified by G8 countries as priority for publication – which are included in the G8 Open Data Charter (see Table 5.4). However there is room, for instance, to invest further efforts to open up government data in areas such as education and public procurement.

Table 5.3. **G8 Open Data Charter: Identified high value data categories for publication by G8 countries**

Data taxonomies	Data categories
Companies	Company/business register
Crime and justice	Crime statistics, safety
Earth observation	Meteorological/weather, agriculture, forestry, fishing, and hunting
Education	List of schools; performance of schools, digital skills
Energy and environment	Pollution levels, energy consumption
Finance and contracts	Transaction spend, contracts let, call for tender, future tenders, local budget, national budget (planned and spent)
Geospatial	Topography, postcodes, national maps, local maps
Global development	Aid, food security, extractives, land
Government accountability and democracy	Government contact points, election results, legislation and statutes, salaries (pay scales), hospitality/gifts
Health	Prescription data, performance data
Science and research	Genome data, research and educational activity, experiment results
Statistics	National Statistics, Census, infrastructure, wealth, skills
Social mobility and welfare	Housing, health insurance and unemployment benefits
Transport and infrastructure	Public transport timetables, access points broadband penetration

Source: UK Government (2013), "G8 Open Data Charter and Technical Annex", Policy paper, Cabinet Office, www.gov.uk/government/publications/open-data-charter/g8-open-data-charter-and-technical-annex.

Table 5.4. **G8 Open Data Charter data categories available on Norway's central OGD portal**

G8 data taxonomies	Norway
Company/business register	●
Crime statistics	●
Safety	○
Meteorological/weather	●
Agriculture	●
Forestry	●
Fishing	●
Hunting	●
List of schools	●
Performance of schools	○
Digital skills	○
Pollution levels	●
Energy consumption	●
Transaction spend	○
Contracts let	○
Call for tender	○
Future tenders	○
Local budget	●
National budget planned	●
National budget spent	●
Zip codes/Postcodes	●
National maps	●
Local maps	●
Aid	●
Food security	●
Extractives	●
Land	●
Government contact points	○
Election results	●
Legislation and statutes	○
Salaries (pay scales)	○
Hospitality/gifts	○
Prescription data	○
Hospital performance data	●
Genome data	○
Research and educational activity	●
Experiment results	○
National Statistics	●
Census	●
Infrastructure	●
Wealth	●
Skills	●
Housing	●
Health insurance and unemployment benefits	●
Ageing society	●
Public transport timetables	●
Broadband penetration	●
Motor vehicle registration statistics	●
Beneficial ownership	○
Lobbying meetings	○
Declarations of interest	○
Natural risk management (incl. data on disasters)	○
Disaster relief data	○
Yes	●
No	○

Note: Data not available for Denmark, Hungary, Iceland, Israel, Latvia and Luxembourg.

Source: OECD (2016b), "OECD Open Government Data Survey 3.0", OECD, Paris, based on Section 1, Question 68. OECD countries: Based on information provided by 29 countries.

Main opportunities and challenges for open government data in Norway

In Norway, the main challenge in regard to OGD is related to the structured and systemic implementation of open government data initiatives in close collaboration with the open data ecosystem (e.g. entrepreneurs, businesses and civil society organisations). While the Digital Agenda includes specific objectives related to OGD (for instance, preparing strategies and action plans for increasing the accessibility of data pertaining to culture, geodata, public expenditure, transport-sector data and research data) (see Box 5.8 above), it is not clear how the aforementioned actors are part of these actions.

Norway has established instruments to support the governance of OGD, such as the 2016 Digital Memorandum (Digitaliseringsrundskrivet) - which instructs Norwegian public sector institutions to take further action to open up government data, the amendments to the FOI act (April, 2017), and those OGD policy objectives included in the Digital Agenda for Norway.

However, the Norwegian government lacks of a formal open data strategy/plan that could set a clear path and strategic actions to be followed by the central government and public sector institutions in order to take OGD to the next level. This would be relevant not only from a national but from a supranational perspective, in light of the current regional objectives in matters related to digitalisation and the digital economy at the Nordic level (see Chapter 1). In view of the lack of a formal stand-alone open government data strategy in the country (OGD is part of the digital agenda), it fails to provide further details on key components related to effectively governing the data value chain at the institutional level (e.g. the availability of data stewards), and it leaves responsibility for implementation to agencies without setting clear leadership roles and a structured strategy or plan of action.

Evidence from the OECD mission to Oslo and the OECD survey point to the fact the OGD is somehow disconnected from the current *de facto* data governance strategy in Norway (strongly linked to the basic registries). In addition, open government data appears to be a priority for the KMD, but evidence from the OECD survey shows that this is not case for other public sector institutions (see the earlier section on main regulations governing the data value chain). There is a need to conceive open government data as an integral part of the overall data governance strategy in the country, and link it with the specific ambitions of public sector institutions (mainly focused on organisational efficiency) and concrete social and policy issues and/or priorities.

Norway is also missing an opportunity to link the open data policy to broader policy areas of work. For instance, OECD and G20 countries, as part of their efforts to use open data in support of anti-corruption efforts, are increasingly embarking on the use of open data as an instrument to increase transparency of public procurement processes, and have created multi-national alliances to spur the use of open data as a driver of more accountable and transparent public procurement processes (see Chapter 3 and Box 5.9).

Box 5.9. **Supporting government openness through the implementation of the Open Contracting Data Standard**

The implementation of the Open Data Contracting Standard (developed by the Open Contracting Partnership) (see Chapter 3) aims to foster public sector transparency, and to fight corruption and nepotism on public procurement processes by following an open-by-default approach during the whole public contracting process. Some countries are already taking steps to support the adoption and the implementation of the OCDS. For instance:

- G20 countries such as Argentina, France, Italy, Mexico, the United Kingdom and the United States (and other eight non-G20 countries) announced their willingness to support the implementation of the Open Contracting Data Standard during the London G20 Anti-Corruption Summit in May, 2016.
- The governments of Colombia, France, Mexico, the United Kingdom and Ukraine created the "Contracting 5 (C5) Initiative", therefore committing to ensure country-level learning on the implementation of open contracting data as well as international knowledge sharing to support other countries in the implementation of open contracting, open data and open source tools. The C5 countries held an inaugural meeting and issued the C5 Declaration at the Open Government Partnership Summit held in Paris in December, 2016.

In addition, some OECD countries have also put in place actions to implement the standard on their procurement processes:

- In December 2015, the **Mexican government** announced its compromise to implement the OCDS for all government contracts, starting with the New Airport of Mexico City. In addition, the Coordination of the National Digital Strategy and the Ministry of Transport and Communications (SCT), in co-operation with other public sector and social organisations, are also working on the implementation of the Open Contracting Data Standard for the development of the Mexican Telecommunication Shared Network – a public-private partnership that represents the largest telecommunication investment in the country to date. Mexico aims to make Open Contracting a mandatory policy across the whole federal level administration by reforming and/or amending public procurement regulations with the objective of publishing as open data, all information related to the whole public procurement process (planning, tender, award, contracting and implementation).
- In **Spain**, the National Commission of Market and Competition (Comisión Nacional de los Mercados y la Competencia, CNMC) is currently working (October, 2016) on recommendations on the publication of public tender information as open data. These recommendations will be included in the updated version of the Guide on Public Contracting of the Spanish Government, thereby setting a precedent to apply the same approach for all stages of the public procurement process.
- The **French government** has developed an ambitious policy concerning public contracting data as a result of an amendment to Article 107 of the French public procurement code (modified by decree) and two subsequent legal modifications that took place in 2017 (a legal decree defining priority data categories related to public procurement, and a second one concerning the identification buyers' platforms). The Etalab – the Taskforce for Open Data and Open Government at the Office of the Prime Minister – is driving experimentation at a local level to implement the open contracting data standard with a multi-level and multi-stakeholder approach that involves all the actors engaged in public procurement processes (e.g. suppliers, public administrations, cities). The public procurement transparency policy is driven by the public procurement dematerialisation policy, which must be fully implemented by October, 2018.

Box 5.9. **Supporting government openness through the implementation of the Open Contracting Data Standard** *(continued)*

Other non-OECD countries have implemented similar actions. In Ukraine (a C5 member), the Prozorro platform was created as an online public procurement system that has included digital government, open data and anti-corruption principles by design. The platform (created in 2015 in co-operation with Transparency International) was created as a result of the collaborative work between private, public and social stakeholders in the country with the purpose of reforming and fighting corruption in public procurement processes. This was achieved by moving away from the mere adoption of ICTs (e-government approach) towards the understanding of digital technologies as levers to transform business models within public sector institutions. The platform was equally conceived as a digital and transforming tool by design; therefore following principles of public engagement and crowdsourcing, while embedding digital technologies such as open source and open contracting data.

Source: Text from OECD (2017b), *Compendium on the Use of Open Data for Anti-corruption: Towards Data-driven Public Sector Integrity and Civic Auditing*, OECD, Paris, www.oecd.org/gov/digital-government/g20-oecd-compendium-open-data-anti-corruption.htm.

Engagement by default: Responding to the demand and leveraging a dynamic open data ecosystem

Results for the third composite of the 2017 OURdata Index (which focuses on measuring governments' efforts to support data re-use) show that Norway's biggest challenge in terms of open government data is related to the sustainable engagement of actors towards the increased re-use of OGD. This is despite Difi's reported efforts to engage external stakeholders.

Difi's Open Data Handbook (Veileder i tilgjengeliggjøring av offentlige data)[10] encourages public sector institutions to perform consultation exercises to inform their open data plans (e.g. to prioritise the publication of OGD), but the implementation of these exercises is at the discretion of public sector institutions.

According to information collected through the 2017 OECD Open Government Data Survey 3.0, the most relevant consultation exercises have been implemented by Difi and not by the vast majority of public sector institutions. Difi's efforts to involve stakeholders were focused on evaluating the opinion of stakeholders (including private sector institutions, the academia, journalists) on the Norwegian Licence on Open Data (NLOD) and the transposition of the 2013 EU Public Sector Information (PSI) Directive, and carrying out formal hearings on the use of the Description of Data Sets and Data Directories (DCAT) for the development of the Norwegian OGD portal. Difi also encourages potential users to request data, and public sector institutions to use FOI requests to inform and prioritise the publication of OGD (an approach also supported by the Digitalisation Memorandum), but this approach is transparency-oriented (reactive release of data) instead of OGD- oriented (dynamic and proactive OGD publication).

Despite Difi's implementation of some exercises focused on identifying specific datasets to prioritise publication in machine-readable and open formats, it is not clear if such efforts are systemic and implemented by public sector institutions, which would contribute to supporting the demand- and user-driven publication of open government data. This is also a missing opportunity as Norway currently lacks a formal open government data infrastructure (e.g. the Strategic Open Data Infrastructure in Mexico; see Box 5.10) that could be used to fulfil overarching policy goals while responding to stakeholders' demands for data.

Box 5.10. Mexico's Strategic Open Data Infrastructure

In 2013, an online public consultation process (that was named Datatrón) was launched by the Mexican government (led by the Office of the CDO). The exercise was launched through the central open data portal in order to assess the external demand for government data. The assessment centred on nine key data categories identified by the Mexican government, including crime and justice, democracy and accountability, economy and public finance, education, energy and environment, geography, social mobility, health, and transport and infrastructure. In 2015, the results of the Datatrón were cross-matched with a second open-ended online public consultation to continue identifying priority datasets to be included in the Strategic Open Data Infrastructure (Infraestructura Estratégica de Datos Abiertos).

From March to May 2015, the Mexican government opened for public discussion a preliminary list of datasets resulting from the above-mentioned exercises. Based on this proposal, users' inputs were useful to prioritise the publication of government datasets, and focus efforts inside the public sector towards the achievement of these goals. As a result of this consultation process, the CDO set the final list of strategic datasets (the data infrastructure) to be open for public access on the central portal. In addition, public institutions were also encouraged to contemplate prioritising the publication of open government data based on citizens' requests to access public sector information.

The Strategic Open Data Infrastructure was useful to better prioritise the allocation of technical, human and financial resources to release government data and, more specifically, to guide the activities of the Open Data Squads – a taskforce within the CDO in charge of providing guidance to public sector institutions in Mexico during the process of opening up their data.

The Mexican government launched a third online consultation exercise from February to March 2017, to update its open data infrastructure, centring on five priority policy areas: anti-corruption, economic development and innovation, public services, climate change and resilience, and human rights. As of June 2017, the results from this exercise were still not available.

Source: OECD (2016c), *Open Government Data Review of Mexico: Data Reuse for Public Sector Impact and Innovation*, OECD Publishing, Paris, http://dx.doi.org/10.1787/9789264259270-en.

There is also an opportunity to increase the design, implementation and sustainability of collaboration and value co-creation initiatives with the participation of actors from the public, private and third sectors.

Notably, the Norwegian Mapping Authority, and not Difi, has taken the lead in this respect. Since 2015, it has organised the #hack4no[11] event, bringing together entrepreneurs, students, and other stakeholder groups, with the objective of increasing the re-use of OGD. These events included the participation of public sector institutions (as data owners). A new edition of #hack4no is expected to take place in 2017. These efforts are in line with engagement initiatives implemented by other OECD countries (see Table 5.5). Some countries, like France, have focused on building capacities within the public sector to organise hackathons that are meaningful and linked to a specific policy issue they want to solve. This is essential to ensure that value is derived as a result of the efforts to engage actors of the ecosystem.

Table 5.5. **How often representatives from central/federal ministries/agencies have been involved in events/activities aimed at promoting the re-use of OGD among businesses since 2015**

	Organise a conference on the opportunities/benefits provided by open government datasets to businesses	Attend conferences organised by a third party to present the opportunities/benefits of open government datasets to businesses	Conduct focus groups/information sessions with business representatives to understand their data needs	Conduct focus groups/information sessions with business representatives to present the benefits/opportunities of open government datasets	Organise hackathon events	Provide funding to a third party to organise hackathon events	Organise co-creation events (e.g. app development contest, data visualisation challenge)	Provide funding for the organisation of co-creation events (e.g. app development contest, data visualisation challenge)
Australia	○	●	⊙	⊙	⊙	●	⊙	⊙
Austria	⊙	⊙	⊙	⊙	⊙	⊙	⊙	⊙
Belgium	⊙	●	○	◉	○	○	○	○
Canada	⊙	⊙	◉	◉	⊙	⊙	○	○
Chile	⊙	⊙	○	○	●	○	⊙	○
Czech Republic	⊙	⊙	⊙	⊙	⊙	○	⊙	○
Denmark	◉	●	◉	◉	●	●	○	○
Estonia	◉	⊙	○	⊙	⊙	⊙	⊙	○
Finland	○	●	●	●	●	●	●	●
France	●	●	◉	◉	●	⊙	●	○
Germany	⊙	●	⊙	○	◉	○	○	○
Greece	◉	●	○	○	⊙	○	⊙	○
Ireland	◉	◉	◉	⊙	⊙	◉	○	⊙
Italy	○	◉	⊙	○	⊙	○	○	⊙
Korea	●	●	●	●	●	●	●	●
Latvia	○	⊙	◉	○	○	○	○	○
Mexico	●	●	●	●	●	●	●	●
Netherlands	●	◉	●	●	●	◉	◉	◉
New Zealand	○	⊙	●	●	◉	◉	⊙	○
Norway	◉	●	◉	◉	●	⊙	⊙	⊙
Poland	◉	◉	◉	◉	⊙	⊙	○	○
Portugal	○	⊙	○	⊙	○	○	○	○
Slovak Republic	⊙	⊙	○	○	⊙	○	○	○
Slovenia	⊙	⊙	○	○	○	○	○	○
Spain	⊙	●	⊙	⊙	○	○	○	○
Sweden	○	⊙	⊙	◉	⊙	◉	○	○
Switzerland	●	●	◉	⊙	◉	⊙	⊙	⊙
Turkey	○	○	○	○	○	○	○	○
United Kingdom	●	◉	●	●	●	●	●	●
United States	⊙	●	●	◉	●	○	●	○
Often (5+ times per year)	●							
Sometimes (1-4 times per year)	◉							
Rarely (1-2 times per year)	⊙							
Never	○							

Source: OECD (2016b), "OECD Open Government Data Survey 3.0", OECD, Paris, based on Section 1,Question 44, "In practice, since January 2015 how often have representatives from Central/federal ministries/agencies been involved in the following events/activities aimed at promoting the reuse of open government data among businesses?"

The Norwegian private sector has also taken a leading role. For instance, in 2016 Telenor – a major mobile operator in the Nordic region – created an initiative to support the development of smart cities and the Internet of Things in Norway.[12] This initiative is implemented in collaboration with StartupLab,[13] a network mainly integrated by private sector actors aiming to support entrepreneurship in the country. Yet, the Norwegian Mapping Authority and the City of Oslo are involved as partners in this initiative.

Some OECD countries have followed a similar approach by creating data and innovation labs at the central level (e.g. Chile and Colombia), and by formalising partnerships with academic institutions in order to develop the data-related skills across key players in the open data ecosystem (e.g. Korea and Mexico). In this line, the case of Spain and the Aporta Initiative is worth mentioning due to its strong focus on the development of a mature infomediary ecosystem in the country (see Box 5.11).

Box 5.11. **Governments as partners: Supporting the development of a mature data ecosystem across OECD countries**

Chile

The Laboratorio de Gobierno (GovLab) is a multidisciplinary institution of the government of Chile that was set up to implement the president's mandate on public sector innovation. Announced by President Michelle Bachelet on 21 May 2014, the Laboratorio has the mission of developing, facilitating and promoting human-centred innovation processes within public sector institutions. The Laboratorio represents the Chilean government's new approach to solving public challenges, which put the citizens right in the centre of public action and transformation processes. The GovLab acts as a learning-by-doing area for civil servants and provides a controlled environment that permits risk-taking and connects a diversity of actors related to public services to co-create and test solutions.

The Laboratorio engages in two main streams of activity:

- Innovation projects and ecosystem: These include actions aimed at supporting public sector institutions to seek innovative solutions that improve the services the state provides to citizens. This includes projects (such as open innovation challenges) with the objective of using the creative intelligence of entrepreneurs, small businesses, students, academics, citizens and non-governmental organisations (NGOs) to come up with solutions to the most urgent challenges of the state. Projects include the new redesign of the electricity bill, and projects in the healthcare sector, social welfare, transport and with the development agency CORFO.
- Innovation capabilities: These include actions focused on developing capabilities of civil servants to initiate and carry out innovation processes within public sector institutions through learning-by-doing experiences. Projects include Experimenta (experiential programme for civil servants), and managing networks of innovations such as the Innovadores Públicos, the Public Innovators Network.

Korea

In March 2016, the Korean government opened the "Open Square D" Centre (OSD) with the objective of providing support to open government data-based start-ups. The OSD is located in Seoul within the Business Incubator Centre of the Sookmyung Women's University. It provides an open space for data entrepreneurs to learn and exchange knowledge on open data in order to move from a business concept to real data monetisation. Beside the potential of the OSD as an open government data-based business community cluster and a business incubator, the centre will equally contribute to the development of skills as a result of public-private partnerships with more established data-driven companies, and the provision of free-of-charge training on open data for students.

Box 5.11. **Governments as partners: Supporting the development of a mature data ecosystem across OECD countries** *(continued)*

Mexico

The Mexican government launched the Open Data Startup Hub "Labora" during the OECD Ministerial for the Digital Economy held in Cancún on 21-23 June 2016, with the objective of supporting the development of skills among entrepreneurs and incentivising the data-driven economy in the country. In addition, Mexico is also trying to develop a data-driven public sector. The idea is to capture the benefits of government data to improve the functioning of the public sector. The "Datalab" initiative – developed in co-operation with the Center for Research and Teaching in Economics (CIDE) - shows the willingness of the Mexican government to bring talent from outside the government to improve public sector capacities to use, re-use and exploit data for better public policies.

Spain

Since 2013, the Spanish government has been organising a yearly forum with the participation of public institutions and business and social organisations. The forum is framed within the actions of the Aporta Initiative – a government initiative implemented by the Spanish Ministry of Industry, Energy and Tourism and the Ministry of Finance, which aims to create a pro-open data government environment, invigorate the national open data ecosystem and increase data re-use by users. The forum (known as Foro CPP-RISP) aims to increase collaboration between business and social user communities and the Spanish government in order to keep building conditions that can contribute to the creation of economic and social value through open data re-use in Spain.

Source: Author, with text from OECD (2016c), *Open Government Data Review of Mexico: Data Reuse for Public Sector Impact and Innovation*, OECD Publishing, Paris, http://dx.doi.org/10.1787/9789264259270-en; OECD (2017e), *Innovation Skills in the Public Sector: Building Capabilities in Chile*, OECD Public Governance Reviews, OECD Publishing, Paris, http://dx.doi.org/10.1787/9789264273283-en.

The data golden cycle: Developing the skills base for a smart and data-driven government

The digitalisation of information and the exponential availability of platforms enabling new forms of machine-human interactions have led to the increased availability of data. These data, when paired with the enhanced availability and use of new digital technologies - such as artificial intelligence, machine-learning and data analytics (including micro, open and/or big data) - are a valuable source of intelligence and knowledge for those actors capable of analysing, understand and using it.

The potential that the use of these technologies brings for governments goes without saying (see Figure 5.10), as highlighted by previous OECD work in this area, e.g. the 2016 *Open Government Data Review of Mexico* (OECD, 2016c) and the OECD (forthcoming) working paper, "A data-driven public sector for sustainable and inclusive governance". In this line, the discussion on the value to be derived by the public sector in relation to the use and re-use of data is not limited to government data, but to a wide array of data produced also by external actors (i.e. a phenomenon also known as big data), and to the strategic and smart adoption of digital technologies for re-using data with the intent to improve public service delivery and data-driven policies.

Figure 5.10. **Opportunities for the data-driven public sector**

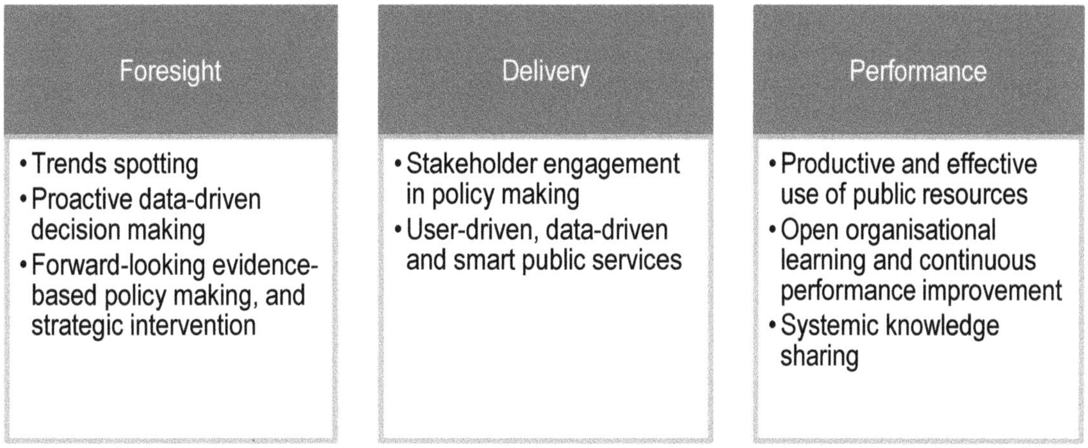

Source: Adapted from OECD (forthcoming), "A data-driven public sector for sustainable and inclusive governance", *OECD Working Papers on Public Governance*, OECD Publishing, Paris.

In Norway, the willingness of the central government to "monitor technology developments in big data and consider the need for a strategy for using big data in the public sector" (KMD, 2016), and the opportunities that public sector institutions see in relation to the development of data-driven services and foresight activities (see the earlier section on the data governance policy in Norway), create a propitious environment for inter-institutional collaboration within the public sector, for innovative partnerships and forms of engagement with the private sector, and for more purposeful public sector experimentation and data-driven innovation. As previously mentioned, ensuring the availability of a supportive leadership and the adequate framework governing the data value chain will play a key role in making the most out of these opportunities.

The above requires understanding how data, machines and humans - as inherent elements of smart and data-driven public sector institutions – interact with each other (see Figure 5.11). Each of these elements has its respective opportunities and challenges:

- **Data**: As the core source of knowledge, ensuring the constant and automated availability of and accessibility to good quality data is strategic to ensure the impact of data-driven initiatives led by public sector institutions. Ensuring data integrity and security during the whole data value chain will play a key role in this respect.
- **Machine**: The strategic adoption of new technologies by public sector institutions is a key, inherent element of the process. This also opens up an opportunity for greater private sector participation as service providers on behalf of the public sector (see Chapter 3).
- **Human**: The role of people goes beyond the one of networked data producers. Human capacities and skills are needed to understand the data collected through

machines, and to turn civil servants into data prosumers. In fact, the development of public officials' systems-based capacities to consume data for the provision of government-to-government shared services can contribute to the creation of systems knowledge across the administration.

Figure 5.11. **Key elements of smart and data-driven public sector institutions**

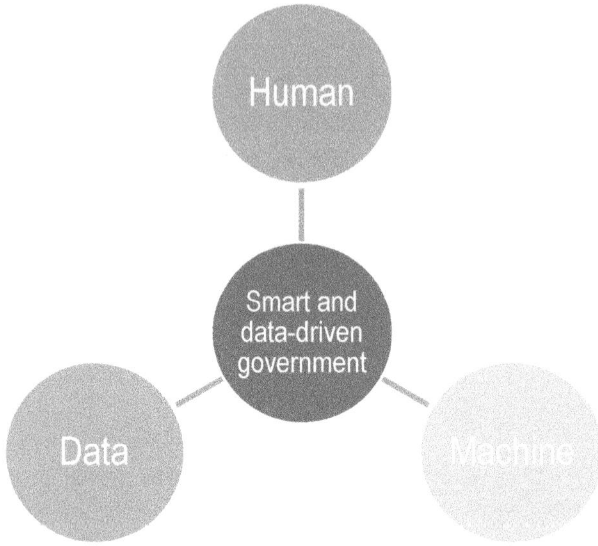

Source: Author (original content created for this review).

While the elements related to the data and machine components can be easily seen as core to digital government and data governance strategies (e.g. procurement and private provision of cloud-based or data analytics services), recognising the importance of developing and/or ensuring the availability of the right set of skills and organisational capacities within public sector institutions is crucial to capitalise on data and digital technologies to fully reap the potential benefits of the first as a strategic asset for the public sector.

As discussed in Chapter 3, the availability of new technologies creates demand for more advanced ICT skills. Therefore, any strategy focused on creating, attracting and retaining digital skills and ensuring a balanced public-private balance in the carrying out ot critical tasks should be part of an integrated strategy focused on the construction of a smart and data-driven public sector.

At the central level, the Norwegian government has not yet prioritised the design of a strategy aimed at developing data skills (e.g. data analysis, data science, coding) across the broad public sector. These results were confirmed with information provided by the Norwegian government also when assessed in relation to open government data through the 2016 OECD Open Government Data Survey (see Figure 5.12).

Figure 5.12. **Existence of a central/federal programme that aims to support open data literacy among public servants in OECD member countries**

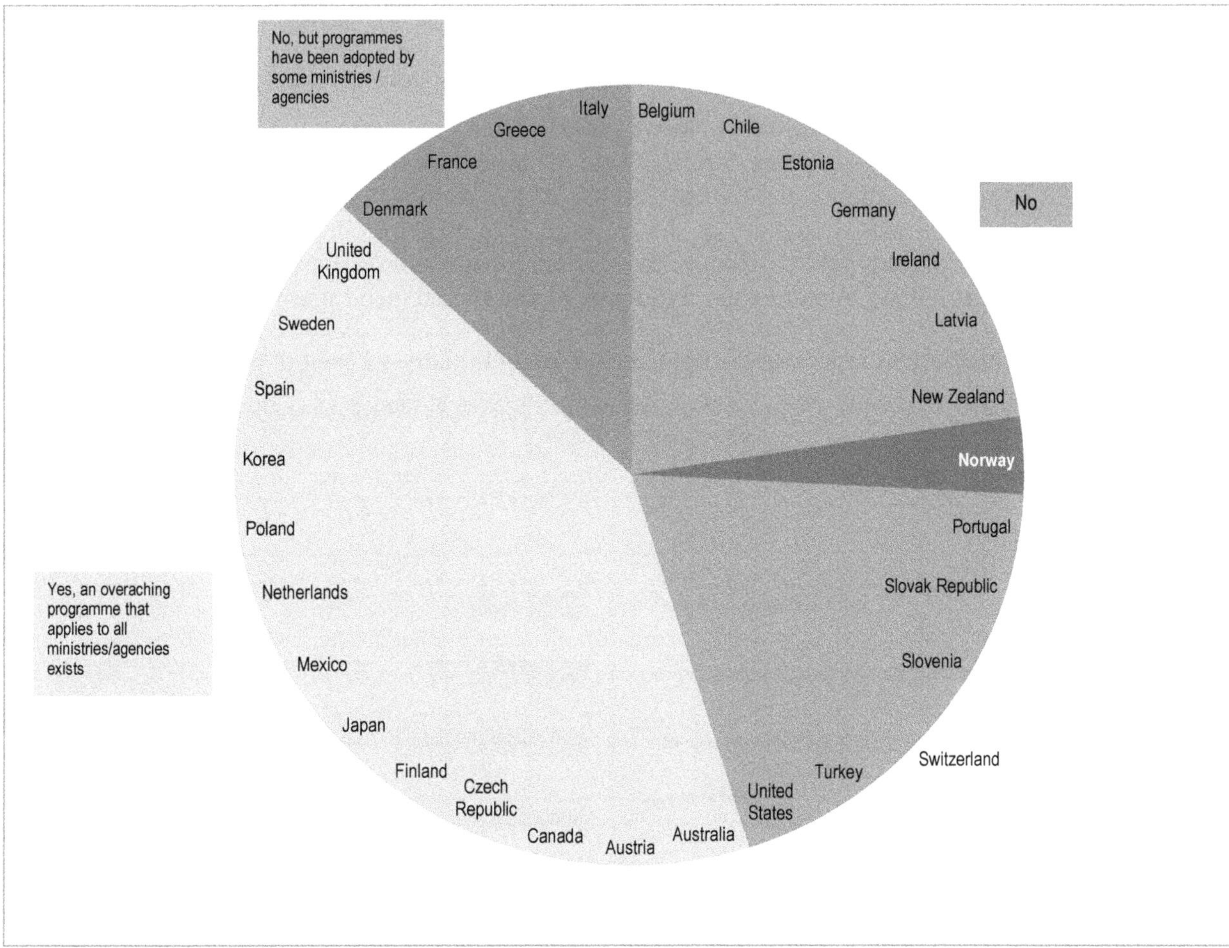

Source: OECD (2016b), "OECD Open Government Data Survey 3.0", OECD, Paris. Based on Section 1, Question 58, Is there a central/federal programme which aims at supporting open data literacy among public servants?

For instance, in Australia, the Department of the Prime Minister and Cabinet has partnered with the Australian Public Service (APS) Commission, other Australian government entities, and the private and academic sectors to develop a holistic approach to improve the overall data skills and capability across the APS. Through this partnership, the APS Data Skills and Capability Framework was developed to empower the Australian Public Service to harness the value of data and increase data literacy across all levels of the APS. Four components form the APS Data Skills and Capability Framework: 1) the Data Fellowship programme; 2) university courses; 3) the APS Data Literacy programme; and 4) data training partnerships. Senior executives across the APS encourage employees to take advantage of these learning and development opportunities.[14] In Colombia, the Programme for Excellence in Government was developed in partnership with the United Nations Development Programme (UNDP) in order to strengthen the design, implementation and development of capacities through training in e-government to civil servants of the country, including all the topics related to open government and open data.[15] Additionally, as part of e-government appropriation initiatives workshops and webinars training sessions on open data have been organised at the mumnicpality level with the participation of CIOs from the central public sector institutions, and civil servants of technology and information (TI) offices. In Mexico, the Office of the President, through the Chief Data Officer, launched the Datalab initiative in 2016 in partnership with the National Lab of Public Policy of the Center for Research and Teaching in Economics (CIDE) to support the use of data for the development, implementation and evaluation of evidenced- and data-driven public policies.

In addition, despite the interest of Norwegian ministries and agencies to explore data-driven solutions and services, only 5 of the total 35 institutions that provided a response to the OECD survey administered for the purpose of this review report the availability of a strategy and/or initiative aimed at developing or enhancing in-house data-related literacy and skills among public officials. In addition, only a minor share of public sector institutions report having implemented initiatives in this regard (see Figure 5.13).

Figure 5.13. **Public institutions reporting the implementation of initiatives aimed to increase data re-use**

% of public sector instittutions responding Yes or No to Question 144: "Has your institution put in place specific initiatives for data re-use aiming to…"

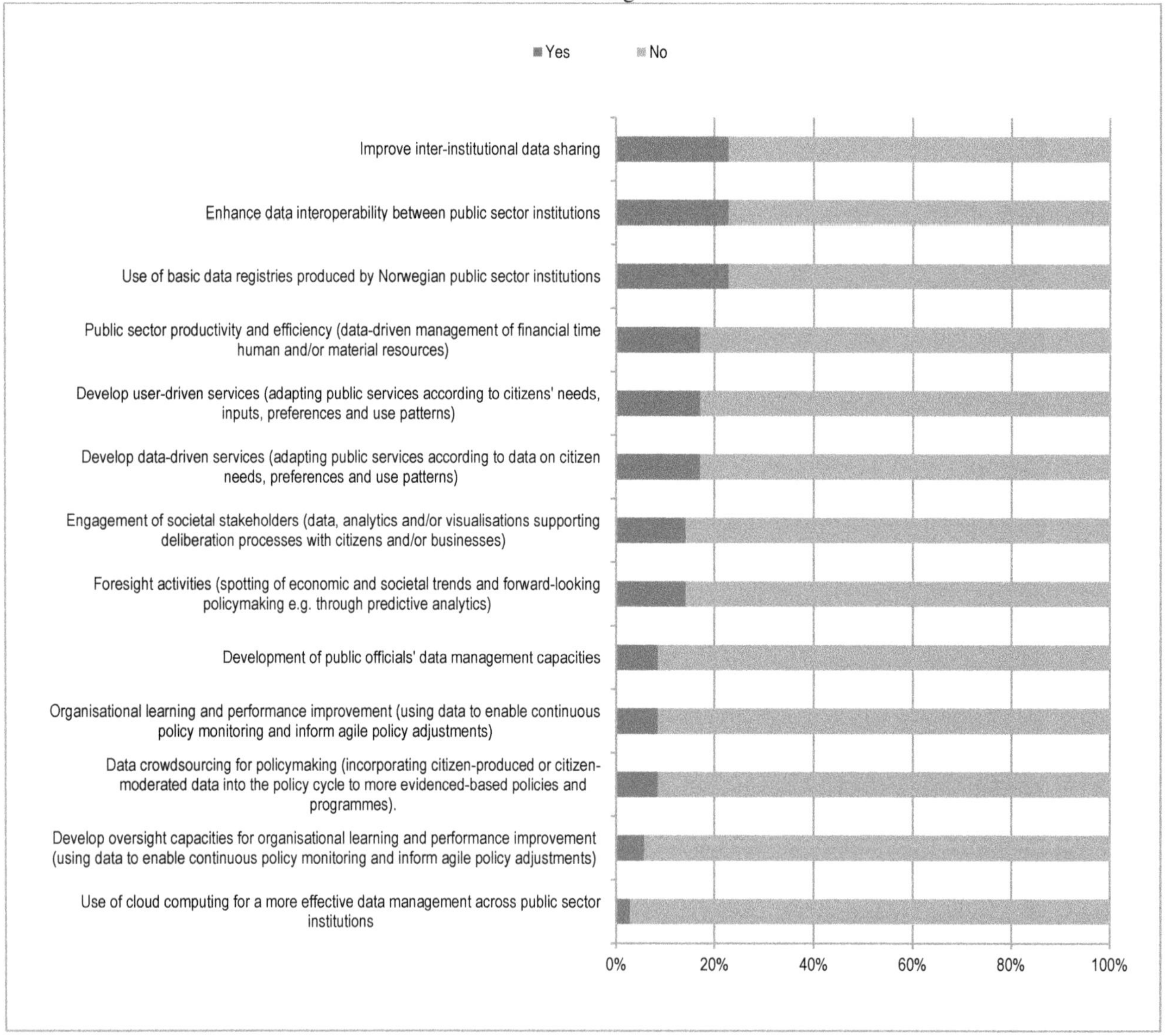

Source: OECD (2017c), "Digital Government Survey of Norway", central version, OECD, Paris.

The evidence above shows that there is a window of opportunity in Norway to design – from an early stage – an inclusive and systemic strategy to develop data-related skills across public sector institutions in collaboration with Norwegian ministries and agencies. Thereby, connecting it with the overall digital government and open government data policy in the country, and contributing to increasing the role of agencies as data and open data prosumers towards the contruction of a smart and data-driven public sector in the country.

Trust in government and citizens' co-responsibility

Anonymity and privacy are valuable assets in the age of digital, global and networked societies. Earlier concepts such as the Internet of Things (the integration and interconnection of smart devices, e.g. home devices) have evolved to the Internet of People (mainly centred on automated and continuous data collection using humans as data sources, e.g. wearable technology). In this context, citizens are rarely aware of how their private data is being used, shared or stored. This scenario underlines the relevance of governments' intervention in order to ensure the protection of sensitive and personal data by public and private actors.

Physical and geographic borders blur in cyberspace; governments are therefore challenged to better regulate, and understand, transnational data management systems. The digital era has equally brought into play new challenging and complex risks. Frequent cyberattacks on key national information technology (IT) infrastructures are the result of, among other factors, the availability of highly intricate, global-wide computer systems that enable anonymity.

In this light, cybersecurity and the protection of personal data and citizens' privacy are a top policy priority for the Norwegian government, ministries and agencies. Among other legal instruments, the 1967 Public Administration Act, the 2000 Data Protection Act, and the 2006 FOI act (see Chapter 1), are the most relevant legal instruments in regard to data protection in the country.[16] The mandate of, and the guidelines (e.g. on data anonymisation and cloud computing) issued by, the Norwegian Data Protection Authority (Datatilsynet) complete the governance framework for secured data transfers and privacy protection in Norway.

At the sectoral and agency level, there is evidence of major advancements in this area. For instance, the Norwegian Ministry of Health and Care Services developed the "Summary Care Record", embedding data access control logs to monitor and register access to citizens' health data. The Norwegian Directorate of E-health developed the "Normen" platform as an operational platform to improve the compliance of data protection regulations within the health sector. The Directorate of eHealth has also developed a governance structure for data protection, including the availability of one Data Protection Officer, and three subordinate Data Protection Managers, in charge of assessing, exploiting and implementing new data protection solutions. The latter is relevant in light of the upcoming (2018) EU regulations on Data Privacy and Protection - which will require the creation of data officer positions across health and care sector institutions at the local level. Other ministries and agencies have also put in place cybersecurity and risk-management systems to secure their systems and data from potential cyberattacks in line with central regulations.

As in many other countries, a key challenge is to ensure that government processes involving the exchange of personal information are designed to ensure that these data are kept safe, secured, accessed and/or modified only by authorised parties (a key element to ensure the data integrity), and anonymised when required.

Data protection and information security are, indeed, one of the five main priorities of Norway's Digital Agenda (see Chapter 2). This follows the digital government principle of privacy by design. This principle calls for the conception and design of secured data management systems and processes that ensure compliance with data protection, anonymisation and privacy regulations.[17] Yet, even more relevant is the role that citizens – as data owners – could play within this process.

On the one hand, at the technical level, it is the role of Norwegian public officials to ensure that data-sharing processes are designed to follow the guidelines and recommendations issued by the Norwegian Data Protection Authority on regulatory compliance. For this purpose, agencies will face the challenge of keeping pace with technological developments in order to spot the need to adopt up-to-date, new data protection technology whenever needed.

At the policy level, increasing and sustaining the evolution from passive citizens' intervention (e.g. through privacy notices and/or automated notifications implying silent consent) to an active citizens' role, co-responsibility and empowerment will be vital to maintain the trust in Norwegian public sector institutions. It is crucial to ensure that citizens are effectively informed on which institutions and public officials have requested or accessed their data, and for what purpose, and draw upon the current IT architecture in place (e.g. eID, mailboxes) to enable citizens to keep track of such activity, as found in Denmark, Estonia and Spain.

On the other hand, further building privacy and data protection co-responsibility between governments and citizens requires returning control to citizens – an approach that in the era of big data and permanent connectivity seems difficult to achieve. Some OECD countries (e.g. the United Kingdom)[18] have underlined the potential role that third parties could play in this regard.

The recent emergence of intermediaries providing personal cloud and fog-based services is a response to an increasing social awareness on data use or misuse by third parties. These services act as an additional encrypted and user-managed database that inter-connects third-parties – e.g. service providers – requesting and/or using citizens' data. The objective is to return the control to citizens over their own data, therefore enabling them to decide how and with whom their data is shared. In this regard, the Norwegian government, through the KMD and Difi, could benefit from further exploring the benefits of these technologies as part of the upcoming digital agenda in the country.

Notes

1. For further information, see www.difi.no/fagomrader-og-tjenester/digitalisering-og-samordning/nasjonal-arkitektur/informasjonsforvaltning/veileder-orden-i-eget-hus.

2. For further information, see www.difi.no/fagomrader-og-tjenester/digitalisering-og-samordning/standarder/standarder/standard-begrepsbeskrivelser.
3. For further information, see www.regjeringen.no/no/dokumenter/retningslinjer-ved-tilgjengeliggjoring-av-offentlige-data/id2536870/.
4. For further information, see www.difi.no/fagomrader-og-tjenester/digitalisering-og-samordning/standarder/standardiseringsradet.
5. See www.altinn.no/en/a-ordningen/ for more information.
6. For further information, see http://inspire.ec.europa.eu/
7. "Sunsetting provides for an automatic annulment of a statutory act after a certain period (typically five to ten years), unless keeping the act in the books is explicitly justified. The logic can apply to specific regulations or to all regulations that are not specifically exempted. For sunsetting to be effective, exemptions and deferrals need to be contained and any regulations being re-made appropriately assessed first. This requires preparation and planning. For this reason, sunsetting is often made equivalent to introducing review clauses." (OECD, 2015b)
8. Based on information provided by the Educational Loan Fund.
9. For further information, see https://data.norge.no/nlod/en/1.0.
10. For more information, see https://data.norge.no/document/del-og-skap-verdier-veileder-i-tilgjengeliggj%C3%B8ring-av-offentlige-data.
11. For further information, see http://hack4.no/.
12. For further information, see www.telenor.com/media/press-release/telenor-supports-norwegian-entrepreneurship-and-artificial-intelligence-research/.
13. For further information, see http://startuplab.no.
14. Information provided by the Australian Government. For further information, see www.dpmc.gov.au/resource-centre/public-data/data-skills-and-capability-australian-public-service.
15. For further information, see http://estrategia.gobiernoenlinea.gov.co/623/w3-article-8304.html.
16. Other data protection regulations are included as part of the Norwegian Penal Code, sectoral and basic registries regulations.
17. See, for instance, the work of the United Kingdom's Information Commissioner's Office on privacy by default and privacy impact assessments at https://ico.org.uk/for-organisations/guide-to-data-protection/privacy-by-design/.
18. See, for instance, the 2017 UK ICO Report on big data, artificial intelligence, machine learning and data protection at https://ico.org.uk/media/for-organisations/documents/2013559/big-data-ai-ml-and-data-protection.pdf.

References

Difi (Agency for Public Management and eGovernment) (2015), *Forprosjektrapport: Evaluering Av Prosjektet "Fjerne tidstyver"*, December, Difi, www.difi.no/sites/difino/files/forprosjektrapport_evaluering_av_prosjektet_fjerne_tidstyver.pdf.

Government of Norway (2006), "Freedom of Information Act", https://lovdata.no/dokument/NL/lov/2006-05-19-16?q=offentleg.

Hilbert, M. and P. López (2011), "The world's technological capacity to store, communicate, and compute information", *Science* 332(6025), pp. 60–65, http://dx.doi.org10.1126/science.1200970.

KMD (Ministry of Local Government and Modernisation) (2016), "Digital Agenda for Norway in brief: ICT for a simpler everyday life and increased productivity", English version, KMD, www.regjcringen.no/en/dokumenter/digital-agenda-for-norway-in-brief/id2499897/sec1.

KMPG (2014), "Barriers to digitizatioen", Executive summary in *KPMG report to the Norwegian Ministry of Local Government and Modernisation*, www.regjeringen.no/globalassets/upload/kmd/aif/dokumenter/barriers_to_digitizatioen.pdf.

OECD (forthcoming), "A data-driven public sector for sustainable and inclusive governance", *OECD Working Papers on Public Governance*, OECD Publishing, Paris.

OECD (2017a), *Government at a Glance 2017*, OECD Publishing, Paris, http://dx.doi.org/10.1787/gov_glance-2017-en.

OECD (2017b), *Compendium on the Use of Open Data for Anti-corruption*: *Towards Data-driven Public Sector Integrity and Civic Auditing*, OECD, Paris, www.oecd.org/gov/digital-government/g20-oecd-compendium-open-data-anti-corruption.htm.

OECD (2017c), "Digital Government Survey of Norway", central version, OECD, Paris.

OECD (2017d), "Digital Government Survey of Norway", public sector institutions version, OECD, Paris.

OECD (2017e), *Innovation Skills in the Public Sector: Building Capabilities in Chile*, OECD Public Governance Reviews, OECD Publishing, Paris, http://dx.doi.org/10.1787/9789264273283-en.

OECD (2016a), "A data-driven public sector for sustainable and inclusive governance", Issues paper produced for the 2016 meeting of the OECD Working Party of Senior Digital Government Officials, 22-23 September, Tallin, Estonia.

OECD (2016b), "OECD Open Government Data Survey 3.0", OECD, Paris.

OECD (2016c), *Open Government Data Review of Mexico: Data Reuse for Public Sector Impact and Innovation*, OECD Publishing, Paris, http://dx.doi.org/10.1787/9789264259270-en.

OECD (2015a), *Open Government Data Review of Poland: Unlocking the Value of Government Data*, OECD Digital Government Studies, OECD Publishing, Paris http://dx.doi.org/10.1787/9789264241787-en.

OECD (2015b), *OECD Regulatory Policy Outlook 2015*, OECD Publishing, Paris, http://dx.doi.org/10.1787/9789264238770-en.

OECD (2014a), "Recommendation of the Council on Digital Government Strategies", OECD, Paris, www.oecd.org/gov/digital-government/recommendation-on-digital-government-strategies.htm.

OECD (2014b), *Spain: From Administrative Reform to Continuous Improvement*, OECD Public Governance Reviews, OECD Publishing, Paris, http://dx.doi.org/10.1787/9789264210592-en.

OECD (2014c), *Regulatory Indicators Data* (dataset), OECD, Paris, www.oecd.org/gov/regulatory-policy/measuring-regulatory-performance.htm.

OECD (2012), "Recommendation of the Council on Regulatory Policy and Governance", OECD, Paris, www.oecd.org/governance/regulatory-policy/2012-recommendation.htm.

Rivera Perez, J.A. (2015), *Beyond Open Data Disclosure: Fostering The Impact Of Open Government Data Towards More Efficient Public Institutions*, London School of Economics and Political Science, Department of Management, London.

Ubaldi, B. (2013), "Open government data: Towards empirical analysis of open government data initiatives", *OECD Working Papers on Public Governance*, No. 22, OECD Publishing, Paris, http://dx.doi.org/10.1787/5k46bj4f03s7-en.

UK Government (2017), "Government Transformation Strategy: Better use of data", Policy paper, Cabinet Office, Government Digital Service, www.gov.uk/government/publications/government-transformation-strategy-2017-to-2020/government-transformation-strategy-better-use-of-data.

UK Government (2013), "G8 Open Data Charter and Technical Annex", Policy paper, Cabinet Office, www.gov.uk/government/publications/open-data-charter/g8-open-data-charter-and-technical-annex.

ORGANISATION FOR ECONOMIC CO-OPERATION AND DEVELOPMENT

The OECD is a unique forum where governments work together to address the economic, social and environmental challenges of globalisation. The OECD is also at the forefront of efforts to understand and to help governments respond to new developments and concerns, such as corporate governance, the information economy and the challenges of an ageing population. The Organisation provides a setting where governments can compare policy experiences, seek answers to common problems, identify good practice and work to co-ordinate domestic and international policies.

The OECD member countries are: Australia, Austria, Belgium, Canada, Chile, the Czech Republic, Denmark, Estonia, Finland, France, Germany, Greece, Hungary, Iceland, Ireland, Israel, Italy, Japan, Korea, Latvia, Luxembourg, Mexico, the Netherlands, New Zealand, Norway, Poland, Portugal, the Slovak Republic, Slovenia, Spain, Sweden, Switzerland, Turkey, the United Kingdom and the United States. The European Union takes part in the work of the OECD.

OECD Publishing disseminates widely the results of the Organisation's statistics gathering and research on economic, social and environmental issues, as well as the conventions, guidelines and standards agreed by its members.

OECD PUBLISHING, 2, rue André-Pascal, 75775 PARIS CEDEX 16
(42 2017 34 1 P) ISBN 978-92-64-27973-5 – 2017

www.ingramcontent.com/pod-product-compliance
Ingram Content Group UK Ltd.
Pitfield, Milton Keynes, MK11 3LW, UK
UKHW051501290926
15471UKWH00008B/1336

9 789264 279735